PENGUIN (◊) CLASSICS

MEDEA AND OTHER PLAYS

EURIPIDES, the youngest of the three great Athenian playwrights, was born around 485 BC of a family of good standing. He first competed in the dramatic festivals in 455 BC, coming only third; his record of success in the tragic competitions is lower than that of either Aeschylus or Sophocles. There is a tradition that he was unpopular, even a recluse; we are told that he composed poetry in a cave by the sea, near Salamis. What is clear from contemporary evidence, however, is that audiences were fascinated by his innovative and often disturbing dramas. His work was controversial already in his lifetime, and he himself was regarded as a 'clever' poet, associated with philosopers and other intellectuals. Towards the end of his life he went to live at the court of Archelaus, king of Macedon. It was during his time there that he wrote what many consider his greatest work, the *Bacchae*. When news of his death reached Athens in early 406 BC, Sophocles appeared publicly in mourning for him. Euripides is thought to have written about ninety-two plays, of which seventeen tragedies and one satyr-play known to be his survive; the other play which is attributed to him, the *Rhesus*, may in fact be by a later hand.

JOHN DAVIE was born in Glasgow in 1950, and was educated at the High School of Glasgow, Glasgow Univeristy and Balliol College, Oxford, where he wrote a thesis on Greek tragedy. From 1975 to 1984 he taught Classics at Harrow, before moving to St Paul's School to become Head of Classics, where he still teaches. He is the author of two articles on the problems of writing favourably about monarchy in a democratic society such as fifth-century BC Athens. He is a member of the Hellenic Society's visiting Panel of Lecturers.

DR RICHARD RUTHERFORD was born in Edinburgh in 1956, and was educated at Robert Gordon's College, Aberdeen and at Worcester College, Oxford. Since 1982 he has been Tutor in Greek and Latin Literature at Christ Church, Oxford. He is the author of a number of books and articles on classical authors, including a commentary on books 19 and 20 of Homer's *Odyssey* (1992), and *The Art of Plato: Ten Essays in Platonic Interpretation* (1995).

EURIPIDES

Medea and Other Plays

Translated by JOHN DAVIE
Introduction and Notes by RICHARD RUTHERFORD

PENGUIN BOOKS

PENGUIN BOOKS

Published by the Penguin Group
Penguin Books Ltd, 80 Strand, London WC2R ORL, England
Penguin Putnam Inc., 375 Hudson Street, New York, New York 10014, USA
Penguin Books Australia Ltd, 250 Camberwell Road, Camberwell, Victoria 3124, Australia
Penguin Books Canada Ltd, 10 Alcorn Avenue, Toronto, Ontario, Canada M4V 3B2
Penguin Books India (P) Ltd, 11, Community Centre, Panchsheel Park, New Delhi – 110 017, India
Penguin Books (NZ) Ltd, Cnr Rosedale and Airborne Roads, Albany, Auckland, New Zealand
Penguin Books (South Africa) (Pty) Ltd, 24 Sturdee Avenue, Rosebank 2196, South Africa

Penguin Books Ltd, Registered Offices: 80 Strand, London WC2R ORL, England

www.penguin.com

This translation first published 1996 as *Alcestis and Other Plays*
Reissued with revised Introduction and updated Bibliography 2003

14

Translation copyright © John Davie, 1996
Introduction and Notes copyright © Richard Rutherford, 1996, 2003
All rights reserved

The moral right of the translator and editor has been asserted

Set in 10.25/12.25 pt PostScript Adobe Sabon
Typeset by Rowland Phototypesetting Ltd, Bury St Edmunds, Suffolk
Printed in England by Clays Ltd, St Ives plc

ISBN-13: 978-0-140-44929-7

Contents

General Introduction

'I portray men as they should be, but Euripides portrays them as they are.' (Sophocles, quoted by Aristotle, *Poetics*, ch. 25, 1460b33–4)

'Whatever other defects of organization he may have, Euripides is the most intensely tragic of all the poets.'
(Aristotle, *Poetics*, ch. 14, 1453a28–30)

'I am really amazed that the scholarly nobility does not comprehend his virtues, that they rank him below his predecessors, in line with that high-toned tradition which the clown Aristophanes brought into currency ... Has any nation ever produced a dramatist who would deserve to hand him his slippers?' (Goethe, *Diaries*, 22 Nov. 1831)

'What were you thinking of, overweening Euripides, when you hoped to press myth, then in its last agony, into your service? It died under your violent hands ... Though you hunted all the passions up from their couch and conjured them into your circle, though you pointed and burnished a sophistic dialectic for the speeches of your heroes, they have only counterfeit passions and speak counterfeit speeches.'
(Nietzsche, *The Birth of Tragedy*, ch. 10)

I

Already in his own lifetime Euripides was a controversial figure. Daring in his theatrical innovations, superbly eloquent and articulate in the rhetoric which he gave to his characters, closely in touch with the intellectual life of his time, he has stimulated

and shocked audiences and readers not only through the unexpected twists and turns of his plots, but also by the alarming
immorality of many of his characters. But before exploring these
and other aspects of his work in more detail, we must briefly
put him in context by giving an outline of the earlier history of
the Athenian genre of tragedy, and the work of Aeschylus, his
great predecessor, and of Sophocles, his older contemporary.

Unlike epic poetry, which was a traditional form familiar
throughout the Greek world, tragedy was a relatively new inven-
tion in the fifth century BC, and one which was particularly
Athenian. Its origins and early development are obscure: if, as
Aristotle believed, it originated in a form of choral song, the
'dithyramb', a song in honour of the god Dionysus, then it had
already been transformed before the time of Aeschylus. Ancient
tradition held that contests between tragic playwrights had
become an established part of the festival known as the City
Dionysia (held in March) some time in the 530s BC, and that
the key figure of these early days was a dramatist called Thespis.
Our earliest surviving tragedy is Aeschylus' Persians, performed
in 472 BC, a full sixty years later. The dramas which have
survived span the rest of the fifth century BC, a period of intense
political activity and social and intellectual change. Hence, generalizations even about the extant dramas will be dangerous,
and we must always bear in mind that we have only the tip of
the iceberg.

The Athenian tragedies were performed in the open air, in a
theatre enormous by modern standards: some experts believe
that it could have contained more than 14,000 people, as it
certainly could after reconstruction in the fourth century.[1] This
large audience was probably composed mainly of men (it is
likely that women could attend, but probable that not many did
so). The stage arrangements were sparse; a building set behind
the main area where the actors moved would represent a palace
or other such building according to the needs of the play. Perhaps on a lower level (though the layout is much disputed) was
the open area called the *orchestra* ('dancing-space'), in which the
chorus stood or danced. The events were conceived as happening
out of doors, theatrically necessary but also more natural in

Mediterranean life. Entrances along passages on either side of the theatre were loosely conceived as leading to different destinations – country or city, army camp or seashore, depending on the plot. Actors were all male (even for female parts), normally Athenian citizens; all wore masks and dignified formal dress; speaking actors were normally limited to three in number, but could take on different roles during the play by changing costume and mask offstage. Stage equipment and props were few; the action was largely stylized, even static, with the more violent action conceived as taking place offstage, then being reported to the actors, often in a long narrative speech. All plays were in verse, partly spoken and partly sung; although Euripides made several strides towards more 'realistic' drama, the effect of a Greek tragedy in his time would still have been to move the audience to a distant world, where great figures of the mythical past fought and disputed over momentous issues.

Every Greek tragedy had a chorus, a team of twelve or fifteen singers representing the community or some other body concerned with the events of the drama. It may be that originally tragedy consisted wholly of choral songs; if so, the key innovation, whether Thespis or another was responsible, must have been the introduction of an actor who engaged in dialogue with the chorus, who could withdraw and take part in events offstage, then return to inform them of developments. Aeschylus is said to have introduced a second actor, Sophocles a third. There the tragedians stopped, though as the century passed the three actors were often expected to play more roles, and 'mute' actors (domestic slaves, attendants or soldiers) were permitted. In general, the importance of the actors and the size of their role in the play increased, while that of the chorus declined; but in the work of the three great tragedians the chorus were never unimportant, and their songs or 'choral odes' do far more than fill in time or allow an interval: these odes comment on the action, react to it and ponder its significance, placing it in a larger perspective, chronological and religious. Some of the finest poetry in Greek tragedy comes in the choral odes.

We tend to think of the theatre as a recreation, and one which is available more or less any night of the year. The position in ancient Athens was quite different. Drama was part of a civic occasion, the festival of Dionysus. Although the city held many religious festivals, tragedies were performed only at a few, and at fixed points in the year. It was not possible for a dramatist to stage anything he liked at any time; he had to apply to the proper authorities and be 'granted a chorus', given permission to compete and financial support (it is true, however, that we also have evidence for theatrical activities in rural Attica, where procedure was perhaps less formal than at the great civic festivals). In the earliest times the playwright would also play a part in his plays, though Sophocles is said to have given this up because his voice was weak. Still more important, the author was also the producer, working together with his actors and choruses and training them. At the City Dionysia three tragedians would compete for the prize every year; each of them would present three tragedies – sometimes but not necessarily a connected 'trilogy'. Aeschylus favoured these trilogies (as his masterpiece, the *Oresteia*, illustrates), but they seem to have gone out of fashion after his death, and the overwhelming majority of surviving tragedies are self-contained dramas. After that each competing dramatist would also put on a 'satyr-play'. This last was a wild and fantastic tailpiece, usually shorter than a tragedy: it always had a chorus of satyrs, the bestial entourage of Dionysus, and usually treated mythological themes in a burlesque and bawdy way. The only complete example to survive is Euripides' *Cyclops*, an amusing parody of the story told in Homer's *Odyssey* about the hero's encounter with the one-eyed monster.

What of the content of the tragedies? Perhaps the most significant fact is that the subjects are almost always mythological.[2] The only surviving exception is Aeschylus' *Persians*, though we know of a few others in the early period. The *Persians* commemorates the victory of the Greeks in the recent war against Xerxes, king of Persia, and in particular the battle of Salamis, which had taken place only eight years earlier. But this exception in a way proves the rule, for the play is not set in Greece, but in the Persian court, presenting the subject from the Persian viewpoint. Nor is it mere jingoism: the theme is almost mythologized, raised to a grander and more heroic plane. No individual Greek is named or singled out for praise: the emphasis falls rather on the arrogant folly of a deluded king, who has led his people to defeat. There is, as always in tragedy, a supernatural element: the ghost of Xerxes' father, summoned back to earth, pronounces stern judgement on his son's rash ambition. In the rest of the tragic corpus, the dramatists use myth to distance their stories in time, and so give them universality. Instead of setting their actors the task of impersonating living generals or politicians confronting contemporary crises, the tragedians, like Homer, show us men and women who are remote from us in their circumstances, yet vividly like us and real in their hopes, fears and desires.

Secondly, Greek tragedy is civic in emphasis: its plots, that is, deal with kings and rulers, disputes and dilemmas which have vital implications for the state as a whole. If Oedipus cannot find the murderer of Laius, the plague which is already devastating Thebes will destroy it. If Odysseus and Neoptolemus cannot recover Philoctetes and his bow, Troy will not fall. Consequently, tragedy normally deals with men and women of high status – monarchs and royal families, tyrants and mighty heroes. Characters of lower rank generally have smaller parts. As we shall see, however, this is one area in which Euripides showed himself an innovator: 'I made tragedy more democratic,' he is made to say in the satirical treatment of tragedy in Aristophanes' *Frogs*, produced after his death.

Thirdly, complementing and often conflicting with the political dimension, the family is regularly the focus for tragic action. Part of the lasting power of Greek drama lies in the vividness with which it presents extreme love and (still more) intense hatred within the family: matricide, parricide, fratricide, adultery and jealousy, even incest and other forbidden passions. Duty to family and duty to the state may come into conflict: can Agamemnon bring himself to abandon the expedition against Troy, or must he take the terrible decision to sacrifice his daughter for a fair wind? Loyalty to kin is central to the *Antigone*; conflicting obligations to different members of the family create many of the dilemmas in the *Oresteia*. The list could easily be extended.

Fourthly, there is the religious aspect. We know too little of early tragedy to confirm or deny the theory that it concentrated mainly on the myths of Dionysus, in whose honour the plays were performed; yet by Aeschylus' time the scope has obviously broadened. But no Greek tragedy is secular. Although the dramatists normally focus on the actions and sufferings of human beings, the gods are always present in the background. In early tragedy they figure quite frequently on stage as characters (as in Aeschylus' *Eumenides*). Sophocles seems to have been much more restrained in this, while Euripides normally confines them to the prologue (where they do not usually meet any mortal characters), or to the conclusion of a play, where a god may appear on a higher level, above the stage-building. Sometimes this seems to be a matter of the god standing on the roof of the building, but more spectacular still was the use of a crane-like device to allow the divinity the power of flight. From this remote position of authority the god would declare his will, *ex machina* as the phrase has it, intervening to resolve or at least impose a conclusion upon the events on earth. Even when gods do not appear, they are frequently invoked, addressed in prayer, called to witness an oath, sometimes questioned or challenged. With the awesome powers of Olympus watching and influencing events, human affairs gain a larger significance: these are not trivial wars or petty crimes, if they attract divine attention and even retribution. Yet because the humans often seem helpless pawns or puppets in the divine game, the greatness of the heroes can seem sadly insignificant, and their proud boasts or ambitions may often be ironically overturned or frustrated. The wiser players on the tragic stage sometimes draw this pessimistic conclusion. 'I see we are but phantoms, all who live, or fleeting shadows,' says Odysseus in Sophocles' *Ajax* (125–6); or, as the chorus sing in his *Oedipus the King*, after the horrible truth is out: 'Alas ye generations of men, how close to nothingness do I count your life. Where in the world is the mortal who wins more of happiness than just the illusion, and after the semblance, the falling away? With your example, your fate before my eyes, yours, unhappy Oedipus, I count no man happy' (1186–96).

One last general point should be made. Greek tragedy was

intended for performance: although texts undoubtedly circu-
lated, the primary concern was production in the theatre.[3] It is
important to try to reconstruct the stage movements, the points
at which characters enter and exit, observe one another, come
into physical contact, pass objects to another person, and so
forth. Major questions of interpretation may hinge on these
seemingly small-scale puzzles: to take an example from the plays
in this volume, does Hippolytus ever address Phaedra or not? It
all depends on how we envisage the staging, and relate it to the
words, of a particular scene (*Hippolytus* 601–68, esp. 650ff.)
Moreover, this performance involved music and dancing by
the chorus, of which we can recover next to nothing – a few
descriptions in ancient prose authors, a handful of papyri with
musical annotation and pictures of dramatic productions on
vases do not get us very far. To compare our situation with that
of an opera-lover confined to studying a libretto would be unfair
to the tragedians, for the spoken dialogue of tragedy is far richer
and more significant, demands far more attention from the
audience, than the interludes between songs in opera. But we
should not forget that, particularly in the choruses and the other
lyrics, we have lost what the original cast and audience would
have regarded as a vital part of the production.[4]

II

To try to sum up the work of Aeschylus and Sophocles in a few
paragraphs is to risk pure banality.[5] The attempt must be made,
however, if we are to see Euripides in relation to his great
predecessors. Seven complete tragedies attributed to Aeschylus
survive, including his great trilogy, the *Oresteia* (*Agamemnon*,
Libation-Bearers, *Eumenides*). One of the others, the *Prometheus Bound*, has recently been subject to close critical scrutiny,
and on the basis of this analysis many authoritative judges think
it spurious, but if so, its author shares something of Aeschylus'
grandeur of conception and magnificence of language. As
already explained, Aeschylus tended to use the trilogy form,
which permitted him, as in the *Oresteia* and in the series of

which the *Seven against Thebes* is the third, to trace the history of a family through several generations, showing how the sins of the elders are re-enacted or paid for by their descendants. Inherited guilt, ancestral curses, persecuting Furies, vendetta and religious pollution – concepts such as these permeate the world of Aeschylean tragedy, a world of dark powers and evil crimes, in which humans must pray and hope for justice and retribution from the gods, but may pray in vain, or find that the gods are slow to respond. Austere in its characterization, eloquent yet exotic in its polysyllabic style, dominated by long and complex choral songs, his drama often seems to belong to an older world. Yet this is only one side of a complex artist; Aeschylus, born in the sixth century BC, is also the poet of democratic Athens, deeply concerned with its ideals of reasoned discussion and decision-making. By the end of the fifth century BC he was established as a classic (his plays were re-performed in recognition of this), though he could also be regarded as remote and difficult. Aristophanes' *Frogs*, which dramatizes Dionysus' quest in the underworld for a great poet to bring back to life, presents Aeschylus as a symbol of the good old days, but also as a composer of grandiose and incomprehensible lyrics. In the next century, Aristotle in the *Poetics* uses examples from Sophocles and Euripides far more than from Aeschylus.

To sum up Aeschylus as a poet of archaic grandeur would, however, be quite misleading. He is capable of much lighter and even humorous passages: particularly memorable are the sentimental reminiscences of Orestes' nurse in the *Libation-Bearers*; or the complaints of the herald in the *Agamemnon* about the awful time the common soldiers had at Troy (it is significant that both of these are lower-class types; the great tragic figures are not allowed these more chatty interludes). More important, in his presentation of the doom-laden world of the heroic age he not only shows us horrific events and catastrophe, but also allows his characters to work towards a difficult resolution. In Aeschylean tragedy there is a strong emphasis on the power of the gods, above all the will of Zeus, who oversees human lives and may bring blessings as well as destruction. Not all the dilemmas faced by Aeschylus' characters are insoluble, although the final outcome may be preceded by further hard choices or disasters. The city of Thebes is saved from invasion, but only through the death of Eteocles, its king. Above all in the *Oresteia*, the one trilogy which we can study as a magnificently unified whole, Aeschylus dramatizes the contrast between a darker world of vendetta and savage intrafamilial conflict and a society in which the rule of law has an important place, where argument and persuasion may prove superior to hatred and violence. It is a society which mirrors or idealizes his own: the refugee Argive Orestes, pursued by the monstrous Furies, finds sanctuary in a mythical Athens where Athena presides over an archetypal law-court. In this trilogy, although the suffering and crimes of the past are not forgotten, the final emphasis is on the enlightened justice of the present, and the reconciliation of opposed factions among the gods promises prosperity in the future. Aeschylus as a boy had seen the overthrow of the Athenian tyrants; he had fought at Marathon, and in his later years saw the transformation of his city into a democracy and the centre of an empire. It is no surprise that ideals of political debate and civic harmony are prominent in his work; but in view of the darker side discussed above, it would be facile to label him an optimist, either about human nature or about human society. The tragic power of his dramas is not diminished by his central recognition that something positive may, in the end, emerge after or out of suffering.

Whereas Aeschylus' characters (the *Prometheus* apart) are above all members of a family or of a larger community, Sophocles tends to focus on individuals set apart from their society or at odds with those who care for them: Ajax, Antigone, Electra, Philoctetes, the aged Oedipus. With him, more than with the other two tragedians, it makes sense to speak of tragic heroes and heroines. Again we have only seven plays, selected in late antiquity for school study, and we know that this represents less than a tenth of his output; moreover, those we have are mostly impossible to date. Obviously, generalizations must be surrounded with cautious qualifications, but we can recognize a number of other differences from Aeschylus (to whom he nevertheless owed much). The abandonment of trilogy form has already been mentioned. The role of the chorus is somewhat reduced, though some of the odes which reflect on human achievement and its smallness in relation to the timeless power of the gods have a poetic splendour to match almost anything in Aeschylus. The characters have more depth and subtlety: as an anonymous ancient biographer said of Sophocles, 'He knows how to arrange the action with such a sense of timing that he creates an entire character out of a mere half-line or a single expression.' Partly because he makes more varied use of the third actor, Sophocles constructs scenes which involve more shifts of attention, more realistic and sophisticated interplay between characters, than we can easily find in Aeschylus. Another difference is in the religious atmosphere. Aeschylus regularly brought the gods on stage and allowed them to converse with humans (the Furies, Athena and Apollo in the *Eumenides*, Aphrodite in the lost third play of the *Suppliants* trilogy); Sophocles does so only rarely, and even then the gap between man and god is emphasized: Athena is remote and haughty with Odysseus in the *Ajax*, Heracles commanding and superhuman in the *Philoctetes*; both are probably out of reach, above the human level. In general, the gods do not communicate plainly or unambiguously with mortals: oracles and prophecies offer mysterious and misleading insights, and even Oedipus, the most intelligent of men, can find that his whole life has been lived on completely false assumptions. The limitations of human knowledge allow ample scope for dramatic irony, where the audience understand the double meanings or the deeper truths behind the superficial sense of the words. Central to Sophoclean tragedy is the gap between reality and appearance, understanding and illusion; his characters often discern the truth about their circumstances, or themselves, only when it is too late to avert disaster.

Sophocles has sometimes been seen as a particularly 'pious' writer or thinker. In part this results from a very partial reading of certain selected passages which have been taken to express the poet's own opinions (always a dangerous method); in part it derives from information about his involvement in Athenian religious life, for instance the cult of Asclepius. But within his plays, although the power of the gods is beyond question, and those who doubt that power or reject their oracles are swiftly refuted, it is hard to see any straightforward scheme of divine *justice* at work. Divine action is characterized as enigmatic and obscure. There is an order in the world, as is shown by the fulfilment of oracles; but the pattern is often too elusive for men to grasp. The gods are not indifferent to humanity: they punish Creon in the *Antigone*, they grant a home and honour to Oedipus at the end of his life (*Oedipus at Colonus*). But there are also mysteries which remain unanswered. Why does Antigone have to die? Why did Philoctetes suffer agonies in isolation on Lemnos for nine years? Any open-minded reader of these plays will acknowledge that Sophocles does not give us a simple or uniform account of human life or of mankind's relation to the gods and fate. Had he done so, the plays would probably not have remained so hauntingly powerful over two and a half millennia.

Sophocles is justly regarded as the greatest master of formal structure – no mere mechanical technique, but a vital aspect of his art. The development of each scene, in each play, is beautifully paced; the contrasts of style and mood between successive scenes, or between one scene and the choral song which follows, are achieved with seemingly effortless brilliance. These skills are combined with deep understanding of character in the scenes between Neoptolemus and Philoctetes, with mastery of tension and irony in the advancing quest which will lead Oedipus to self-discovery. On a more minute level of style, the *Oedipus the King* also shows his subtlety of technique in the exchange which culminates in the revelation of the hero's identity (1173–6): here each line is divided between Oedipus and the herdsman whom he is questioning, and as the truth becomes plainer Oedipus' questions become shorter and more faltering, the servant's responses fuller and more desperate. This flexible handling of dialogue form is only one small example of the complete command Sophocles has over his medium. Appalling hatred and unbearable loss are expressed in formal verse of wonderful lucidity and sharpness; only rarely do the eloquent lines dissolve into incoherent cries of pain, as they do when Philoctetes is overcome by his repulsive wound.

III

We turn now to our main subject, the third of the great tragedians. It is far too commonly supposed that Euripides comes 'after' Sophocles, and this can easily lead to a simplifying formula which sees Aeschylus as primitive, Euripides as decadent, and Sophocles as the apex of perfection in between. In fact, although Euripides was clearly younger, he and Sophocles were competing together, often against one another, for most of their lives, and Sophocles died within a year of his rival. Both were very much younger than Aeschylus, though they will certainly have seen some of his later productions. Sophocles in fact competed against Aeschylus with his first production, in 468 BC, and won; Euripides first put on a tetralogy in 455 BC with a less satisfactory result, coming third. We do not know his competitors on that occasion. From that point on Euripides was constantly in the public eye, putting on a total of around ninety plays up to his death in 406 BC (his last plays, including the *Bacchae*, were produced posthumously).

We know very little about his life, and what comes down from antiquity is often unreliable (a great deal seems to be derived from the comic treatment of the dramatist by Aristophanes). There is a long-standing tradition that he was unpopular and unsuccessful in his career. We are told that he was melancholy, thoughtful and severe, that he hated laughter and women, that he lived in a cave looking out to the sea from Salamis, that he had a substantial library. None of this amounts to much more than doubtful anecdote. A more concrete statement, which probably rests on inscriptional evidence, is that he won the first prize four times (once posthumously) in his whole career. This sounds more dramatic than it is, since prizes would be awarded to the tetralogy of plays as a whole: in other words, sixteen out of about ninety plays were winners. Even with this reservation, however, there remains a contrast with the other two tragedians: Aeschylus and Sophocles were each victorious with over half their plays. In the end Euripides is said to have emigrated to Macedonia, where King Archelaus was gathering a circle of poets and intellectuals to give tone to his court. It may be doubted whether he left Athens purely because he felt unappreciated; the hardships of life in a city engaged in a long war which it now looked likely to lose might be a more pragmatic explanation. He died in Macedonia, an event again elaborated in wild anecdotes (he was allegedly torn to pieces, like Actaeon in myth, by a pack of hunting-dogs). We should not attach too much importance to the figure about his victories, for it is clear that he was repeatedly granted a chorus, and that the Athenians enjoyed and were fascinated by his work. The constant parodies and references to his plays in Aristophanes' comedies are not only satirical criticism but a kind of tribute to a playwright whose work he obviously knew intimately and whose significance was beyond question.

We happen to have more plays by Euripides than by the other two tragedians put together: the total is nineteen, but that includes the satyr-play *Cyclops* and also the *Rhesus*, a play widely thought to be a fourth-century BC imitation. This larger figure is partly accidental, the result of the hazards of transmission through the ages, but partly reflects the popularity of Euripides in the educational tradition – his language is easier, his speeches were more suitable for aspiring orators to study, and his plays, with their heady mixture of intellectual and emotional appeal, might be found more immediately accessible.[6] We can also put fairly firm dates to a good many of the plays, because of information which survives in copies of the original inscriptions recording victories in the contests and citing the names of annual magistrates of Athens. Where external evidence for dating is lacking, the date of a play can be determined within limits by 'stylometry', that is, the statistical analysis of the poet's linguistic and metrical habits, using the firmly dated plays as a framework.[7] This means not only that we can say something about Euripides' development as a poet, but also that it is possible to identify, or at least speculate about, passages which touch on or allude to Athenian politics and other contemporary events. Although this approach can frequently be overdone, and the tragedies are not allegories of history, it is a mistake to rule out such allusions on principle.[8]

None of the plays we possess in entirety is from the earliest stage of Euripides' career; the first, the *Alcestis*, was produced in 438 BC, when he was already in his forties. The great majority of surviving plays come from the last three decades of the fifth century BC, the period of the great war between Athens and Sparta, a time in which the cultural and political prominence of Athens was still conspicuous but no longer unchallenged, and by the end of the period increasingly under threat. Euripides did not live to see the defeat of Athens, but several of his later plays suggest growing pessimism about political and military leadership, about civic deliberation, and about the conduct of the victors in wartime. These are not novel themes, in poetry or in life, but they have an added resonance in the light of fifth-century BC history.

The sheer range and variety of Euripides' plays are extraordinary. Perhaps if we had as many of Aeschylus' or Sophocles' plays, they would seem equally difficult to categorize; but it is tempting to see Euripides as particularly innovative and trendsetting. Like Sophocles, he seems to have worked mainly on sequences of self-contained plays, though it looks as if the *Trojan Women* was the third of a trilogy concerning the Trojan war from its origins to its conclusion. Unlike Sophocles, he does not generally take a single heroic figure to form the focus of a play – only the *Medea* easily fits this pattern. There is a strong tendency to divide the play between major characters: thus, in the *Alcestis* the heroine gives way to Heracles, the sufferer to the doer; in the *Hippolytus* Phaedra dominates the first half of the play, Hippolytus the second; in the *Bacchae* the action is polarized, with the mortal Pentheus and the disguised god Dionysus in conflict throughout. Other plays extend this experimentation to the overall structure. Thus in the *Andromache* we begin, as we might expect, with the widow of Hector in difficulties, but as the action advances Andromache is forgotten and other events follow, with other characters taking the limelight. In the *Trojan Women* the continuous presence of Hecabe, the grieving queen of Troy, seems to mark her out as the 'heroine', or at least the principal sufferer, but she is a figure who can achieve nothing. As the play unfolds we are shown a series of scenes which embody the suffering and ruin accompanying the fall of Troy, a sequence which adds up only to further misery. Other plays multiply characters and divide our attention still more: the *Helen* has eight human characters with full speaking parts, the *Orestes* nine, the *Phoenician Women* eleven.

The plays of Euripides, although they still work within the traditional range of myths, do not generally dramatize heroic initiatives and triumphant achievements. His are tragedies of suffering rather than of action (the *Medea* again is a special case, a partial exception). Phaedra, Andromache, Hecabe, the Trojan women, the chorus of mothers in the *Suppliant Women*, the guilt-ravaged Orestes, are all presented as victims, whether of war or other persecution, human folly or divine antagonism. Even when they do attempt to take the initiative, to assert themselves through action, the consequences are rarely presented positively. Phaedra's efforts to preserve her good name bring about Hippolytus' death without achieving her objective; Electra and Orestes in the *Electra* destroy their mother, but with psychologically devastating results for themselves; in the *Orestes*, the young man's matricide makes him an outcast, and his efforts to take revenge on his mother's sister Helen are first frustrated, then turned to near-farce. Even when Euripides is reworking material which had been treated grimly enough by Aeschylus, he regularly gives his own version a new twist. The brutal sacrifice of Iphigenia at Aulis, so that the Greek fleet may sail for Troy, was presented by Aeschylus in an unforgettable choral song as a terrible necessity, an agonizing decision reluctantly taken by Agamemnon, and one which will have momentous consequences. In Euripides' version, Agamemnon and Menelaus chop and change, other members of the expedition seem to have more authority than they have, Iphigenia herself changes her mind, and, most disturbing of all, there is the offstage presence of the army, an uncontrollable mob of soldiers panting for blood. The *Iphigenia at Aulis* is a fast-moving and constantly attention-grabbing play, but one in which the high seriousness of the Aeschylean ode is dissipated, and the tragic sacrifice becomes wasteful self-deception. As A. P. Burnett put it: 'In these plays the poet shows men scaled for comedy trying to live in a world still ruled by the gods of tragedy.'[9]

Some of the ways in which Euripides made old subjects new have already been mentioned. This practice was not simply a perverse desire on his part to alter tradition. Between 480 and 430 BC some 500 tragedies would have been staged; a middle-aged man in his audience might have seen over two hundred.[10] The Athenians, like any audience, enjoyed innovation: indeed, originality and novelty were at a premium in the second half of the fifth century BC, as new ideas and new literary styles made their appearance in Athens. Euripides was in part responding to audience demand (though it is only fair to add that a sizeable portion of his audience would be more conservative, and that Sophocles clearly did not feel the need to innovate so ostentatiously). By the middle stage of Euripides' career Aeschylus looked archaic: in his *Electra*, the younger tragedian unmistakably parodies a recognition-scene from Aeschylus' *Libation-Bearers*, in which the discovery of a lock of hair at Agamemnon's tomb was taken as evidence of Orestes' return. It is interesting to note that the grounds for criticism are improbability, lack of realism and violation of common sense. Aeschylus and his audience had been above such concerns; by Euripides' time it was more natural to apply to tragedy at least some of the standards of everyday life.[11] Nevertheless, the parody is two-edged: it turns out that the Euripidean Electra's scepticism is misguided, and the deduction from the Aeschylean tokens remains valid. The allusion to Aeschylus need not be merely dismissive.

Innovation can also be observed in the composition of his plots. It is natural for us to think of the myths as fixed and organized, as they are in the modern summaries which we find in handbooks; but in fact the fluidity of the legends is surprising, and the tragedians already found variations in the epic and lyric accounts which they inherited. Euripides often uses less familiar versions of myths, or combines stories normally kept apart. Although the loss of so much earlier literature makes firm assertions dangerous, it seems likely that he is modifying the legend in making Medea kill her own children deliberately (in an earlier version it was the Corinthians who took their revenge upon her offspring). In the legends of Heracles it was normally held that the hero's labours were a kind of penance for killing his children in a fit of insanity. Euripides reverses the sequence, making Heracles return home to his family triumphant after his labours are ended – then the crowning horror, madness and slaughter, follows. In the *Helen* he adopts the bizarre version which made Helen a prisoner in Egypt throughout the Trojan war, while Greek and Trojan armies fought for ten years over a phantom. The unexpected becomes the rule, in both plot and characterization: women behave manfully, slaves show nobility and virtue, barbarians express civilized sentiments.

Even when he is closer to the traditional versions, he often introduces new characters or explores the implications of legends with a fresh eye: thus, in the *Orestes* Menelaus, Tyndareus, Hermione and Orestes' friend Pylades all have prominent roles, and the effect is quite different from earlier versions of this myth. Characterization can also be modified: in Aeschylus' *Seven against Thebes*, Eteocles, king of Thebes, is a noble figure, though labouring under a curse; in Euripides' *Phoenician Women*, he becomes a power-crazed tyrant. In the *Electra* of Euripides it is even possible to sympathize with Clytemnestra and Aegisthus, the murderers of Agamemnon. Sharp changes of direction and unexpected shifts of personality are also common: in the *Andromache*, Hermione at first seems a cruel and malicious princess, but later becomes a sympathetic victim. In the *Medea*, the heroine vacillates throughout much of the play: loving mother or merciless avenger, which side of her character is to prevail? Aristotle in his *Poetics* (ch. 15) found fault with these startling reversals of character, singling out the *Iphigenia at Aulis* for criticism: 'the girl who pleads for her life is quite different from the later one', he complains, referring to the scene where Iphigenia, after earlier begging for mercy, resolves to sacrifice herself in the name of Greece. Euripides also plays variations on his own earlier work: our extant *Hippolytus* is a second version, in which the portrayal of Phaedra is made more sympathetic and her character more complex.

In some ways Euripides can be seen as a more self-consciously literary dramatist than his fellow tragedians. It is not accidental that it was he who was said to have a large library. He seems regularly to modify the conventions of his genre and adapt the work of his predecessors, sometimes even drawing attention to the changes he has made. The parody of the Aeschylean recognition-scene has already been cited; similarly, later in the *Electra*, the trapping and killing of Clytemnestra within the hovel in which Electra and her husband have their home is a re-enactment of the killing-scenes within the palace of Agamemnon in Aeschylus' trilogy: humbler setting, unheroic characters, dubious morality all work together. In the *Helen*, the heroine proposes that they contrive an escape by pretending Menelaus is dead and mourning him. Is that the best you can do, asks Menelaus; 'there's a certain old-hat quality in the proposal' (1056). The point is that the trick has been tried often before in tragedy: the character is given the critic's fastidiousness. Aeschylus and Sophocles are also experienced in reshaping and adapting traditional motifs, but Euripides goes far beyond them in playing with conventions and exploiting the spectator's awareness of the dramatic situation. While shocked and moved by the events on stage, we are nevertheless frequently reminded that this is 'only' a play.[12]

As the example from the *Helen* just quoted suggests, Euripides' plays are not devoid of lighter, humorous touches. Indeed, his wide repertoire includes not only starkly 'tragic' plays in the stricter sense, such as the *Medea*, but also dramas which are harder to categorize. The *Alcestis*, with its fairy-tale plot and happy resolution, seems to belong to a kinder and less threatening world than most tragedies. Later plays, notably the *Iphigenia among the Taurians* and especially the *Helen*, have often been classed as tragi-comedies. In both plays, after many misfortunes, the principal characters are reunited in a far-off setting (Helen is held captive in Egypt, Iphigenia in the Crimea), recognize one another after many false steps, and plan a successful escape back to Greece, outwitting their barbarian opponents. Hair-breadth escapes and cliff-hanging moments are common, as when Iphigenia is about to sacrifice her unrecognized brother to the goddess Artemis. We know that similar scenes occurred in lost plays by Euripides: in the *Cresphontes*, a mother is on the point of killing her son with an axe, but the danger is averted, the potential tragedy dissipated.

There is much here which looks back to the *Odyssey*, with its complex plot full of deceptions and recognitions. Moreover, plays of this kind also look forward to later comedy, the types of plot favoured by Menander, Terence and eventually Shakespeare (not to mention Oscar Wilde).[13] These plays are sometimes called escapist, misguidedly: there remains a strong sense of suffering and waste in the past, and they undoubtedly still qualify as tragedies. But they do show the versatile Euripides experimenting with new types of play, and these experiments are accompanied by a lighter and more ironic tone, providing a very different kind of pleasure from the cathartic experience produced by the *Oresteia* or the *Oedipus*. Euripides is plainly interested in variations of tone, juxtaposing scenes of very different emotional intensity. A 'comic' element may be found even in much grimmer plays, but there it is often used to reinforce the seriousness of the rest of the action. The self-pity and bad temper of the downtrodden Electra, for example, provide some humour as we sympathize with her husband, the long-suffering farmer; but their conversation also contributes to our understanding of Electra's tortured psyche. Far more macabre is the delusion of Heracles, who believes he is journeying to Mycenae, arriving there, punishing Eurystheus – when all the time he is in his own home, slaughtering his sons. The effect is intensely powerful: this madness would be funny if it were not so horrible.

In reading a plain text, and still more a translation, of Euripides, it is easy to overlook the formal and musical aspects of the dramas. Here too we can see that he went beyond the earlier conventions of the genre, in ways which were exciting to the audiences, but also often controversial. Greek tragedy is broadly divisible into spoken verse and sung verse: the former is the medium in which the actors converse with one another or with the chorus-leader, the latter is most commonly found in the songs of the chorus. Already in Aeschylus there are plenty of exceptions: actors can sing solo parts or participate in lyric dialogue. In the *Agamemnon*, the prophetess Cassandra voices her god-given insight in emotional song, to the bewilderment of

the chorus; still more wild and agitated are the lyric utterances
of Io, tormented by pain, in the *Prometheus*. But Euripides
seems to go further in giving his actors lyric passages, often
highly emotional and linguistically rich (no doubt these were
also striking in their musical accompaniment). The solo passages, arias or 'monodies', are often virtuoso pieces, and must
have made huge demands on an actor: examples are rarer
in our earlier plays, but there are several in the *Hippolytus*.
From the later plays the most memorable examples include
Creusa's lament for the child she exposed years ago and now
believes dead, the ecstatic suicide-song of Evadne, and (as in
Aeschylus) the prophetic raving of Cassandra (*Ion* 859–922,
Suppliant Women 990ff., *Trojan Women* 308ff.). In the *Orestes*
of 408 BC we find the prize example, a *tour-de-force* narrative
of the attempt on Helen's life, sung by a Phrygian eunuch in a
state of extreme panic, exotically foreign in its linguistic and
rhythmical looseness, and no doubt accompanied by violent
gestures and mime. The brilliant lyric parody in Aristophanes'
Frogs (1309–63), which lifts lines from the *Orestes* and elsewhere, shows how extraordinary audiences found his style in
these arias. Other formal features of the drama would take too
long to illustrate, but the general impression is of sharper and
more prosaic or argumentative dialogue style combined with a
more self-consciously 'poetic', decorative, image-laden, almost
romantic style in lyrics.[14]

Several other aspects of Euripides' work can also be illumi-
nated by Aristophanes' *Frogs*, in which he and Aeschylus compete against one another in the underworld. Although it is unsafe
to use this play to establish Aristophanes' own aesthetic position,
it is first-rate evidence for at least some of the things in Euripidean
drama which made the greatest impression on contemporary
audiences. In the *Frogs*, Euripides is made to boast that

as soon as the play began I had everyone hard at work: no one standing
idle. Women and slaves, master, young woman, aged crone – they all
talked ... It was Democracy in action ... I taught them subtle rules
they could apply; how to turn a phrase neatly. I taught them to see, to
observe, to interpret; to twist, to contrive; to suspect the worst, take

nothing at its face value . . . I wrote about familiar things, things the audience knew about . . . The public have learnt from me how to think, how to run their own households, to ask, 'Why is this so? What do we mean by that?' (*Frogs* 948–79, tr. D. Barrett)

In Euripidean drama others besides kings and heroes play major roles; a large number of plays are named after, and focused on, female characters. Indeed, it has been pointed out that most of Euripides' *thinkers* are women: certainly Creon, Jason and Aegeus are easily outclassed by Medea, and in both the *Trojan Women* and the *Helen* Menelaus is inferior to his quick-witted wife.[15] Lower-class characters are more prominent and more influential: the Nurse in the *Hippolytus* is a perfect example. In the *Electra*, the downtrodden princess is married to a mere farmer, who respects her in her adversity and has not slept with her. The farmer comes from a noble family now impoverished; his low status is contrasted with his honourable behaviour, but the latter still has to be explained by his noble birth. In both the *Hecabe* and the *Trojan Women*, the decent herald Talthybius is sympathetic to the captive women, and shocked at the misdeeds of his social superiors. Mention should also be made of the many messengers in Euripides, several of whom are vividly and sympathetically characterized.

The other point which the passage in the *Frogs* emphasizes is the way these characters talk. Here we come close to one of the central aspects of Euripides' work, his fascination with argument, ideas and rhetoric. In the later fifth century BC professional teachers were instructing young men, in Athens and elsewhere, in the art of rhetoric, which in a small-scale democratic society could justly be seen as the key to political success. Types of argument were collected, methods of refutation categorized. It was possible, one of these experts claimed, 'to make the worse case defeat the better'. Euripides gives his characters the inventiveness and articulacy which these teachers sought to impart. This is particularly clear in the so-called *agon* ('contest'), at least one example of which can be found in most of his plays. The *agon* is a scene in which two (occasionally more) characters express their antagonism in long, highly argumentative and sometimes ingenious speeches: rhetorical skill is combined with energetic emotion. Examples are Jason versus Medea, Theseus versus Hippolytus, Helen versus Hecabe (*Medea*, *Hippolytus*, *Trojan Women* respectively). These scenes sharpen our understanding of the issues, and often challenge us to adjudicate between the parties involved. There is rarely a clear winner, either on the arguments or under the prevailing circumstances in the play: often considerations of power and self-interest matter more than who is in the right. As a result, tragic conflict-scenes rarely lead to a resolution, but tend rather to heighten the antagonism of those involved.[16]

Perhaps all drama suggests larger issues beyond the particular experiences enacted on stage, but Euripides' plays articulate these more abstract and generalizing concerns to an unusual degree. Although the characters on stage are not mere types – what could be called typical about Medea or Heracles? – their situations and dilemmas often suggest larger questions, more general themes and problems inherent in human life and society. When does justice become revenge, even savagery? Can human reason overcome passion? Should right and wrong be invoked in inter-state politics, or is expediency the only realistic criterion? The audience, like the characters, must often have been uncertain which side was in the right, and their attitude would naturally change as the drama unfolded. Many, perhaps most, Athenian theatre-goers would also have served as jurors in the law-courts (Athenian juries were often very large, 500 or more); many would also have voted on proposals in the democratic assembly. They were used to moral and verbal contests, real and fictional, public and private, forensic and literary. Indeed, Athenians were notorious for their addiction to debate: the contemporary historian Thucydides makes a politician call them 'spectators at speeches', a telling paradox.[17] It is no coincidence that this 'agonistic' aspect of Athenian society is so vividly reflected in the dramas. Euripides may have taught the audience to be glib and clever, but he was responding to a development already well advanced.

Perhaps no question has bulked so large in criticism as the nature of Euripides' beliefs, his philosophy. This may seem

strange: why should we expect a dramatist to adopt a philosophic position, still less to maintain it from play to play?
The reason that this issue seems to many people particularly
important is that Euripides frequently introduces abstract ideas
or theoretical arguments, sometimes drawing attention to the
oddity of his character's language or thought. In the *Suppliant
Women* the Athenian Theseus and the Theban herald argue at
length about the relative merits of democratic and monarchic
government. Even if we allow that Theseus, the favourite hero
of Athens, is no ordinary monarch, the anachronism involved
in placing such a debate in the heroic age is obvious. In the
Hippolytus, Phaedra discourses on the power of passion and
how it can overwhelm the mind's good resolutions: her calm-
ness, and the abstract tone of her words, seem strange after her
earlier frenzy. More striking still are the many passages in which
characters question the nature, or the very existence, of the
Olympian gods. In the *Trojan Women*, Hecabe, in need of
inspiration in the *agon*, prays as follows:

O you who support the earth and have your seat upon the earth,
whoever you are, difficult to fathom and to understand, Zeus, whether
inflexible law of nature or man's mind, I call upon you. Following your
path soundlessly you direct the affairs of men in accord with justice.

  (884–8, tr. S. Barlow)

These lines echo both traditional prayer-formulas and contemporary science; they involve contradictory conceptions of the
supreme deity; they even hint at the theory that gods are merely
externalizations of human impulses. Little wonder that Menelaus remarks in response, 'What's this? How strange and new
these prayers to the gods!'

In passages of this kind Euripides plainly shows his familiarity
with the philosophic or metaphysical teachings of a number of
thinkers: Anaxagoras, Protagoras, Gorgias and other figures
known to us particularly through the writings of Plato and
Aristotle. Influence from philosophy or abstract prose has
occasionally been detected in Aeschylus and Sophocles, but any
such cases in their work are rare and unobtrusive; with Euripides

we are dealing with something new. This introduction of modern ideas coheres with his general tendency to make the characters of myth less remote and majestic, more like ordinary mortals with human weaknesses. Unsettling and bizarre these passages may seem, but they are clearly meant (as in the plays of Ibsen and Shaw) to surprise and stimulate: it would be absurd to suppose that Euripides did not realize what he was doing, or that he was incapable of keeping his intellectual interests out of his tragedies.[18]

Ancient anecdote claimed that Protagoras, an agnostic thinker, gave readings from his work in Euripides' house, and that Socrates helped him write his plays. Although these stories are rightly now recognized as fictions, the frequency with which Euripides introduces philosophic or religious reflections still needs explanation. An influential tradition of criticism has maintained that Euripides was a disciple of one or other of these thinkers, and that his dramas represent a concerted endeavour to open his countrymen's eyes to the moral defects of men and gods as represented in the traditional myths. In the earlier part of the fifth century BC, the lyric poet Pindar had questioned a myth which told of divine cannibalism, and in the fourth century BC Plato was to censor epic and tragedy in the name of morality. The myths were also criticized by Euripides' contemporaries on grounds of rationality and probability: how could sensible people take seriously stories of three-headed hounds of Hades, or other monstrous creatures? There is, then, no reason to doubt that Euripides could have seen reasons to be sceptical about some of the myths: he makes Helen doubt whether she was really born from a swan's egg, and Iphigenia question whether any deity could conceivably demand human sacrifice (*Helen* 18, 259; *Iphigenia among the Taurians* 380–91).

It is much less plausible to suppose that he was urging total scepticism about the gods or the supernatural, and proposing some alternative philosophic or humanist view in their place. It is difficult for the modern student to appreciate how different Greek religious thought and practice were from the Judaeo-Christian tradition.[19] There was no creed, no sacred books, no central priestly establishment. The city performed its sacrifices and paid honour to the gods, as had always been done; sometimes new gods were admitted to the pantheon; but cult was not the same as myth, and it was well known that myths contradicted one another and that poets made up many stories – many lies, as the Athenian Solon once said. To express doubts about one particular myth did not shake the foundations of religion. Outright atheism was rare and freakish. The more open-minded attitude of the great traveller Herodotus may have been more usual: he declared that all men were equally knowledgeable about the divine.[20]

Certainly there are serious difficulties in treating Euripides as an unbeliever on the evidence of his plays. This is not simply because, alongside the more questioning attitudes in the passages quoted, we find many speakers expressing profound faith and devotion, and choral odes which invoke the Olympians in magnificent poetry: one could always argue (though with some circularity) that these characters possessed only partial or erroneous insights into religion. More important is the fact that without the existence of the gods the plays simply do not work. How is Medea to escape if the sun-god, her grandfather, does not send his chariot to rescue her? How will Theseus' curse destroy his son if Poseidon is a mere fiction? How will the plot of the *Alcestis* even begin to work unless death is something more than natural, unless there is a personified being against whom Heracles can do battle? A full discussion would also have to consider the numerous scenes in which gods appear at the end of plays to bring events under control: rationalizing interpretations in such cases truncate the dramas.

But if Euripides the 'anticlerical' atheist cannot stand, neither can he simply be forced into the straitjacket of 'traditional' piety, even if that piety is defined in terms flexible and sophisticated enough to include Aeschylus and Sophocles. There remains overwhelming evidence that Euripides, in this as in other respects, was an innovator: just as he introduces new and often unfamiliar characters into traditional myths, or views familiar tragic situations from unexpected angles, so he combines traditional mythical and theatrical conventions about the gods with disturbing new conceptions and challenging ideas.

Sometimes the contradictions become acute and paradoxical, as in a notoriously baffling passage of the *Heracles*. In this play Heracles, son of Zeus by the mortal woman Alcmene, has been brought to his knees by the goddess Hera, who persecutes him because she resents Zeus' adulteries. Theseus, befriending Heracles and seeking to comfort him, refers at one point to the immorality of the gods, whereupon Heracles bursts into a passionate rejection of this concept:

I do not believe that the gods indulge themselves in illicit love or bind each other with chains. I have never thought such things worthy of belief and I never will; nor that one god treats another as his slave. A god, if he is truly a god, has no need of anything; these are the wicked tales of poets. (*Heracles* 1340–46)

This outburst comes near to rejecting the very premises that underlie the play and Heracles' own experiences within it. Is Euripides showing us something about Heracles' psychology? Insisting, in Plato's manner, on the moral inadequacy of the myths? Alluding to the poetic and fictional quality of his own play? Or all of these at once, and more? The passage, and the issues it raises, are likely to remain controversial.[21]

Although all such labels are bound to oversimplify a many-sided artist like Euripides, we may find more valuable than 'atheist' the term proposed by E. R. Dodds, one of the most gifted interpreters of Greek literature in the twentieth century, who dubbed Euripides 'the irrationalist'.[22] By this Dodds meant that Euripides was interested in and impressed by the achievements of human reason, not least in the fields of rhetorical argument and philosophic theory, but in the end felt that they were inadequate both as explanatory tools and as instruments to enable mankind to deal with the world. Reason versus passion, order versus chaos, persuasion versus violence – these antitheses are present in all Greek tragedy, but Euripides seems more pessimistic about the limits of man's capacity to control either himself or society.[23] The demoralizing and brutalizing effects of a prolonged war surely play a part in the development of his outlook: the *Suppliant Women, Hecabe* and *Trojan Women*, or a decade later the *Phoenician Women* and the *Iphigenia at Aulis*, all dramatize the suffering and callousness which war makes possible or inevitable. Even *Helen*, for all its playful irony and lightness of touch, implies a bleak and pessimistic view of human action: the Trojan war, far from being a glorious achievement, was fought for a phantom; and although Menelaus and Helen are finally reunited, that partial success cannot compensate for the countless lives thrown away on the plains of Troy.

On this reading, Euripides does not assert the independence of man from divine authority; he is neither an agnostic nor a humanist. Rather, he acknowledges that there are forces in the world which mankind cannot understand or control. They may sometimes be described in the language of traditional religion, or referred to by the names and titles of the Olympians, though even then he often suggests some new dimension: 'She's no goddess, then, the Cyprian, but something greater', cries the Nurse when she learns of Phaedra's desire (*Hippolytus* 359–60). At other times he will make his characters speak of Nature, or Necessity, or Chance; as one of them asks in the *Hecabe*, 'O Zeus, what am I to say? Do you watch over men or are we fools, blind fools to believe this, and is it chance that oversees all man's endeavours?' (488–91). Or again, a speaker may throw out the suggestion that 'it is all in the mind': 'when you saw him your mind *became* the goddess. All the indiscretions of mortals pass for Aphrodite . . .' (*Trojan Women* 988–9). The supernatural, however it is defined, embraces those things which are beyond human grasp. The author of the following speech, again from the *Hippolytus*, may not have been a conventional worshipper, but he understood how to communicate religious longing.

It's nothing but pain, this life of ours; we're born to suffer and there's no end to it. If anything more precious than life does exist, it's wrapped in darkness, hidden behind clouds. We're fools in love – it's plain enough – clinging to this glitter here on earth because we don't know any other life and haven't seen what lies below. (*Hippolytus* 189–96)

No play of Euripides raises these questions more acutely than the *Bacchae*, almost his last and surely his greatest tragedy. It is also his most enigmatic work: it has been read as evidence of a change of heart, a conversion of the ageing playwright to the truths of religion, while others have preferred to see it as a denunciation of ecstatic cult, expressing the tragedian's deep distrust of irrational action.[24] It would be quite impossible to do justice to the play here; what can be done is to sketch a few of the ways in which, for all its special qualities, it is quintessentially Euripidean.

The *Bacchae* describes the coming of Dionysus, still a new god in the mythical world of the play, to his native city of Thebes, accompanied by a chorus of loyal bacchants. The god seeks recognition in his own land, but comes in disguise, as gods often do, to test the citizens; even the chorus suppose him to be a human priest. The youthful king Pentheus, ignoring good advice from older heads, proceeds to defy the god, little knowing the power he is confronting. At first Dionysus plays the part of an innocent captive in Pentheus' power, answering his questions and leading him on; but he soon escapes from captivity and in a series of scenes gradually gains an ascendancy over the king. In the end Pentheus is completely in his power (magic? hypnosis? or something in Pentheus' own heart that answers the Dionysiac summons?). The god, still not revealing his identity, leads him to the mountains where the Theban women are running wild in bacchic frenzy. A messenger reports the horrifying outcome: Pentheus is dead, literally torn to pieces by the women, with his own mother Agave in the lead; in her madness she believes she has slain a wild beast. The Bacchic chorus rejoice that their divine master has been vindicated; but even they feel some pity and distress when Pentheus' mother brings on the head of her son and is slowly coaxed back to sanity and misery by her father Cadmus. The whole royal house is to be punished for their unbelief; Dionysus, appearing finally without disguise, *ex machina*, drives Cadmus and Agave into exile, and his pitiless speech contrasts with the tender parting of father and daughter. The cult of Dionysus will now be celebrated in Thebes, but its inauguration has been achieved through the slaughter of the opposing king.

The theme is traditional. Tragedy may have originally focused on Dionysiac subjects; in any case, we know that Aeschylus wrote a trilogy on how the god overcame his early opponents, which Euripides seems to have imitated. In this play Euripides to some extent abandons many of the stylistic and rhetorical features which made his late work so striking: there is no *agon*, for example, and the choral odes are more directly relevant to the play as a whole. Other aspects discussed above are well represented, however: the touches of sophistic argumentation (especially in the pompous lecture by the prophet Tiresias, who claims to know the 'true' nature of Dionysus); the brilliantly vivid and often gruesome narrative of the messenger; the macabre black humour of the scene in which Dionysus clothes Pentheus in female Bacchic dress, and in which the king preens himself on his new outfit, unaware that he is being attired as a ritual victim.

Furthermore, the overall treatment of the theme is very different from anything we can imagine from Aeschylus' hand. The play could have been a straightforward tale of hubris punished, an evil man struck down by a proud but just god. What is different in the *Bacchae* is the presentation of Pentheus as a weak and unstable young man, psychologically more interesting than the standard tyrant-figure. As already mentioned, the scenes between him and Dionysus are hard to interpret: on the one hand the god is playing with the foolish king like a cat with a mouse, but on the other Pentheus seems eager to fall in with Dionysus' suggestions, pruriently keen to visit the maenads, perhaps even sexually attracted by the almost feminine beauty of the stranger. Euripides, as we have seen, is interested not only in the decisions and actions of his characters, but also in their inner psychology. As for the god himself, unusually present on stage throughout, he too is hard to evaluate. The chorus sing beautifully of the delights of Dionysiac worship: 'O blessed he who in happiness knowing the rituals of the gods makes holy his way of life and mingles his spirit with the sacred band, in the mountains serving Bacchus with reverent purifications' (73–7). We recognize here the playwright's understanding of religious devotion, just as we do in the lines in which Hippolytus prays to his beloved Artemis (73–87), or in the lines of choral ecstasy from the lost *Cretans* (fragment 472). But the joy of union with nature is the inverse side of the madness that leads a mother to slay her own son – this, too, at Dionysus' bidding. Dionysus values honour from mankind, and relishes his revenge: is this what a god is truly like? The broken Cadmus entreats the god for mercy at the end of the play, in terms which echo the words of earlier plays.[25]

CADMUS:

Dionysus, we beseech you. We have done wrong!

DIONYSUS:

You were late to understand us. When you should have, you did not know us.

CADMUS:

This we have come to recognize; but your reprisals are too severe!

DIONYSUS:

Yes, because I am a god, and you insulted me.

CADMUS:

Gods should not resemble men in their anger!

DIONYSUS:

Long ago Zeus my father approved these things.

(1344–9, tr. G. S. Kirk)

It is not the business of a tragedian to solve the riddles of the universe, but to dramatize human experience in such a way as to arouse his audience's compassion and extend their imaginative understanding. This, and much else, is what Euripides offers to spectator and reader alike.

NOTES

1. On the festivals and theatrical conditions see above all A. W. Pickard-Cambridge, *The Dramatic Festivals of Athens* (2nd edn Oxford 1968); more briefly E. Simon, *The Ancient Theatre* (Eng. tr. London and New York 1982), pp. 1–33; O. Taplin, *Greek Tragedy in Action* (London 1978), ch. 2. A readable account of the theatrical context is by R. Rehm, *Greek Tragic Theatre* (London 1992).

2. For an excellent discussion of the types of myths favoured, see B. M. W. Knox, *Word and Action: Essays on the Ancient Theater* (Baltimore 1979), ch. 1.

3. O. Taplin, *The Stagecraft of Aeschylus* (Oxford 1977); D. Bain, *Actors and Audience* (Oxford 1977); D. Mastronarde, *Contact and Discontinuity* (Berkeley 1979); M. R. Halleran, *Stagecraft in Euripides* (London and Sydney 1985); R. Rehm, op. cit.

4. See M. L. West, *Ancient Greek Music* (Oxford 1992). On dance see A. W. Pickard-Cambridge, op. cit., ch. 5.

5. For fuller essays see R. P. Winnington-Ingram and P. E. Easterling in *The Cambridge History of Classical Literature*, vol. 1, ed. P. E. Easterling and B. M. W. Knox (Cambridge 1985); also the pamphlets by S. Ireland and R. Buxton in the *Greece and Rome New Surveys* series (Oxford).

6. Revivals of older tragedies became a regular feature at the festivals from 386 BC onwards: see A. W. Pickard-Cambridge, op. cit., pp. 99–100. Euripides' plays were frequently chosen. For the possibility of performances outside Athens already in the fifth century BC, see P. E. Easterling, *Illinois Classical Studies* 19 (1994), pp. 1–8.

7. This work is highly technical, but the essentials can be gleaned from A. M. Dale's introduction to her commentary on the *Helen* (Oxford 1967), pp. xxiv–xxviii.

8. See further G. Zuntz, *The Political Plays of Euripides* (Manchester 1955), chs. 1–3, esp. pp. 78–81. Some more recent approaches, which all seek in different ways to put tragedy in an Athenian context, can be found in the collection *Nothing to do with Dionysos?*, ed. J. Winkler and F. Zeitlin (Princeton 1990), and in *Greek Tragedy and the Historian*, ed. C. B. R. Pelling (Oxford 1997).

9. From the jacket blurb of *Catastrophe Survived* (Oxford 1977).

10. I draw here on R. P. Winnington-Ingram, 'Euripides, *poietes sophos* [intellectual poet]', *Arethusa* 2 (1969), pp. 127–42.

11. In Aristophanes' *Clouds*, originally produced in 423 BC, the rebellious Pheidippides is asked by his father to sing a passage of Aeschylus, and scoffs at the idea, dismissing the older poet as a bombastic and incoherent ranter. When asked to produce a modern alternative, he shocks his father by reciting a passage from Euripides' *Aeolus* defending the merits of incest!

12. This aspect of Euripides has been emphasized in recent years, sometimes to excess: see e.g. S. Goldhill, *Reading Greek Tragedy* (Cambridge 1986), esp. ch. 10.

13. Knox, *Word and Action*, pp. 250–74 ('Euripidean comedy').

14. Good summary, with further references, in C. Collard, *Euripides (Greece and Rome New Surveys* 14, Oxford 1981), pp. 20–29.

15. The reference to Euripides' 'thinkers' comes from E. R. Dodds' essay 'Euripides the Irrationalist', *Classical Review* 43 (1929), pp. 87–104, reprinted in his collection *The Ancient Concept of Progress and Other Essays* (Oxford 1973), pp. 78–91. On women in Athenian literature and society see further J. Gould, 'Law, custom and myth; aspects of the social position of women in classical Athens', *Journal of Hellenic Studies* 100 (1980), pp. 38–59; S. Goldhill, op. cit., ch. 5; and the essays in A. Powell (ed.), *Euripides, Women and Sexuality* (London 1990).

16. For a very helpful essay on this side of Euripides, see C. Collard in I. McAuslan and P. Walcot (eds.), *Greek Tragedy* (*Greece and Rome Studies* 2, Oxford 1993), pp. 153–66; also M. Lloyd, *The Agon in Euripides* (Oxford 1992).

17. Thucydides iii, 38, 4. It is particularly striking that the word translated as 'spectator' is the regular term for a member of the theatrical audience.

18. A. N. Michelini, *Euripides and the Tragic Tradition* (Madison, Wisconsin and London 1987), part 1, gives a well-documented history of the debate over Euripides' views. A seminal work, still enjoyable and stimulating, is G. Murray's short book *Euripides and his Age* (London 1913).

19. See the useful collection of essays edited by P. E. Easterling and J. V. Muir, *Greek Religion and Society* (Cambridge 1985), esp. J. Gould's contribution, 'On Making Sense of Greek Religion'.

20. Herodotus ii, 3, 2. On this subject in general, J. Mikalson, *Athenian Popular Religion* (Chapel Hill 1983) and *Honor thy Gods* (Chapel Hill and London 1991) are valuable collections of material, but tend to draw too firm a line between what happens in life and what appears in literature.

21. T. C. W. Stinton, *PCPS* n.s. 22 (1976), pp. 60–89, reprinted in *Collected Papers on Greek Tragedy* (Oxford 1990), pp. 236–64; H. Yunis, *A New Creed: Fundamental Religious Beliefs in the Athenian Polis and Euripidean Drama* (Göttingen 1988), esp. pp. 155–71.

22. E. R. Dodds, op. cit.

23. Classic (over-)statement in K. Reinhardt, 'Die Sinneskreise bei Euripides' in *Tradition und Geist* (Göttingen 1960), also available in a French translation (*Éschyle; Euripide*, Paris 1972).

24. E. R. Dodds' commentary on the Greek text of this play (2nd edn 1960) remains essential for serious study; see also R. P. Winnington-Ingram, *Euripides and Dionysus* (Cambridge 1948).

25. See esp. *Hippolytus* 114–20.

Note on the Text

We have no manuscripts in Euripides' hand, or going back anywhere near his own time. If we had, they would be difficult to decipher, and would lack many aids which the modern reader takes for granted: stage directions, punctuation, clear indications of change of speaker, regular divisions between lines and even between words. In fact, although some parts of his plays, mostly short extracts, survive in papyri from the earliest centuries AD, our complete manuscripts of the plays translated in this volume go back no further than the tenth century. Moreover, the textual evidence for the various plays differs greatly in quantity. Three plays were especially popular in later antiquity, namely the *Hecabe*, the *Phoenician Women* and the *Orestes* (the so-called 'Byzantine triad'). These survive in more than 200 manuscripts. Others, including *The Children of Heracles*, are represented in only one manuscript and its derivatives. The *Alcestis*, the *Medea* and the *Hippolytus* fall in between, each surviving in a number of manuscripts of varying date. In a different category come the many quotations from Euripides in other classical authors, which sometimes preserve different readings from those in the direct tradition of Euripidean manuscripts.

This situation is not unusual in the history of classical authors. No ancient dramatist's work survives in his own hand: in all cases we are dealing with a text transmitted by one route or several, and copied many times over. In an age which knew nothing of the printing-press, far less the Xerox machine, all copying had to be done by hand, every copy in a sense a new version. The opportunities for corruption of the text – that is, the introduction of error – were numerous. The reasons for such corruption include simple miscopying or misunderstanding by the scribe, omission or addition of passages by actors in later productions, accidental inclusion of marginal notes or quotations from other plays, and very occasionally bowdlerization of 'unsuitable' passages. Problems of this kind were already recognized in antiquity: efforts were made to stabilize the texts of the tragedians in fourth-century BC Athens, and the ancient commentaries or 'scholia' to some of Euripides' plays make frequent comments on textual matters, for instance remarking that a line is 'not to be found' in some of their early manuscripts, now lost to us. In the same way, when a modern scholar produces an edition of a Euripidean play, there are many places where he or she must decide between different versions given in different manuscripts. Sometimes the choice will be easy: one version may be unmetrical, ungrammatical or meaningless. But often the decision may be more difficult, and in many cases it is clear that no manuscript preserves the lines in question in the correct form. Hence, the editor must either reconstruct Euripides' authentic text by 'conjecture', or indicate that the passage is insolubly corrupt, a conclusion normally signalled by printing daggers ('obeli') on either side of the perplexing passage.

A translator is in a slightly more fortunate position than an editor. The editor must make a decision on what to print at every point, and uncertainty may prevail as to the exact wording even when the overall sense is fairly clear. In this translation James Diggle's excellent Oxford Classical Text has normally been followed: when he has marked a word or phrase as probably or certainly corrupt, we have usually adopted a conjectural reading, whether made by him or by a previous editor, even though we often agree that there can be no certainty that this is what Euripides actually wrote. In cases where the corruption is more extensive, we have tried to give a probable idea of the train of thought. These problems arise particularly in choral and other lyric passages, where the language is less close to everyday speech, and where unusual metre and dialect often misled copyists.

Many of the smaller problems involving variations of words or uncertainty over phrasing will be unlikely to cause difficulties to readers of this translation. More noticeable are the occasional places where it seems that something has dropped out of the text; usually this can be explained by the accidents of miscopying or by damage to some of the manuscripts from which our texts descend. The problem is not acute in these plays, but there are several gaps in our text of *The Children of Heracles*, and one important possible case must be suspected at the end of the play, where the chorus's rapid assent to Alcmene's proposal seems unnatural, and brings events to a surprisingly sudden conclusion. In the notes to each play problems of this kind are usually indicated.

The other main problem which affects criticism of Euripides is that of interpolation. This is the term used to describe the inclusion of alien material in the original text, expanding and elaborating on the author's words. Sometimes the new material betrays itself by its very unsuitability to the context, and we may suppose that it has been included by accident (for instance, parallels from other plays were sometimes copied out in the margin, then found their way into the text in subsequent copies). Sometimes lines may be present in one manuscript but omitted in others: if they seem superfluous in themselves, they may well be a later addition. Sometimes a speech may seem unnecessarily wordy, and we may suspect that it has been expanded without feeling certain; here textual criticism merges with literary judgement. It has often been suggested that some passages in the plays have been 'padded out' by actors seeking to improve their parts: although this tendency has probably been exaggerated, it would be a mistake to rule it out altogether. One speech which has fallen under suspicion on these grounds is Medea's famous soliloquy as she wavers over the killing of her children (*Medea* 1019–80: the boldest critics would excise all of 1056–80). On the whole we agree with Diggle's judgements in these four plays, and have omitted from the translation a fair number of short passages which he considers interpolated. In the case of Medea's soliloquy, however, expert authorities have been unable to reach agreement, and in view of the central importance of the scene, we have included the whole of the speech despite the doubts which may be reasonably felt as to the authenticity of parts.

FURTHER READING

W. S. Barrett, *Euripides: Hippolytus* (Oxford 1964), pp. 45–84
(a detailed account, requiring some knowledge of Greek and
technical terms).

C. Collard, *Euripides, Greece and Rome New Surveys* 14
(Oxford 1981), p. 3 (a good one-page summary with
bibliography).

L. D. Reynolds and N. G. Wilson, *Scribes and Scholars: A Guide
to the Transmission of Greek and Latin Literature* (3rd edn,
Oxford 1991).

M. L. West, *Textual Criticism and Editorial Technique* (Stutt-
gart 1973), part I.

Chronological Table

As explained in the Introduction, not all of the plays of Euripides (and fewer still of Sophocles) can be firmly dated. This table shows all of the extant Greek tragedies for which we have fairly certain dates, and also lists most of Aristophanes' surviving comedies and some major historical events to put them in context. Conjectural dates are given with question-marks, and are usually fixed by analysis of metrical technique: they may well be three or four years out either way.

Year BC

c. 535–2 Thespis competes in
first tragic competition

    490 Darius' invasion of
       Greece
    480–79 Xerxes' invasion

472 Aeschylus *Persians*
468 Sophocles' first victory,
on his first attempt
467 Aesch. *Laius, Oedipus,
Seven against Thebes,
Sphinx*
463? Aesch. *Suppliants,
Aigyptioi, Danaids,
Amymone*

    c. 462 Radical democracy
      established at Athens

458 Aesch. *Agamemnon,
Libation-Bearers,
Eumenides, Proteus*

456 Death of Aeschylus
455 Euripides' first
   competition; third prize
438 Eur. *Alcestis*
431 Eur. *Medea*

431 War begins between
   Athens and Sparta
430 Great plague at Athens

c. 430? Eur. *The Children of
   Heracles*

429 Death of Pericles

428 Eur. *Hippolytus*
   (surviving version)

427 Aristophanes' first play
   (now lost)
425? Eur. *Andromache*

425 Arist. *Acharnians*
424 Arist. *Knights*

pre-423? Eur. *Hecabe*
423? Eur. *Suppliant Women*

423 Arist. *Clouds* (original
   version)
422 Arist. *Wasps*
421 Arist. *Peace* Death of
   Cleon; peace of Nicias

c. 417 Eur. *Heracles, Electra*

416 Athenian massacre on
   Melos

415 Eur. Trojan trilogy,
   including *Trojan Women*

414 Arist. *Birds*
413 Athenian expedition to
   Sicily ends in disaster

pre-412? Eur. *Ion, Iphigenia
   among the Taurians*
412 Eur. *Helen*
412? Eur. *Cyclops*
   (satyr-play)

411 Arist. *Lysistrata, Women
   at the Thesmophoria*
   Oligarchic revolution in
   Athens

c. 409? Eur. *Phoenician Women*

409 Soph. *Philoctetes*

408 Eur. *Orestes*

406–5 Death of Euripides in Macedonia; death of Sophocles

after 406 Eur. *Iphigenia at Aulis, Bacchae* (posthumously produced)

405 Arist. *Frogs*

404 End of war, with Athens defeated

401 Soph. *Oedipus at Colonus* (posthumously produced)

399 Execution of Socrates

Translator's Note

A new translation of an author as great as Euripides needs little justification, perhaps, but it may be useful to point out certain respects in which this translation differs from those of Philip Vellacott, which Penguin published in four volumes between 1953 and 1972. In these, for the most part, the translation was deliberately broken up into verse-like lines, creating a certain stateliness that reflected the dignity of the original but often resulted in the kind of English that could only exist on the printed page. My aim has been to produce a version that conforms far more to how people speak, and for this the medium of continuous prose was essential.

A further consequence of the earlier approach is that all the characters speak the same form of stylized English, whether they are princes or slaves. By adopting continuous prose I have tried to achieve a tone that is more relaxed, less stylized and less close to the Greek word-order, while remaining true to the original. There is a wider range of tones and moods in recognition of the fact that, for all the uniformity of the Greek, not every character maintains a wholly dignified tone. Some speak in a more colloquial and fast-moving style, even verging on the humorous (e.g. the Nurse in the *Hippolytus*), others require a more dignified style because they are arrogant or demented or divine.

In the lyric passages, especially the choral odes, I have aimed at a certain archaic formality of language in recognition of their emotional or religious content, but the overriding concern has been to let the freshness and beauty of the poetry come through to the reader as directly as possible. These elements of song in

Euripides' work were much admired by his contemporaries and by later generations and here, if anywhere, the translator's responsibility weighs particularly heavily.

Euripides is intensely interested in human nature in all its different forms and a modern translation must therefore try to take some account of the richness of his character portrayal and psychological insight. It is this belief that underpins my attempt throughout these plays to find and express variety of tone; I have tried to think of the words as being spoken by real persons rather than literary creations, remembering the remark attributed to Sophocles that, whereas in his plays he showed men as they should be, Euripides drew them as they are.

No dramatist of any age can be content to live solely within the confines of the printed page, and it is gratifying that my translations of two plays, *Trojan Women* and the *Bacchae*, have been used for performances on the London stage. I hope that other plays in these versions may catch the eye of modern producers and that the reader who comes fresh to Euripides in this volume may feel that his voice deserves to be heard more in the modern theatre.

My collaborator, Dr Richard Rutherford, and I are both grateful for advice and encouragement from Professor Pat Easterling, and particularly for her careful scrutiny of the General Introduction. At a late stage Dr Oliver Taplin also read this section and suggested a number of improvements. There is a debt of some thirty years' standing I should like to record here and that is to the man who introduced me to Euripides at school, Mr Robert Grassom: I hope he approves of my efforts. My thanks go also to Robin Waterfield, whose suggestion it was that I attempt this translation, and to my wife, Philippa, for her patience and support. Finally, I would like to thank Dr Rutherford for his contribution of introductory essay and notes, and for his thoughtful and prompt checking of my versions: his scholarly eye rescued me several times from 'translationese', and any remaining imperfections should be laid firmly at my door.

I would like to dedicate this book to Philippa, Lorna and Andrew.

ALCESTIS

Preface to *Alcestis*

The *Alcestis* is the first surviving play by Euripides, but by this stage he was an experienced dramatist, seventeen years from his first competition. The story it treats – the self-sacrifice of Alcestis to save her husband, and her rescue from death by Heracles – is not one of the central heroic myths of Greek tradition: in its domestic scope no less than its miraculous ending, it is tangibly different from the plays which dramatize the grim events of the Trojan or Theban wars. There is a flavour of 'fairy-tale' or naive story-telling about it, especially in the personification of Death as a monstrous physical abductor, but also in the concept of Admetus being allowed to live if he can find a substitute. Parallels of various kinds have been found in other cultures, and it seems likely that Euripides has taken a simpler and more magical myth, intensified the emotional content and given the characters greater dignity. It is also possible that he was innovating in bringing Heracles into the tale. If so, the effect is to connect the story with the larger world of heroic legend, and to give an almost timeless fable a more precise chronological niche in relation to the labours of Heracles.

We happen to know, from a summary which precedes the play in our manuscripts, that the *Alcestis* was produced as the fourth of a tetralogy of plays, occupying the slot normally filled by the single 'satyr-play', a shorter, more frivolous and boisterous type of drama which featured the wild and bawdy antics of Silenus, drunken companion of Dionysus, and of his company of goat-footed satyrs. The replacement of the satyr-play by a tragedy is exceptional, and we have no way of knowing what motivated this change of normal practice. The 'pro-satyric' role of the *Alcestis* has sometimes been invoked to explain some of its curious features, but the only convincing point concerns the lively scene in which the gluttonous Heracles is seen drunk and inappropriately cheerful, a common motif in lighter genres. Even here, however, the humour is kept within bounds: when Heracles learns the actual situation he sobers up at once, and his thoughts turn to how he can aid his friend in his hour of need.

The sequence of events is handled with characteristically Euripidean flair. The situation is already well advanced, with Admetus and Alcestis married for some time, and with children; the play opens on the day on which it has been determined that Alcestis must die. The prologue presents a clash between light and dark, the kind Apollo, friend of Admetus, confronting the implacable and hideous figure of Death. On the human plane, the first part of the play movingly portrays, in both song and dialogue, the self-sacrifice of Alcestis: through their reactions we see what she means to the Maidservant, to Admetus, to the household. Finally the moment comes: she is dead. Admetus must now try to come to terms with his loss.

At this point Heracles appears on the scene. The audience has been expecting this, since Apollo mentioned his approach in the prologue; but it comes as a surprise and an unwelcome development to Admetus, who feels he must conceal his grief and allow Heracles the hospitality that he naturally expects of a friend. The simple drama of Alcestis' sacrifice and its aftermath thus becomes complicated by delicate questions of tact and morality. Much more serious moral questions are brought into the open, and explored in vicious argument, in the scene which follows, between Admetus and his father Pheres. This is clearly a Euripidean innovation: he has taken the assumptions of the story (that others refused to die for Admetus, then Alcestis agreed), and subjected them to realistic scrutiny: what would the consequences be for the surviving members of the house-hold? His answer is dramatically effective: bitter resentment on Admetus' part, scorn and rejection of his complaints by his father. But it is typical of a tragic debate of this kind that there is no clear winner: it is inevitable that the audience must ask further questions about Admetus' character, and about his acceptance of Alcestis' sacrifice. The debate temporarily shifts the emphasis of the play from plangent emotions to animated and articulate argument.

We have already considered the lively scene between the boozy Heracles and the outraged servant, which serves to inform Heracles of his host's loss. While he sets out to remedy that loss, the procession of mourners returns to the house, and both Admetus and the chorus are overwhelmed by grief. Now at last it is clear to the bereaved king how fruitless is the life which Alcestis has won for him: 'This truth has just come home to me' (940). The chorus, sharing his grief, sing of necessity and death: but, as they end their ode, Heracles appears on the scene with a veiled figure. As he gently reproaches Admetus for failing to be open with him, and goes on to explain about his business elsewhere, the audience are conscious that this figure must be Alcestis; but Heracles does not simply announce this. Instead he plays a game with Admetus, delaying the revelation of the joyous truth. Greek audiences obviously relished scenes of this kind: there are close parallels in the *Odyssey* as well as in other tragedies. The conclusion is never in doubt, but the way in which Admetus has first to go back on his resolve and allow another woman into the house is curious and may seem disturbing. Condemnation of Admetus as a weak or cowardly character would be misguided, but it does seem that the playwright has introduced complexities and nuances which were surely alien to the story as he found it.

The *Alcestis* is a play much concerned with the themes of harmony and hospitality within the house. Alcestis is devoted to her husband and her children, but her supreme act of devotion must be to leave them. In return for her self-sacrifice she asks that he will never remarry (remarriage in the event of a wife's early death would seem normal to an Athenian audience), and he pledges eternal devotion. In contrast stands the bitter invective which Admetus directs at his father, who replies in the same terms. Pheres will not be welcome at the funeral; Admetus goes so far as to reject and sever relations with both his parents (esp. 734ff.). The extraordinary situation has drawn Admetus closer to his wife and set him at odds with his surviving family; moreover, his future will be a life of mourning, almost a living death. As for the other theme, Admetus' hospitality to Apollo won him a gift which proved to be a cause of misery; his hospitality to Heracles seems at first ill-judged but leads to his wife's salvation; his reluctant agreement to take care of the unrecognized Alcestis during Heracles' absence is again inappropriate in a house of mourning, yet precedes the revelation that restores his life to its former state. Although it is possible for a Greek tragedy to end happily, with the issues resolved (witness the *Oresteia* and the *Helen* among others), the preceding events normally involve deep and prolonged suffering. Here the misery is short-lived, and, exceptionally, the inevitability of death itself is averted. With the original terms of the bargain forgotten, Admetus and Alcestis are allowed a cloudless future. The end of the play reminds the modern spectator of the similarly miraculous reunion in *The Winter's Tale*, where the statue of the dead Hermione turns out to be the woman herself, alive. This gentler and un-tragic finale dispels the misery of earlier scenes, and probably also softens the effect of the conflict between father and son; we are not intended to think of Admetus' household as sundered irreparably. Euripides has created a varied and emotionally satisfying play, one which certainly touches on moral questions (especially in the debate between Admetus and Pheres), but which does not treat them with the same painful intensity as in his later and more ambitious dramas.

Characters

APOLLO
DEATH
CHORUS *of elders of Pherae*
MAIDSERVANT *of Alcestis*
ALCESTIS, *wife of Admetus*
ADMETUS, *king of Pherae*
YOUNG BOY AND GIRL, *children of Admetus*
HERACLES
PHERES, *father of Admetus*
SERVANT *of Admetus*

[*The scene is set before the house of* ADMETUS, *king of Pherae. The god* APOLLO *emerges, wearing his bow and quiver.*]

APOLLO: House of Admetus! Here I brought myself to accept such food as a common labourer gets, yes, I, a god! This was caused by Zeus: he had killed Asclepius, my son, flinging a fiery thunderbolt at his chest, and in my anger at this I killed the Cyclopes who fashion Zeus' fire; to punish me for this my father forced me to work in the employ of a mortal man. I came to this country and tended cattle for a stranger and to this day I have kept this house free from harm.

In the son of Pheres I found a man whose goodness matched   10
his servant's loyalty and I forestalled his death by playing a trick on the Fates.[1] These goddesses granted my request that Admetus should escape imminent death if he gave another dead person in exchange to the spirits below. He went round all his kinsfolk, sounding them out, but only in his wife did he find a willingness to quit this light and die for him. She is inside the house now, supported in his arms as she struggles   20
for breath, for on this day fate has ruled she must die and bid farewell to life.

Now I must leave this house where I have known such kindness or risk pollution[2] from death within its walls.
[*Enter* DEATH, *a black-robed, winged figure with a sword. As yet he does not see* APOLLO.]
Already I see Death[3] drawing near, priest of the dead, who means to lead her down to the house of Hades. He is punctual; he has kept watch for this day that must end her life.

DEATH [*suddenly noticing* APOLLO *and uttering a cry of frustration*]: What brings you to the palace? Why do you frequent this place, Phoebus? Is this more of your flouting of the law, limiting and putting a stop to our infernal rights? Was it not enough for you to prevent Admetus' death by using a cunning trick to entrap the Fates? Have you now even armed your hand with a bow to mount guard over this woman in turn, Pelias' daughter, who promised to ransom her husband's life by giving her own?

APOLLO: No need for alarm; justice and sound arguments are my weapons.

DEATH: Justice is your weapon? Then why the need for a bow?

APOLLO: It has always been my custom to carry this weapon.

DEATH: Yes, and to give this house your protection whether justified or not.

APOLLO: Yes, my protection: it is a friend whose sufferings touch my heart.

DEATH: Do you really mean to rob me of this second life?

APOLLO: Did I use force to take the first one from you? I think not.

DEATH: Then why is he in the land of the living instead of below the earth?

APOLLO: He gave his wife in his place, the woman you have come now to fetch.

DEATH: And I will carry her off, make no mistake, into the land beneath the earth.

APOLLO: Take her and go! I doubt if I will persuade you . . .

DEATH: To kill my allotted victim, you mean? That's my office, surely!

APOLLO: No, to defer the penalty of death for your intended victim.

DEATH: Now I understand your argument and your interest in this!

APOLLO: Then is there any possibility of Alcestis reaching old age?

DEATH: There is not; you must realize that I, too, take pleasure in receiving due respect.

APOLLO: And yet you would gain a single life, no more.

DEATH: When my victims are young, the prize I win is greater.

APOLLO: Even if it is an old woman who dies, her funeral will be costly.

DEATH: Why, Phoebus, it's for the benefit of the rich, the law you advocate!

APOLLO: What do you mean? Have I underestimated your intelligence?

DEATH: Those with the means would pay for the privilege of dying old.

APOLLO: You are determined, then, to refuse me this favour?   60

DEATH: I am; you know my nature.

APOLLO: Yes, one that men and gods regard with loathing.

DEATH: Not everything to which you have no right is yours for the having!

APOLLO: You will do as I say, yes, for all your cruelty! [*Aside:*] Such is the man who shall come to Pheres' house, sent by Eurystheus to fetch a team of mares from Thrace's wintry regions.[4] He shall indeed wrest this woman from you by force, once he has received hospitality in this house of Admetus. [*He again addresses* DEATH *directly:*] And as for any gratitude you might have had from me, there shall be none; you will   70 surrender her just the same and you will have my hatred.
[*Exit* APOLLO.]

DEATH: No lack of words there but little good will they do you! The woman will descend to Hades' dwelling, come what may. I am advancing on her now to initiate the ritual with my sword. For once this weapon has shorn a lock of hair from the victim's head, so consecrating it, that life is sacred to the gods below.
[*Exit* DEATH *into the palace. As he disappears, the* CHORUS *makes its entrance. They are elderly citizens of Pherae. In the first half of the ode there are various changes of speaker, indicated by a dash at the start of the line.*]

CHORUS: What does it mean, this stillness before the palace? Why has a hush fallen on the house of Admetus?

– Moreover not a friend is at hand to tell us if we should   80 mourn the queen as one already dead or if she yet lives and sees this sunlight, the daughter of Pelias, Alcestis, whom I and all men think the noblest wife a husband ever had.

[*Strophe*:] – Does anyone hear the sound of mourning inside the palace or of hands beating breasts or of wailing, as if all were over?

90 – Why no: there is not even a servant posted at the door. O healing Apollo, show yourself amid the waves of ruin!

– They would surely not be silent if she were dead.

– No corpse has yet left the house.

– How do you know this? I am not so sure. What makes you so confident?

– Would Admetus have buried such a noble wife with none to mourn her? I think not.

[*Antistrophe*:] – I see no bowl of spring-water before the door
100 as custom prescribes when someone dies.

– And there is no shorn lock of hair lying on the threshold in token of mourning for the dead or any sound of women beating their breasts.

– And yet this is the appointed day –

– What's that you say?

– When she is bound to pass beneath the earth.

– You touch my heart; you touch my mind.

110 – When the good suffer ruin, tears are owed by those whose loyalty has stood the test of time.

[*Strophe*:] There is no land where a pilgrim might voyage, be it Lycia or the waterless tract where Ammon has his shrine,[5] to win release for this poor lady's life. Relentless is her fate and it draws near. I know of no altar of the gods where I
120 should go with sheep for sacrifice.

[*Antistrophe*:] She alone, if only Phoebus' son[6] yet lived to look upon this light, would have escaped the murky abode and gates of Hades and returned to us; for he used to raise the dead, until the flaming thunderbolt hurled by Zeus ended
130 his life. But now what hope of her life can I still entertain?

[*Enter from the house a* MAIDSERVANT.]

CHORUS-LEADER: But here comes one of the servants from the house, her eyes full of tears. What shall I hear has happened? It is excusable to grieve if one's master meets any misfortune;

but we would like to know whether the lady yet lives or has   140
perished.

MAIDSERVANT: You may describe her both as living and as
dead.

CHORUS-LEADER: How could the same person be both dead
and alive?

MAIDSERVANT: She's already drooping and struggling to
breathe.

CHORUS-LEADER: Then there is no more hope that her life will
be saved?

MAIDSERVANT: No; this is the day and destiny drives her hard.

CHORUS-LEADER: Is she receiving the proper rites?

MAIDSERVANT: Yes, clothes and jewellery are ready for her
husband to set beside her in the grave.

CHORUS-LEADER: Poor man, he has been a fine husband! To
lose a wife like this!

MAIDSERVANT: The master doesn't know this yet; suffering will
teach him her worth.

CHORUS-LEADER: She can count on this: death will only add to   150
her renown as the noblest wife by far of all beneath the sun.

MAIDSERVANT: None could be nobler. Who will dispute it?
What words can describe her, this paragon among women?
How would a woman give greater proof of honouring her
husband than by freely giving her life for his? This, of course,
the whole city knows; but it will amaze you to learn of her
behaviour in her own home.

When she realized that the appointed day had come, she
washed her white body with water from the river, then,   160
selecting garments and jewellery from her cedar-wood
chambers, she dressed herself worthily of the occasion and,
standing before Hestia's altar,[7] she made this prayer: 'Lady, I
now take my journey below the earth and so kneel before you
for the last time. Care for my children, I beg you, who will
have no mother. Join them in wedlock, my boy to a loving
wife, my girl to a noble husband. Spare them an untimely
death such as their mother's and grant them happiness so that
they end their lives untouched by sorrow in the land of their
forefathers.'

170   Then she approached all the altars in Admetus' house and, covering them with garlands, she made her offering of prayers, breaking off shoots of myrtle from their branches. She gave way to no tears, no sighs; there was no loss of colour in that lovely face at the thought of the horror to come. She rushed next into her bedroom and up to her bed; then it was the tears came and with them these words: 'O my bed of marriage, where once I gave myself, a virgin, to the husband for whom I now die, farewell! I do not hate you. Yet you and you alone

180   have caused my death; for it is my reluctance to betray you and my husband that brings about my death. Some other woman will become your owner – she could not be more true to her husband, but perhaps she may be more fortunate.'

She threw herself on the bed, kissing it, and the whole coverlet grew wet from the tears that streamed from her eyes. But when she had had her fill of weeping, she tore herself away from the bed and stumbled out with head lowered. Many times she tried to leave the chamber and turned back, flinging herself again upon the bed. Her children were clinging

190   to their mother's dress, crying. Then she picked them up and hugged them as she made her farewells to each in turn, telling them she had to die. All the servants throughout the palace were shedding tears of pity for their mistress. But she held out her right hand to each of them and there was none so humble that she refused to address him or hear his reply. Such, then, is the scene of misery in Admetus' house. Had he been the one to die, he would be gone from us, but now that he has eluded death, he has inherited such anguish as he shall never forget.

CHORUS-LEADER: No doubt this misfortune is reducing
200   Admetus to tears, if fate is to rob him of his noble wife?

MAIDSERVANT: He weeps all right and holds his dear wife in his arms, begging her not to abandon him, but what he asks is impossible; she is dying, worn down by her malady. She languishes, a pitiful weight in his arms, but still with the meagre breath left to her she wants to gaze upon the sun's

210   rays. I will go with the news that you are here; not everyone feels such regard for a royal master that he stands loyally by

him when disaster strikes. Yours is a friendship my master
and mistress have known for many a long year.

[*The* CHORUS *now sings a short ode to which, as before,
different members contribute, before the entry of the royal
couple. In the duet that follows these lyrics are prolonged
pathetically by the singing of* ALCESTIS, *which contrasts with
her husband's spoken appeal to her not to die.*]

CHORUS [*Strophe*]: O Zeus, can there be any way out of our
troubles, any release from the fate that has befallen our king
and queen?
– Will someone announce the news or should I already
take a knife to my hair and wrap myself in grief's black
clothes?
– A terrible predicament, friends, yes, terrible, but still we
will pray to the gods; mighty indeed is their power.   220
– Lord Healer,[8] devise some plan for Admetus to thwart this
evil!
– Grant this prayer, yes, grant it! In the past you did this; this
day also be our rescuer from death and keep bloody Hades
at bay!
[*Antistrophe:*] – Son of Pheres, I pity you! What ill-fortune is
yours, robbed of your wife!
– Ah! This is enough to make a man fall on his sword, more
than enough to make him end his life in a swinging noose!
– Aye, this very day you will see dead the woman you loved   230
as no husband ever loved a wife.
– Look! Look! She is coming now from the palace, she and
her husband!
– Cry out, O land of Pheres, make lament for the finest of
womankind wasting away from sickness to infernal Hades
below the earth!

[*The* KING *and* QUEEN *and their children begin to enter
slowly. Attendants follow behind, bringing on a couch for*
ALCESTIS.]

   Never shall I say that marriage brings more joy than pain.
Past experience is my evidence and the sight of what the king   240
is suffering here; he is about to lose the best of wives and to
endure in the years left to him a life that is no life.

[ALCESTIS *sings an ecstatic monody. She shows no awareness of* ADMETUS' *desperate appeals.*]

ALCESTIS [*Strophe*]: O sun and light of day! Eddies of cloud that race across the heavens!

ADMETUS: They look on you and me, two sorry creatures, who have done the gods no wrong to make them want your death.

ALCESTIS [*Antistrophe*]: O earth and high-roofed palace in my native Iolcus, with its marriage bed!

250   ADMETUS: Rouse yourself, my poor lady, do not desert me! Beg the mighty gods to show pity!

ALCESTIS [*Strophe*]: I see it, the two-oared boat, I see it on the lake! He has his hand on the pole, Charon, the ferryman of the dead! Already he is calling me: 'Why do you linger? Make haste! You hold us back!' So he impatiently urges me to hurry.

ADMETUS: Oh, no! This voyage you tell me of is one that wounds my heart! My wretched lady, what a fate we endure!

[ALCESTIS *rises from the couch as if under some compulsion.*]

ALCESTIS [*Antistrophe*]: Someone is leading me, leading me
260   away (do you not see him?) to the hall of the dead, staring at me from under dark-gleaming brows, a winged figure – Hades!

[*To the vision:*] Oh, what will you do? Let me go! What a journey I am going on! How it appals me!

ADMETUS [*attempting to calm her*]: A pitiful one for those who love you but most of all for me and our children; they too share in this sorrow.

[ALCESTIS *sinks back wearily on the couch and addresses the servants, who have been trying to restrain her during the stress of her trance.*]

ALCESTIS [*Epode*]: Let go of me, let go of me now; lay me down, I have no strength to stand. Hades is near and night's darkness
270   steals over my eyes. O children, children, you have a mother no more, no more! Look long upon the light, children, and fare you well!

ADMETUS: Oh, what misery! These are words that wound my ears, worse to bear than any death! In the name of the gods, in the name of the children you will turn into orphans, do not bring yourself to abandon me but rise up, be brave! When

you are dead, I can have no life; on you depends my life, my
death, for I cannot be untrue to the love we share!

ALCESTIS: Admetus, you see how things stand with me.[9] I want   280
to tell you my wishes before I die. Because I put you first,
because I chose that you should look upon this light at the
cost of my own life, I am dying, for your sake, though I
might have lived, marrying any man of Thessaly I wished and
enjoying the luxury of a royal home. But I had no desire to
live without you at my side, with children who were orphaned,
and I did not grudge the loss of my youth with all the joys it
brought me. And yet they betrayed you, the parents who gave   290
you life, though they were of a good age to die and to save a
son's life – a glorious end to their days. They had no other
child but you, no hope of producing other children after you
had died. We could then have gone on living, we two, for the
rest of our years; you would not be grieving as now, a husband
turned widower, a father with motherless children. No, some
god caused this to turn out as it has.

Very well; it is for you now to remember what I have done
for you. What I shall ask of you is not in any sense an equal   300
return (for nothing is more precious than life) but it is fair, as
you yourself will grant.

These children are loved as much by you as by me, for you
are a responsible father. Allow them to become masters in my
house. Do not marry again and give them a stepmother to
ill-treat them, your children and mine, someone who will love
them less than I and eye them with jealousy. Do not do such
a thing, I beg you! A stepmother approaches the children she   310
inherits like an enemy, yes, a viper would show them more
affection. A boy, of course, has a tower of strength in his
father; [*turning to her daughter:*] but what of you, my child,
how will you grow happily from girl to woman? What kind
of woman will you find your father's new partner to be? I fear
she may spread some scandalous report about you when you
are on the verge of womanhood and blight your marriage.
For never will you have your mother to prepare you on your
wedding day, to speak words of encouragement in your ear
during childbirth, when nothing can match a mother's care.

320 For I must die; and this evil comes upon me, not tomorrow or the day after, no, in a moment you will speak of me as one already dead. [*To the whole family:*] Goodbye! Be happy! You, my husband, can be proud that you won a noble wife, and you, my children, that you were born of a noble mother.

CHORUS-LEADER: Have no fear; I do not hesitate to speak on his behalf. He will do this, unless his wits desert him.

ADMETUS: So it shall be, never fear, so it shall be! For while you lived, no other woman had my heart and in death you
330 alone shall be called my wife. No woman of Thessaly shall ever take your place or speak to me as bride to husband. There is none so noble in birth, none of a beauty to match your excellence. I am well content with the children I have and I pray to the gods I may have some joy in them; in you my joy has been little enough. Not merely for a year will I endure my grief for you; no, my lady, as long as my life continues, it shall be my burden and I shall loathe the woman who gave me birth and I shall hate my father. Theirs was a love that lived in words, not actions. But you, you have saved
340 me by sacrificing in return for my life your most precious possession. Should I not then weep to lose such a wife as you?

I will put an end to them,[10] the noisy gatherings of guests, the dancing and drinking, the garlands and music that used to fill my house. Never could I now touch my lyre, never follow the heart's prompting to sing to the Libyan flute; you have taken away my joy in life. I shall have sculptors fashion with cunning hands a statue in your image[11] and on our bed it shall lie outstretched. This I will clasp and fold in my arms;
350 I will call your name and imagine it is my darling wife I hold in my embrace, when it is not – cold comfort, it is true, but yet I would be easing the burden on my heart. In my dreams you would flit to and fro, bringing me joy; for joy it is to see a loved one, even in dreams, for as long as the vision lasts.

Oh, had I Orpheus'[12] words and music, so that I might charm Demeter's child or her lord by my songs and so win
360 you back from Hades, I would make the descent and neither Pluto's hound would stop me nor spirit-guiding Charon at his oar until I had set you, living, in the light above! But at

least wait for me to join you, when I die, and prepare a home
for us to share together. I will instruct these children to place
me in the same cedar coffin as you and to lay my body side
by side with yours. I have no wish to be parted ever from you,
the only one who was true to me, not even in death.

CHORUS-LEADER: And be sure that I will share your bitter load
of grief for this woman, as friend to friend; it is her due.   370

ALCESTIS: Children, you heard your father, you heard him say
that never would he marry another woman to be a second
mother to you, never would he dishonour me.

ADMETUS: And I repeat it now, and will be true to my word.

ALCESTIS [*releasing the children from her embrace*]: On these
terms receive our children from my hands.

ADMETUS: I do receive them, a precious gift from precious
hands.

ALCESTIS: Now you must take my place and be a mother to our
children.

ADMETUS: Indeed I must do this, now that you are to be taken
from them.

ALCESTIS [*losing control*]: O children, the very time I should be
living, I depart for the world below!

ADMETUS: Oh, then what shall I do, alone without you?   380

ALCESTIS: Time will soften the blow for you; one who is dead
is as nothing.

ADMETUS: Take me with you, in heaven's name, take me below!

ALCESTIS: It is enough that I am dying in your place.

ADMETUS: O spirit that guides my fortune, how noble a wife
you will be taking from my side!

ALCESTIS: Darkness is coming upon my eyes, they grow heavy.

ADMETUS: Then my life is finished, if you really mean to leave
me, my lady!

ALCESTIS: You may speak of me as gone, dead and gone!

ADMETUS: Lift your face! Do not abandon your children!

ALCESTIS: It is not by my wish, assuredly. Goodbye, children!

ADMETUS: Look at them, look!   390

ALCESTIS: My life is over.

ADMETUS: What are you doing? Are you deserting us?

ALCESTIS: Goodbye! [*She dies.*]

ADMETUS: Oh, misery! I am ruined!

CHORUS-LEADER: She has gone, Admetus' wife is no more.
[ONE OF THE CHILDREN[13] *now sings a short monody of grief.*]

CHILD [*Strophe*]: Oh, what has happened to me? Mama has gone below, she is no longer under the sun, Father. She has left me here to live an orphan's life – how could she? Look,

400   look at her eyelids and limp hands! Listen to me, Mother, listen, I beg you! It's me, Mother, it's me calling you, me, your little chick pressing on your lips!

ADMETUS: She doesn't hear, doesn't see; a terrible blow has struck the three of us.

CHILD [*Antistrophe*]: She has left me, Father, my darling mother; I am young and all alone. Terrible are the sufferings

410   I have known and you, dear Sister, have shared them with me. O Father, all for nothing did you marry, all for nothing; you have not reached the goal of old age with her, for she has perished before then; you are gone, Mother, and so ruin has come upon our house.

CHORUS-LEADER: Admetus, you must bear what has happened here. You are not the first or last man on earth to lose a noble wife. Recognize that we are all death's debtors.[14]

420 ADMETUS: I know it; this evil has not swooped upon me without warning; my awareness of it has long been torturing me. But attend on me; I will arrange the funeral for this dead lady. Stay here and sing to the god who rules below the hymn that needs no offerings of wine. I command all Thessalians who are my subjects to share in my grief at this woman's loss by cropping their hair and wearing the black dress of mourning. And you who harness teams of four or keep single horses, cut back their manes from their necks with your knives. Let there

430   be no sound of flutes or the lyre throughout the town until twelve moons have waxed and waned. For never shall I consign to the grave another so dearly beloved, so loving to me. She deserves my devotion, for she alone has died for me.
[*Servants carry the body of* ALCESTIS *into the palace.* ADMETUS *follows slowly with the children.*]

CHORUS [*Strophe*]: Daughter of Pelias, fare you well in Hades'

home, when you dwell in that sunless house! Let Hades, the
dark-haired god, know, and the old man who sits at oar and   440
rudder as he ferries the dead, that he has taken in his two-
oared craft across Acheron's lake the noblest by far, by far,
of womankind.

[*Antistrophe:*] Many a time will they sing of you, the servants
of the Muses, celebrating your name on the seven-toned shell
of the mountain tortoise and in songs unaccompanied by the
lyre, in Sparta when the cycle of seasons brings round the
Carnean month, when the moon rides high the whole night   450
long, and in Athens the brilliant, the fair of fortune. Such a
theme for song has your death bequeathed to bards.[15]

[*Strophe:*] Oh, would that it lay in my power, would that I
could bring you back safe to the light, by boat over the
infernal river from the abode of Hades and Cocytus' stream!
For you alone, you, dear lady, had the courage to redeem   460
your own husband from Hades at the cost of your own life.
Lightly, I pray, may the earth lie upon you, lady! Should your
husband ever choose a new bride, truly he would earn my
hate and your children's!

[*Antistrophe:*] His mother would not, for her son's sake, hide
her body in the earth, nor would his father; wicked pair, they
had not the heart to protect their own son, for all their old,
grey hair. But you, a young woman with a young husband,   470
you are gone from us, giving your life for him. Had I but the
good fortune to gain such a loving partner in wedlock –
seldom in life does this occur – truly, then, would she share
my life to the end and bring me only joy.

[*As the* CHORUS' *song dies away, the hero* HERACLES *enters
abruptly. His club and lionskin cloak reveal his identity to
them.*]

HERACLES: Friends, good citizens of this land of Pherae, have I
the luck to find Admetus here at home?

CHORUS-LEADER: The son of Pheres is indeed inside the palace,
Heracles. But tell me, what is the need that sends you to the
land of Thessaly, that you should visit our city of Pherae here?   480

HERACLES: I am performing a task set me by Eurystheus of
Tiryns.[16]

CHORUS-LEADER: Where are you going? What is this errand that binds you fast?

HERACLES: I go to Thrace, to capture Diomedes' team of four mares.

CHORUS-LEADER: But how will you succeed? Surely you know how he treats guests?

HERACLES: I do not; I have not yet set foot in the land of the Bistonians.

CHORUS-LEADER: You must fight him for ownership of the mares; there is no other way.

HERACLES: No way either for me to turn my back on labours once set.

CHORUS-LEADER: Then it is kill him and return or be killed and remain there.

HERACLES: This will not be the first such contest I have risked.

490 CHORUS-LEADER: What would you stand to gain if you defeated their master?

HERACLES: The mares; I'll drive them off to Tiryns' king.

CHORUS-LEADER: No easy task to put a bit between those jaws!

HERACLES: Easy enough, unless it's fire they breathe from their nostrils.

CHORUS-LEADER: No, but they seize men in their jaws and in no time tear them to pieces!

HERACLES: That's what beasts of the mountain feed on, not horses!

CHORUS-LEADER: Their stalls spattered with blood, that's the sight awaiting you.

HERACLES: And the man who bred them, whose son does he claim to be?

CHORUS-LEADER: The son of Ares, master of the Thracian shield in all its gold.

HERACLES: This task you speak of fits well with my destiny (a
500   path ever hard to tread, ever leading uphill), if I am to do battle with all the sons of Ares' loins; first came Lycaon, then Cycnus, and now a third time I enter the lists, to fight it out with those horses and their master. But no man lives who shall ever see Alcmene's son tremble to face an enemy.

[*Enter* ADMETUS *from the palace, his head shorn as a sign of mourning.*]

CHORUS-LEADER: Why, here is Admetus in person, ruler of this land, coming out of the palace.

ADMETUS: Welcome, son of Zeus, sprung from the blood of Perseus!

HERACLES: All happiness to you as well, Admetus, king of   510
Thessaly!

ADMETUS: I wish it could be mine. But you mean kindly, I know it well.

HERACLES: This display of grief with your head shorn, what does it mean?

ADMETUS: I am going to bury this day one who has died.

HERACLES: God keep misfortune from your children's heads!

ADMETUS: They are alive and inside the house, the children I fathered.

HERACLES: If it is your father who has died, well, the years have been kind to him.

ADMETUS: He lives yet, Heracles, and so does my mother.

HERACLES: It's not your wife, it's not your Alcestis who has died?

ADMETUS: There are two answers I might give you about her.

HERACLES: What are you saying? Is she dead or still alive?   520

ADMETUS: She is both alive and dead,[17] and this is what breaks my heart.

HERACLES: I remain in the dark; your words are confusing.

ADMETUS: Are you aware of the fate she must undergo?

HERACLES: I am; she has undertaken to die in your place.

ADMETUS: How, then, can she still be alive, if she has agreed to this?

HERACLES: Ah, yes! But you musn't shed tears for your wife before the time. Put that off until the hour comes.

ADMETUS: One that is doomed is dead; he may be here but he no longer lives.

HERACLES: Being alive and being dead are regarded as two separate things.

ADMETUS: That's your view of the matter, Heracles; I see it differently.

530   HERACLES: But why is it that you are weeping? Which of your
        friends has died?
      ADMETUS: A woman;[18] we were just talking about a woman.
      HERACLES: An outsider or some relation by blood?
      ADMETUS: An outsider but in another sense closely tied to my
        house.
      HERACLES: Well, how did she come to die in your house?
      ADMETUS: After her father's death she lived here as an orphan.
      HERACLES: Admetus, my poor fellow, I wish I had not intruded
        on your grief!
      ADMETUS: What are you hinting at? What is it you mean to do?
      HERACLES: I have other friends who can give me hospitality;
        I'll go to them.
      ADMETUS: That is out of the question, my lord; heaven forbid
        such a disgrace!
540   HERACLES: When a family is in mourning a visit from a stranger
        is hardly welcome.
      ADMETUS: The dead have died; please come into my home.
      HERACLES: It does little credit to a man that he sits and eats
        heartily while his host is in tears.
      ADMETUS: The guest rooms where we will take you are in a
        separate wing.
      HERACLES: Let me depart and I will be infinitely in your debt!
      ADMETUS: Never; you simply cannot go to another man's house
        to find welcome. [*To a servant:*] You there, take this gentle-
        man to the guest rooms that are away from the house, open
        them up and instruct the staff to provide a good quantity of
        food! [*To other servants as* HERACLES *leaves:*] Shut the doors
        to the central court and make them fast! When guests are
550   feasting they should not have their enjoyment marred by the
        sound of groans.
      CHORUS-LEADER: What are you doing? With such a calamity
        weighing on you, Admetus, have you the heart to entertain
        guests? Why are you so foolish?
      ADMETUS: But if I had driven from my home, from my city, the
        stranger who came to me, would you have praised me more?
        Of course not! It would hardly have dulled the edge of my
        misfortune and I would have been shown up as a bad host.

My sorrows would then be crowned by this new one, my house being called inhospitable. In my own experience this man is an excellent host, whenever I visit the parched land of Argos. 560

CHORUS-LEADER: Why, then, were you trying to conceal what the gods have done to you, when, in your own words, your visitor is a friend?

ADMETUS: He would never have consented to set foot in my house, had he known any hint of my troubles. I imagine some will think me mad for behaving like this and will disapprove. But this house of mine has never scorned a visitor by turning him away and it never will.

[*Exit* ADMETUS *into the palace.*]

CHORUS [*Strophe*]: O house ever welcoming to strangers, house of an ever generous master, in you Pytho's lord saw fit to 570 make his home, Apollo himself, supreme in the lyre; in your pastures he deigned to become a herdsman, piping to your flocks over the sloping hills tunes to stir their hearts to wedlock.

[*Antistrophe:*] Delighting in this music, spotted lynxes mingled with them as they grazed and a tawny troop of lions came down, forsaking Othrys' glen; and to your lyre, 580 Phoebus, the dappled fawn did dance, stepping dainty-footed from the high-crowned firs, drawn for joy to the spell of your melodies.

[*Strophe:*] So it is that Admetus dwells in a domain rich in flocks beside Boebe's lake with its lovely waters; so, that he 590 sets the boundary of his tilled acres and spreading plains where the sun stables his horses under the gloom of the Molossian sky, while eastward his rule extends to the Aegean sea, where Pelion looks down on the havenless shore.[19]

[*Antistrophe:*] Now once more he has opened wide his house in welcome to a guest, though tears moisten his eyes as he weeps within his palace over the body of his beloved wife, but lately dead. Such is the man's noble spirit; it compels my 600 respect even when it leads him astray. All qualities belong to noble men; I wonder at his wisdom. In my heart abides the trust that all will be well with this god-fearing man.

[ADMETUS *comes out of the palace with servants, who carry* ALCESTIS *on a bier. They set this down shortly when* PHERES *enters to pay his last respects.*]

ADMETUS: Men of Pherae, your attendance here shows your goodwill. These servants are now bearing on high my dead lady, together with all that becomes her, to the funeral pyre.
610 I ask you to follow custom and salute the departed as she goes forth upon her final journey.

CHORUS-LEADER: I see your old father approaching at a slow pace and with him men carrying in their hands gifts to adorn your wife, proper offerings for the dead.

[*Enter* PHERES *with servants.*]

PHERES: My son, I am here to share with you the burden of this sorrow. You have lost, and no man will deny it, a noble and virtuous wife. But for all its bitterness this is a stroke of fortune you must bear. Accept now these gifts; let them share her journey to the world below. All honour is owed to her
620 body, the woman who gave her life for yours, my son, who saved me from childlessness and would not allow me to waste away in a sorrowful old age, bereft of you. By performing this noble act of sacrifice she has made the lives of all women shine with a greater glory. [*He extends a hand towards the body in formal salutation.*] Farewell, my lady! You saved this man from death and raised up our family when we were fallen; may it go well with you in Hades' halls! A marriage such as this profits a man, or he had better avoid marriage.

ADMETUS: It was not at my invitation that you came to this
630 funeral; I do not count your presence here as a friend's. Never will these gifts of yours be worn by her; she shall go to her grave needing nothing from you. Then was the time for you to share my grief, when I was dying. But you kept your distance and let another die, though she was young and you were old. And will you now weep and wail over her corpse? You are not, then, it seems, my true father, any more than she is my mother, the woman who has this name, who claims she gave me birth; no, some slave has that honour and I was secretly placed at your wife's breast to be nursed. When it
640 came to the test, you showed your true colours; I no longer

regard myself as your son. What man on earth could match
your cowardice? Though as old as you are, as close to life's
end, you lacked the will, the courage to die for your son,
renouncing this privilege to the woman who lies here, whose
blood is not ours! She alone is the one I would be right to
think of as my mother and my father.

And yet what honour might have been yours, had you faced
the challenge and died for your son, having, in any case, only   650
a brief span of life left? Again, all the happiness a man has
the right to expect has been yours. Your best years were spent
in kingship and you had in me a son to inherit your house, so
that you were not going to die childless and leave an orphaned
home for other hands to pillage. You are in no position to
claim it was my lack of reverence for your years that made
you give me up to death; I have always treated you with the   660
utmost respect. And this is the thanks you have given me in
return, you and my mother!

Well, lose no time in fathering sons to support you in old
age, to see to your shroud in death and organize the burial of
your corpse. For never will these hands of mine lay you in the
grave. Indeed, I am dead, as far as you are concerned. If I look
upon the sunlight because I found someone else to deliver me
from death, then I say it is that person whose child I am, that
person who will receive my loving support in old age. How
insincere they are, these prayers for death voiced by the
elderly, these complaints they make against old age and the   670
tedious passing of the years! If death draws near, not one of
them wants to die; old age is suddenly a burden that weighs
lightly on their shoulders.

CHORUS-LEADER: That is quite enough from you both! Are
    our present sufferings not sufficient? Young sir, do not pro-
    voke your father's anger.

PHERES: Boy, who is it you suppose you are heaping these
    insults on, some slave from Lydia, perhaps, or Phrygia,[20]
    purchased with your money? Do you not know I am a Thessal-
    ian and free-born, the true-born son of a Thessalian father?
    It is too much, this insolence of yours! But you will not get
    away with it, you will not simply hurl these insults at me, you   680

young puppy, and walk away! I brought you into this world and raised you up to be master of this house; I am under no obligation to die for you. I have inherited no such tradition from my ancestors, that fathers should die for their sons; it is not one recognized by Greeks. For yourself you were born to know misfortune or, it may be, happiness. I have not withheld from you what you were entitled to receive from me. You have many subjects and I will bequeath to you broad acres of land, no less a patrimony than my father gave me.

690 So, tell me, how have I wronged you? What am I robbing you of? Do not die for me and I shall not for you! You are happy to see the sun's light; do you imagine your father is not? It's a long time, I reckon, I'll be spending dead, a long time, and only a short one alive, but all the more precious for that. You certainly were shameless enough in struggling out of death's clutches; you are alive, after eluding your appointed fate, but you killed her. And then you talk of *my* cowardice, you despicable creature, when you have been found inferior to a woman who has given her life for you, her fine young husband! What a brilliant solution to the problem of dying –
700 you simply persuade your wife of the day to die for you each time! And then, when your relatives refuse to do this, do you turn it into a criticism of them, when you are a coward yourself?

[ADMETUS *can no longer contain himself and tries to speak.*] Be quiet! Think about this: you love your own life; well, so does every man. You can heap insults on my head but they will return, multiplied, to vex your ears with their truth!

CHORUS-LEADER: You have both uttered quite enough abuse against each other, now and before. Pheres, you are advanced in years; check this torrent of abuse against your son.

ADMETUS: Talk away; I have had my say. If it distresses you to hear the truth, you should not have treated me the way you did; you are at fault.

710 PHERES: It would be a greater fault, if my life had been given for you.

ADMETUS: Is there no difference between a man dying in his prime and in old age?

PHERES: It's one life we have to make do with, not two.

ADMETUS: Well, I wish you a longer life than Zeus!

PHERES: What? Cursing your own father when he's done you no wrong?

ADMETUS: Yes; I noticed you were in love with longevity.

PHERES: But isn't she taking *your* place, this dead lady you mean to bury?

ADMETUS: Proof of your spinelessness; how I despise you!

PHERES: I'm not responsible for her death; you can't say that.

ADMETUS: Oh, hasten the day when you will need help from me!

PHERES: Try wooing many more girls, so you can cause more deaths! 720

ADMETUS: You are the one who refused to die, so yours is the shame there.

PHERES: It is precious, this light the god sends, yes, precious.

ADMETUS: And yours is a craven spirit, unworthy of a man.

PHERES: But this is no old man's corpse you are carrying out to burial – no chance for you to mock that!

ADMETUS: But death will claim you one of these days and what a shameful spectacle that will be!

PHERES: Men's rebukes will not concern me when I am dead.

ADMETUS: Oh, excellent! Do the old have *any* sense of shame?

PHERES: She was not shameless but witless in your hands.

ADMETUS: Leave me! Let me bury my dead!

PHERES: I will leave you. You are the one who took her life and 730 you will bury her. But there will be a reckoning; you will yet answer to her relatives. Acastus is surely a man no longer if he fails to avenge his sister's blood.

[*He turns abruptly and starts to leave, together with attendants.*]

ADMETUS [*shouting after him*]: Yes, go on your way, you and the woman who shares your home! Go to enjoy a childless old age though you have a child of your own, for this is what you deserve! Never will the pair of you ever more come under the same roof as me! If the law permitted me to disown you, to deny by proclamation any tie of hearth or home between us, this I would have done. But now let us proceed – the

740   misery facing us must be borne – so that we may set the dead
        on the pyre.

        [ADMETUS *and the cortège begin to leave in procession*.]

CHORUS: Ah, my lady, so steadfast in your courage, so noble
        that you surpass all other women, farewell! May Hermes of
        the nether world and Hades give you kindly welcome, and, if
        even there virtue has its reward, may you benefit from this
        and attend upon Hades' bride!

        [*They turn and leave, following* ADMETUS *and the funeral
        procession. When the scene is empty a* SERVANT *comes out
        of the palace and addresses the audience*.]

SERVANT: I've known many strangers to come to Admetus'
        house before now, from every sort of place, and I've served
750   them at dinner; but I've never yet shown hospitality to a
        greater rogue than today's guest. In the first place, he saw the
        master was in mourning but in he came, crossing the doorstep
        bold as you please. Then, realizing our situation, did he show
        any tact and put up with whatever we served him? Not a bit
        of it! Anything we didn't put in front of him, he insisted on
        having it produced. He took the ivy-wood cup in his hands
        and gulped down neat the dark grape's juice until the wine's
        flame wrapped him in its warmth. He crowned his head with
        myrtle sprays and began crooning in a tuneless bray. Two
760   strains could be heard: he kept singing away, caring nothing
        for the troubles in Admetus' home, while we servants wept
        for our mistress but kept our tear-stained cheeks hidden from
        the guest, remembering Admetus' instructions. So here I am
        now, waiting upon a stranger in the house, some damned
        thief or brigand, while she has left this house, my own dear
        mistress, and I didn't even follow her body or stretch out a
        hand in farewell or join in the voices of lament! To me and
770   all who serve in this house she was a mother; she calmed her
        husband in his angry moods and saved us from trouble time
        and again. Who can blame me for hating this stranger who
        has intruded on our sorrow?

        [HERACLES *emerges from the palace, garlanded and drunk*.][21]

HERACLES: Here, my man, why do you look so solemn? What's
        troubling you? It's not sour looks a guest should get from

servants but a decent, affable greeting. Now here I stand
before your eyes, a friend of your master, but what's your
welcome? Scowls and frowning looks – you're too wrapped
up in someone else's trouble! Come over here and I'll improve
your education. You know how it is with life on this earth? I   780
doubt it – how should you? Just listen to me. Death's a debt
all men must pay; there's not a living soul knows for sure if
tomorrow's morn will see him alive or dead. As to how
fortune's plans will turn out, it's far from clear – no amount
of teaching or practice can give you that knowledge. So heed
my words and learn from me: be happy, drink, think each
day your own as you live it and leave the rest to fortune. Give
honour, too, to Cypris,[22] kindest, sweetest of deities to mortal   790
men; she is a gracious goddess. As to everything else, pay it
no attention and do as I say, if you think I'm talking sense; I
think I am. Let's have no more of this extravagant grief. Come
and drink with me! I know just the thing to shake you out of
this tense frame of mind, these frowning looks – sinking a
good few cups of wine, that'll change your attitude! We're
mortal men and ought to think mortal thoughts. Life for all   800
you sour-faced enemies of pleasure, if you want my opinion,
is not really life, it's a chapter of sorrows.

SERVANT: I know this; what we're going through at the moment
doesn't call for laughter and celebration.

HERACLES: But the woman who died wasn't a member of this
family. Your mourning is excessive: the master and mistress
of this house are still alive.

SERVANT: How do you mean, *alive*? Don't you know what has
happened in this house?

HERACLES: Of course, unless your master has misled me
somehow.

SERVANT: His hospitality goes too far, too far, I say!

HERACLES: Should a stranger's death have made him refuse me   810
the welcome of his house?

SERVANT: Stranger? Oh yes, indeed, absolutely; she was a
stranger!

HERACLES: Nothing serious has happened, surely, that he has
not told me of?

SERVANT: Go on your way and good luck to you! It is for us to care about our master's misfortunes.

HERACLES: These words do not indicate the troubles of a stranger.

SERVANT: Otherwise I should never have resented the sight of you making merry.

HERACLES: What? Have I been deceived by my host?

SERVANT: When you came here this house was in no position to give you welcome.

820 HERACLES: Is it one of his children he has lost, or his old father?

SERVANT: It is his wife Admetus has lost, stranger.

HERACLES: What are you saying? And after that you gave me the hospitality of the house?

SERVANT: Yes; he was ashamed to show you the door.

HERACLES: Poor man, what a wife you have lost!

SERVANT: It is not just the queen who has perished, so have we all.

HERACLES: Of course I did notice; I saw the tears in his eyes, his shorn head, his expression. But he convinced me with his explanation that it was a stranger's corpse he was taking to burial. Despite my own misgivings I went blundering inside
830 and began drinking in the house of my hospitable friend, when this had happened to him! And do I now feast and drink with a garland on my head? [*He throws down his drinking-cup and tears off the garland he is wearing, disgusted with himself, then rounds on the servant.*] And you, to think that you kept quiet, when such a disaster had fallen on your house! Where is he burying her? Where shall I go to find him?

SERVANT: Straight along the road that leads to Larisa, just as you leave the outskirts of the city, you will see a tomb of dressed stone.

[*He leaves the stage.*]

HERACLES: Come, my heart, that has endured so much, come hand of mine, now show what kind of son Electryon's daugh-
840 ter, Alcmene of Tiryns, bore to Zeus! Now must I save the woman who has lately died; now must I give Alcestis her place once more in this house and pay this debt of gratitude to Admetus. I will go and keep watch for Death, the black-

winged lord of the dead; I fancy I will find him near her tomb,
drinking the blood of beasts sacrificed there. And if I rush
upon him from my place of ambush and seize him, pinning
him in my encircling arms, no man shall free him from that
rib-crushing hold until he gives the woman up to me. But if I
fail to catch my prey and he does not come to taste the gory   850
offering, I will go to the sunless dwelling of the Maid and her
lord[23] and there ask for Alcestis to be returned. I have no
doubt I will bring her back to this world and place her in the
hands of my host, who welcomed me into his home. Fortune
had dealt him a heavy blow but he refused to turn me away.
Out of respect for me and because he has a noble heart he
kept me in the dark. What man of Thessaly could have greater
regard for guests? Who that lives in Greece? Admetus has a
generous soul; he will have no cause to say his kindness met   860
with ingratitude.

[*Exit* HERACLES. *The funeral procession with* ADMETUS
returns.]

ADMETUS:[24] Oh, how hateful to me is this homecoming, how
hateful the sight of these widowed halls! Ah, the pain, the
misery I feel! Where should I go? Where remain? What shall
I say? What not? Oh, if only I might die! It was a grim fate
that my mother brought me into the world for. I envy the
dead; theirs is the lot I crave, theirs the home where I long to
dwell. For it gives me no pleasure to look upon the sun's light
or to feel the ground under my feet. Such is the hostage that   870
Death has stolen from me and handed over to Hades.

CHORUS [*Strophe*]: Go forward, go forward; enter your home.

ADMETUS: Oh, misery!

CHORUS: Your sufferings merit such groans.

ADMETUS: What pain!

CHORUS: Yours has been a painful path, I know it well.

ADMETUS: I am so wretched!

CHORUS: You are not helping the one who is below.

ADMETUS: I cannot bear this!

CHORUS: Never again to look into the face of a beloved wife!
It is cruel.

ADMETUS: There you touch on what has wounded my heart;

what greater sorrow can a man endure than the loss of a
880   loving wife? I should never have taken her as my wife, never
shared this home with her! How I envy them, those men who
have never married, never had children! They have only one
life; bearing its sorrows is a burden a man can endure. But to
have to witness disease striking down one's children, or bridal
beds marred by death, is past enduring, when a man can live
his whole life childless and unwed.

CHORUS [*Antistrophe*]: Fortune has come upon you, fortune
the wrestler that none can throw.

ADMETUS: Oh, misery!

890   CHORUS: There is no boundary that you can set to your sorrows.

ADMETUS: What pain!

CHORUS: They make a heavy burden, and yet –

ADMETUS: I am so wretched!

CHORUS: Endure! You are not the first man to lose –

ADMETUS: I cannot bear this!

CHORUS: – a wife. Disaster in mortal life has many forms; she
crushes now one man, now another.

ADMETUS: Ah, the long days of sorrow and grief for those we
love below the earth! Why did you stop me from flinging
myself into the hollowed trench that is her grave, from lying
dead beside her whose worth no other woman can match?
900   Then Hades would have had not one life but two, most
faithful souls who crossed his infernal lake together.

CHORUS [*Strophe*]: I had a relative whose son, an only child,
died in his house, a youth well worth the weeping. But in spite
of all, he bore his misfortune with restraint, childless though
910   he was, though he was now declining towards grey hair and
no longer in his prime.

ADMETUS [*pausing at the entrance to his palace*]: Ah, house of
mine, how am I to enter you, how live under your roof, now
that fortune has dealt me this new blow? What misery! This
is a transformation indeed! On that day I went inside you
with Pelian torches and wedding songs, clasping my dear
wife's hand in mine, and a happy, shouting throng accompanied us, congratulating the dead woman and me: 'What a
920   well-born pair they are! How splendid a match!' But now

those wedding songs have given way to cries of sorrow, those bright clothes to mourning's dusky garments that usher me inside, to the embrace of my empty bed.

CHORUS [*Antistrophe*]: This grief has come upon you suddenly, in the midst of your happiness, when you did not know what sorrow was. Yet you have saved your own life. Your wife has died but left her love behind. This is not strange; many men 930 have already lost their wives to the strong arms of death.

ADMETUS: Friends, I count my wife's fate happier than my own, though it may not seem so. No pain will ever touch her now, nothing tarnish her good name, no more troubles weigh her down. But I, the man who cheated fate, who should not be living, will drag out my days in anguish. This truth has just 940 come home to me. For how will I find the strength to enter this house? And if I should, is there anyone to gladden my heart by our exchange of greetings? There is none. Where shall I turn? The loneliness inside will drive me out, whenever I see our bed with no wife to share it and the chair she used to sit on and, throughout the house, the floor unswept. The children will fall at my knees, weeping for their mother, and the servants sigh for the kind mistress they have lost.

So much for what will happen in my house. Outside there 950 will be Thessalian weddings and gatherings full of women to drive me indoors once more. I will not be able to bear the sight of them, my wife's friends, all as young as her. And this is what will be said about me by someone who wishes me ill: 'There he is, the one who flouts decency by still living! The man who lacked the courage to die, who gave in exchange the woman he married and, like a coward, has given Hades the slip! And now should he be called a man? He hates his parents, though it was he who refused to die!' This is the kind of talk I will be subjected to, crowning my other sorrows. Why, then, my friends, should I choose to live rather than die, 960 when both fortune and men's tongues deal me such wounds?

CHORUS [*Strophe*]: Much learning have I perused, high in the heavens let my thoughts soar, with many a doctrine grappled, but nothing have I found stronger than Necessity.[25] And there is no remedy, either in the Thracian texts that the voice

of Orpheus[26] prescribed or among the herbs that Phoebus
970   shredded as antidotes and gave to the sons of Asclepius[27] to
cure the many ills of man.

[*Antistrophe:*] This goddess alone has no altars, no images
for men to approach; to sacrifices she is indifferent. Dread
lady, I pray you may not visit me with greater force than my
years have so far seen. For whatever purpose Zeus sets in
980   motion, he accomplishes with your aid. Even the iron the
Chalybes forge you tame by force, while nothing earns respect
from your unbending will.

[*Strophe:*] You, also, Admetus, the goddess has caught in the
grip of those hands from which there is no escape. But be
resolute; for never by weeping will you bring the dead up
990   from the world below. Even children of the gods pass away
into the darkness of death. She had our love when among us
and will not forfeit that love now that she is dead. Noblest of
all her kind is the woman you took as your own dear wife.

[*Antistrophe:*] Not as a mound covering the dead and gone
must men think of your lady's tomb; no, let her be honoured
as are the gods, winning reverence from the wayfarer. As he
1000   sets foot on the winding path, he shall say these words: 'This
woman once died for her husband and now belongs to the
company of immortal spirits. Hail, gracious lady, and grant
me your blessing!' Such will be the prayers addressed to her.

[ADMETUS *has remained motionless throughout this ode of
consolation. The* CHORUS *now alerts him to the return of*
HERACLES, *who is leading a veiled woman.*]

But here, it seems, is Alcmene's son, making his way
towards your home!

HERACLES:[28] A man should speak freely to a friend, Admetus;
if he nurses any grievances, he shouldn't keep them to himself
1010   and say nothing. Now, when I arrived in your hour of need,
I expected to be counted as a friend. But you did not reveal
that the body you had to bury was your wife's, oh no, you
entertained me in your home, saying it was some neighbour's
misfortune that touched your heart. And I wore a garland on
my head and poured libations to the gods in a house where
disaster had struck! I hold you to blame, yes, I do, for treating

me like this. Yet I do not want to cause you pain when you
are in enough distress. I will tell you why I turned back and
am here again.

Take this woman and keep her safe for me until my return   1020
with the Thracian mares, once I have killed the ruler of the
Bistonians. Now if things turn out for me as I trust they won't,
for I hope I do return here, I give you this woman to serve in
your house. It was hard work that caused her to come into
my hands; I discovered that some men had organized a public
competition, a proper trial of strength for athletes, in which
I won this woman and carried her off as the prize of victory.
The winners in the lighter events had horses to lead off, while
those who came first in the heavy events, such as boxing and   1030
wrestling, were awarded cattle, and with these came a woman
for good measure. As I was in this fortunate position, it would
have shown a lack of propriety to forgo this honourable prize.
So now, as I said, you must take care of this woman. It was
no act of theft on my part that brings her here with me; I won
her at the cost of some effort. Perhaps in time you will actually
thank me.

ADMETUS: It was not out of disrespect to you or because I
thought it any cause for shame that I concealed from you my
wife's wretched fate. But it would have been crowning one
sorrow with another if you had left my house to seek hospital-   1040
ity under another man's roof; it was enough that I should
weep at my own misfortune. As to this woman, if at all
possible I beg you, my lord, bid some other man of Thessaly
take charge of her, someone who has not known suffering
such as mine. You do not lack friends among the Thessalians;
do not remind me of my miseries. I would not be able to see
her in my house and hold back the tears. I am sick at heart;
do not add a further sickness to this one. For my calamity is
a burden I can scarcely bear.

Where would a young woman live in my house, anyway?
She is young, as her clothes and jewellery indicate. Is she to   1050
live under the same roof as men, then? How will she keep her
virginity if she consorts with young men? It is no easy thing,
Heracles, to restrain a young man in his prime. It is your

interests I am thinking of here. Or am I to admit her to my
dead wife's chamber and keep her there? How am I to allow
her a place in that lady's bed? I fear a double reproach: some
Thessalian may charge me with betraying my benefactress in
seeking the arms of another young woman, while she who
1060   has died (who deserves my devotion) haunts me; I must show
the utmost care in what I do.

     Whoever you are, lady, let me tell you that you are the
same in stature as Alcestis and resemble her in form. Oh no!
In heaven's name take this woman out of my sight! Do not
wound a wounded man! In looking at her I seem to see my
own wife. She makes my heart start pounding; tears break in
springs from my eyes! Oh, this is wretchedness, only now do
I taste the real bitterness of this grief!

1070 CHORUS-LEADER: I cannot speak well of what has befallen
you; but we must bear with patient hearts whatever gift the
god has bestowed.

HERACLES: If only I had the power to bring your wife from
the dwellings of the dead into the light and to do you this
kindness!

ADMETUS: You would wish it so, I have no doubt. But how can
this be? The dead cannot return to the light.

HERACLES: Then set limits on your grief; endure as a man
should.

ADMETUS: It is easier to give counsel than to suffer and be
strong.

HERACLES: What good would it do you, if you are bent on
mourning for ever?

1080 ADMETUS: I know this for myself, but a kind of passion drives
me on.

HERACLES: Yes, love for a departed one compels tears.

ADMETUS: She has made a ruin of my life, more than I can
say.

HERACLES: You have lost a noble wife; who will deny it?

ADMETUS: And with her lost any further pleasure in life.

HERACLES: Time will soften the blow of this grief; now it is still
reaching full strength.

ADMETUS: Time will do this, if by time you mean my death.

HERACLES: Marriage to a new woman will cure you of this longing.

ADMETUS: Stop there! What a thing to say! I would never have thought it of you!

HERACLES: What? You're not going to marry? You will sleep alone?

ADMETUS: There is no one who will ever share my bed again.   1090

HERACLES: You don't imagine you are helping your dead wife at all, do you?

ADMETUS: Wherever she is I must honour her.

HERACLES: Admirable! Admirable! But people will think you a fool.

ADMETUS: May I die if I ever betray her, dead though she is.

HERACLES: Show your generous heart now; receive this woman into your home.

ADMETUS: I beg you, by Zeus who fathered you, no!

HERACLES: You will be making a mistake if you don't do this.

ADMETUS: And if I do I will be putting my heart on the rack.   1100

HERACLES: Do as I say; perhaps this kindness will turn out to your advantage.

ADMETUS: Ah, I wish you had never won her in that contest!

HERACLES: But I did win her and you share the victory with me.

ADMETUS: You are kind; but let the woman go on her way.

HERACLES: So she shall, if she must; but first consider if she must.

ADMETUS: She must, unless this means that I incur your anger.

HERACLES: I know what I'm doing; that's why I'm insisting like this.

ADMETUS: Well, have it your way; but you are doing me no kindness by behaving like this.

HERACLES: One day you'll thank me for it; just humour me.

ADMETUS [to servants]: Take her inside, if I am to receive her   1110
into my house.

HERACLES: I would rather not entrust the woman to your servants.

ADMETUS: Then escort her into the house yourself, if this is what you think best.

HERACLES: No, I'll place her in *your* hands.

ADMETUS: I will not touch her; my house stands there; let her enter.

HERACLES: To your right hand and no other I entrust her.

ADMETUS: My lord, you force me to do this against my will!

HERACLES: Be brave! Stretch out your hand and touch the stranger.

ADMETUS [*extending his hand with eyes turned away*]: There, I am reaching out, as if I were beheading the Gorgon.[29]

1120 HERACLES [*approaching the woman and lifting her veil*]: Look at her and see if she bears any resemblance to your wife. Forget your sorrow and be happy.

ADMETUS: Gods! What shall I say? This is a wonder beyond hope! Is it my wife I see here, truly my wife, or merely a vision of joy, sent by a god, that mocks me and fills me with wonder?

HERACLES: No vision is before you; it is your wife you see.

ADMETUS: I fear this may be some phantom from the shades.

HERACLES: Do not make your guest out to be a conjurer of spirits!

ADMETUS: But am I looking at my wife, the woman I buried?

1130 HERACLES: You must not doubt it; but I do not wonder at your distrusting this turn of events.

ADMETUS: May I touch her, speak to her as to my living wife?

HERACLES: Speak to her. You now have all your heart desired.

ADMETUS: O my dearest wife! That face, that form I love! You are mine again, when I had lost all hope and never thought to see you more!

HERACLES: She is yours; I pray the gods do not grudge you this joy.

ADMETUS: Noble son of sovereign Zeus, all happiness be yours! May the father who sired you keep you safe! For you and you alone have raised my fortunes from misery. How was it you succeeded in restoring her from the shades to this light?

1140 HERACLES: I fought for her in combat with the god who governs the dead.

ADMETUS: This duel with Death, where do you say you fought it?

HERACLES: Hard by her grave; I leapt out at him and held him fast.

ADMETUS: But the lady stands here speechless. Why is this?[30]

HERACLES: It is forbidden for you to hear her words until her dedication to the gods below has been annulled and the third day has come. But lead her inside and continue, Admetus, to do what is right in treating your guests as the gods would wish. And now farewell; I shall go and perform for the royal son of Sthenelus[31] the task prescribed.   1150

ADMETUS: Stay with us and share the hospitality of this house.

HERACLES: And so I shall – another day; for the moment I must press on.

ADMETUS: Well, I wish you success and a speedy homecoming. To the citizens of Pherae and all the rest of my kingdom I proclaim that dancing is to be held in honour of this happy outcome and altars are to steam with oxen sacrificed in thanksgiving to the gods. For now we have found the way from our past ill-fortune to a better future. Good fortune is mine and I will not deny it.

[*He turns and, holding* ALCESTIS, *makes his way into the palace.*]

CHORUS: Many are the forms the plans of the gods take and many the things they accomplish beyond men's hopes. What   1160
men expect does not happen; for the unexpected heaven finds a way. And so it has turned out here today.[32]

MEDEA

Preface to *Medea*

The *Medea*, a play of dark revenge and child-slaughter, is one of the most powerful and horrific of all the Greek tragedies. It is dominated by the figure of Medea herself, the foreign princess who aided Jason in the past and whom he now spurns. Medea is by far the most dynamic character in the play, easily out-classing and outwitting the men whom she manipulates. It is easy to see why Euripides' first audiences could brand him a misogynist (in Aristophanes' play *Women at the Thesmophoria*, the women of Athens complain that he constantly blackens and slanders their sex). But it must also be stressed that Euripides is extraordinarily acute and often sympathetic in his presentation of women, their situation and their psychology. Medea's speech to the chorus of Corinthian women (230ff.) is a prime example of the dramatist's willingness to see, and give a voice to, the women's case.

It is probable, though not absolutely certain, that Euripides was the first to make Medea kill her own children deliberately. Other versions were current and may well be earlier: in one, she killed them inadvertently, in an effort to give them immortality; in another, the Corinthians killed them in anger at the revenge Medea had taken upon their princess. In our texts of the play Medea does not reveal this part of her plan until a fairly late stage (792); the chorus, who have been happy to support her in her efforts to punish Jason, now recoil in horror, but are bound by their earlier oath of silence. There have been some hints earlier that Medea may do some harm to the children (e.g. 37ff.), but her intentions are at first not made explicit. These adjustments make Medea's action all the more terrible; the tragic effect is further heightened by her own hesitation and self-torture as she prepares herself for the deed.

As often in Euripides, some of the issues of the play are aired at length, and with vigorous rhetoric, in the *agon*, the debate between Medea and Jason, in which the latter inadequately defends his betrayal of his wife. It is unusual for Euripides to make a debate of this kind so clear-cut; most readers will agree that Medea wins hands-down. The amazement and outrage of Aegeus when he hears of Jason's behaviour seem to confirm this verdict. But Euripides' interest in this play is not primarily in the conflicting rights and wrongs of the participants, but rather in the psychology of Medea: what kind of a woman, even in such circumstances, could bring herself to kill her own infant children? Her situation is viewed from several perspectives: as an ordinary woman, suffering from the same disadvantages as everyday Athenian wives; as a stranger in a foreign land; as a cunning woman, one of exceptional quickness and intelligence; as a barbarian witch, skilled in potions and poisons; and as an avenging daemonic figure. The last aspect is dominant in the shocking finale. Some have felt that the mixture is too rich, that Medea does not come together as a coherent and believable personality; but this may be the result of applying over-rigid criteria of consistency and plausibility. Certainly, the part offers abundant scope for an actor or actress, who may choose to emphasize different aspects of her complex character.

The practicalities and conventions of the Greek stage discouraged the presentation of violence and death before the eyes of the audience: neither the destruction of Creon and his daughter nor the infanticide could be enacted in all their horror. In the case of the revenge on Creon's daughter, Euripides uses another regular device, the messenger speech: an eye-witness narrates the events to the gloating Medea. This speech is a *tour de force* of gruesome detail, and the messenger's dismay provides a perfect foil to Medea's exultation. Still more memorable is the long soliloquy (1021–80) in which Medea prepares herself for the child-killing, tenderly addresses and caresses her children, repeatedly falters in her determination, and finally dismisses thoughts of mercy. Euripides presents this inner conflict with a sharper eye and with more dramatic shifts of attitude than Aeschylus in his treatment of Orestes' dilemma in the *Libation-Bearers*, and even surpasses Sophocles' sensitive portrayal of Deianira in the *Women of Trachis*. Perhaps the most striking feature of the play is the clarity with which Medea sees the full horror of her revenge, yet proceeds to execute it; though she speaks of her anger and her fury, these emotions are combined with a terrible lucidity and resolution.

Vengeance is a recurrent theme in Greek myth and hence in tragedy: the *Oresteia* is a pre-eminent example. Euripides often returns to this theme: besides his own treatments of the Orestes legend, we may single out *Hecabe*, in which the Trojan women blind Polymnestor and kill his young sons as punishment for his treachery. As in the *Medea*, there is no doubt that the revenge is just, but the way in which it is exacted, and the viciousness of the avenger, must shock and disturb the spectator. It is no accident that so many avengers are women (compare also Alcmene in *The Children of Heracles*): in mythical drama, the weaker sex assert their power and often gain the upper hand over their supposed masters. Aeschylus' husband-slaying Clytemnestra had set the pattern. The dramatist draws on myths, on earlier drama, and on the conflicting attitudes of his own society, then reshapes this material into a form which will arouse the pity and fear of his audience. We cannot expect to deduce Euripides' own views about women, or extract a simple moral imperative, from the tightly knit structure of the *Medea*.

The finale of the play is a further shock. When Jason and his followers arrive seeking Medea, she finally appears above them, beyond their reach. How this was staged is uncertain, but she is presumably on the roof of the stage-building, or on the 'crane' which often conveys divine figures. The end of a play is a common place for the appearance of a deity (e.g. Artemis in the *Hippolytus*), and Medea seems to occupy that role here: she speaks with super-human authority and remoteness, prophesies Jason's death, dictates the form of a future cult. She is in fact the granddaughter of the sun, and it is he who has sent a chariot on which she can escape. Triumphant and malevolent, she shows no sign of grief or regret (despite her own earlier anticipations,

1067–8; 1249–50). This astonishing scene disappoints any hope that the gods might step in to restrain Medea, or to punish her (the chorus had invoked the sun himself in these terms, 1251ff.). Medea, descendant of the gods, here transcends all human limits: it seems that someone who has done such a deed cannot be human, but must be something more (or less?). Yet the bitterness with which Jason reproaches her shows that she is not beyond human judgement. In this final scene Euripides even makes us feel some pity, improbably, for Jason. Nor is the tale of Medea ended; she will go on now as planned to find refuge in the Athens of King Aegeus (1384–5; cf. 824ff.). In every way the ending of the *Medea* is disturbing: the horror of the action, the consequences for Athens in its mythical past, the disruption of simple expectations about human crime and divine punishment. If both civilized Athens and the heavenly gods protect Medea, how can we make sense of the world? Here and elsewhere, Greek tragedy offers the audience no easy answers.

Characters

[*The scene is set before the house of* JASON *in Corinth.*]

NURSE:[1] Oh, if only it had never gone to the land of Colchis, the ship *Argo*, winging its way through the dark-blue Clashing Rocks! If only that pine in Pelion's glens had never fallen to the axe and furnished with oars the hands of those heroes who went to get the golden fleece as Pelias commanded! For never then would my mistress Medea have sailed to the towered city of Iolcus, her heart transfixed by desire for Jason; never would she have persuaded Pelias' daughters to kill their father or now be living in this land of Corinth with her 10 husband and children, an exile who has won a warm welcome from her new fellow-citizens and who seeks to please her husband in all she does. This is what keeps a marriage intact more than anything, when a husband can count on complete support from his wife.

But now everything has turned to hatred and where love was once deepest a cancer spreads. Jason has betrayed my lady and his own children for a princess' bed; he has married the daughter of Creon, ruler of this land. And Medea, poor 20 lady, dishonoured in this way, cries out, 'What about his oaths? His right hand that clasped mine and pledged his heart? You gods, I call you to witness Jason's gratitude to me!' From the moment her husband's criminal behaviour came home to her, she has remained where she lies, all thought of food dismissed, surrendering herself to anguish and melting each passing hour with tears, not raising an eye or turning her face from the ground. A rock or wave of the sea would pay more attention to the counsel of friends than she does.

30 All she does is occasionally turn her white neck away to speak
bitter words to herself: 'O Father dear,[2] my country, my
home, I have betrayed you all in coming here with a man who
now treats me with contempt!' Misfortune has taught her,
poor lady, the misery of losing one's country. She hates her
children[3] and takes no pleasure in seeing them. My fear is
40 she may hatch some unheard-of scheme. She is no ordinary
woman; no one making an enemy of her will win an easy
victory, take it from me.

But here are the children coming, finished with their running around; their mother's troubles don't enter their heads;
grief knows no place in a child's mind.

[As the NURSE ends her speech MEDEA's two SONS come in
with their TUTOR.]

TUTOR: Old servant of my mistress' house, why are you standing
50 all alone like this at the door, muttering to yourself about
your troubles? Surely Medea would want you waiting on her
at this time?

NURSE: Old man, tutor to Jason's children, when the dice of life
fall badly for a master, a good slave's heart shares the pain.
Take me, I'm so upset by what's happened to my mistress I
just had to come out here and tell earth and sky!

TUTOR: You mean the poor lady still continues with her
laments?

60 NURSE: How naive you are! This sorrow's just beginning, not
half way yet!

TUTOR: How stupid of her! She's my mistress, I know, and I
shouldn't call her that, but wait until she learns the disaster
she faces now.

NURSE: What is it, old fellow? Out with it, please!

TUTOR: Nothing. What I said there, I take it back.

NURSE: Oh, I beg you, we're both slaves together, don't keep
me in the dark! I won't say a word about it, if necessary.

TUTOR: I'd gone over to the draughtsboards, you know the
spot, where the old fellows sit and play, round Pirene's holy
spring, and there I heard someone say it (no one thought I
70 was listening): these children are to be driven out of Corinth,
and their mother with them; it's the will of Creon, king of

this land. Now I don't know how true this story is; I'd be glad if it were false.

NURSE: I know Jason has a quarrel with their mother, but will he tolerate this treatment of his children?

TUTOR: Old ties of affection give way to new; this house has no claims on that man's heart now.

NURSE: That's scuppered us, then, if a new wave is going to crash over us before we've managed to bale out the old one!

TUTOR: Well, your task in this is to do nothing and keep quiet 80 about my story; this is no time for the mistress to know this.

NURSE: You young ones, do you hear how your father treats you? Death's not good enough for him – oh, no, I mustn't say that of my master. But where he should be showing love he's proving a traitor and that I can say!

TUTOR: Is he so different from the rest of mankind? Has it only just dawned on you that no one loves his neighbour more than himself? Have these children not lost their father's love because he now loves elsewhere?

NURSE: Inside with you, children, it will be all right, into the house! And you do all you can to keep them out of the way; 90 don't let them near their mother while she's in this depression! I've already seen her glaring at them like a bull, as if she wanted to do something awful. I'm sure of one thing, that anger of hers won't die down until someone's felt the force of her thunderbolt. I pray her victims are enemies, not those who love her!

MEDEA [*from inside*]: Oh, I am wretched, pity me for my sufferings! Oh, if only I could die!

NURSE: There you are, my poor little loves! Wasn't I right? Your mother has a troubled heart, and an angry one, too. Inside 100 the house with you quick and no delay! Don't let her catch sight of you or approach her! Watch out for that savage temperament of hers, that stubborn will and unforgiving nature! Off with you right now, go in and quickly! It's clear that this anger of hers will grow; soon enough her grief like a gathering cloud will be kindled by it and burst in storm. What action will she take then, that proud, impassioned soul, so ungovernable now that she has felt the sting of injustice? 110

MEDEA: Ah, my sufferings, my wretched sufferings, they invite
a world's tears! O cursed children of a hateful mother, I want
you to die along with your father, and all the house to go to
ruin!

NURSE: Oh, mercy! I can't bear it! What makes you blame the
children too for their father's crime? Why do you hate them?
Oh, you poor dears, I've a terrible fear in my heart that you'll
come to some harm! They have frightening natures, those of
120   royal blood; because, I imagine, they're seldom overruled and
generally have their way, they do not easily forget a grudge.
Better to have formed the habit of living on equal terms with
your neighbours. Certainly, what I want for myself is to grow
old in secure and modest circumstances. For moderation in
the first place sounds more attractive on the tongue and in
practice is by far the best for a man. Excess, though, means
no profit for man and pays him back with greater ruin,
130   whenever a house earns heaven's anger.

[*The* CHORUS *of Corinthian women now enter the orchestra
and begin to sing in lyric exchange with the* NURSE, *interrup-
ted twice by* MEDEA's *outbursts from inside the house.*]

CHORUS: I heard the voice, I heard the shouting of the unhappy
Colchian. Has she still not softened? Tell us, old woman. I
heard laments coming from inside the two gates of the fore-
court and I take no pleasure, woman, in the sorrows of the
house, as I have chosen to give it my loyal friendship.

NURSE: There is no house; all that is now ended. Its master is
140   the captive of a princess' bed, while the mistress pines her life
away in her bedchamber, refusing to let a single friend bring
any comfort to her heart.

MEDEA [*screams*]: If only a flaming bolt from heaven would
pierce my head! What benefit is it to me to continue living?
Oh, the pity of it, the pity! Oh, to die and so find rest, leaving
behind loathsome life!

CHORUS [*Strophe*]: Did you hear, Zeus and Earth and light,
150   how sad a lament she sings, the sorrowful wife? Why this
longing for the bed that others abhor, poor, rash creature?
Will you hurry to the end that is death? Do not pray for that!
If your husband worships a new bride, do not let this fault

in him vex you. Zeus will aid you in seeing justice done. Do not grieve so much for a husband lost that it wastes away your life.

MEDEA: O great Themis and lady Artemis, do you see what I 160 suffer, though I bound my accursed husband by weighty oaths? How I wish I might see him and his bride in utter ruin, house and all, for the wrongs they dare to inflict on me who never did them harm! O Father, O land of Colchis, forsaken by me to my shame when I took my own brother's life!

NURSE: Do you hear what words she speaks, how she calls upon Themis, who listens to prayer, and upon Zeus, the appointed 170 steward of mortal oaths? The mistress will not lightly abandon her rage, it cannot be.

CHORUS [*Antistrophe*]: If only she would come before our eyes and hear the sound of these words that have been spoken, in the hope that she might give up this anger that weighs on her heart and alter her mood. Let it never be said I have failed to lend a helping hand to friends. Go and bring her here from 180 the house. Tell her that we also wish her well and lose no time before she does some harm to those inside. This sorrow of hers sweeps on violently.

NURSE: I'll do this, though I doubt whether I'll win my mistress round. It's no easy task but I'll do you this further kindness. And yet that fierce look she throws at any servant who approaches her with a message, it reminds me of a lioness with cubs! Blockheads, witless fools, that's all you can call 190 them, those men of earlier days who thought up songs to cheer our lives at feasts and banquets and at dinner, without one of them ever inventing music of song or tuneful lyre to banish the hateful sorrows we mortals know, those that lead to death and the cruel strokes of fortune which overthrow homes.

And yet how much our lives would be improved if we could cure these ills by the remedy of song! When they find 200 themselves at rich banquets, why do men raise their voices in unnecessary song? The fine food served in plenty before their eyes gives them pleasure enough. [*Exit* NURSE.]

CHORUS: I heard the sound of heartfelt lamentation, as she

bewails her piteous sorrows and cries out against her wicked husband, traitor to her bed. She calls upon the gods to witness how unjustly she is treated, on Themis, child of Zeus, protec-
210   tress of oaths, who brought her over the salty depths by night to where Greece faces the waters that lock the boundless Euxine.

[*The doors of* JASON's *house open to reveal* MEDEA. *Slowly she walks out with the* NURSE *behind her and begins to address the* CHORUS *in measured tones.*][4]

MEDEA: Ladies of Corinth, I have come out of doors in case you may be blaming me in some way; for I know that arrogance is a common trait in people whether it is noticed or kept private, but it happens too that some win a bad reputation for idleness simply through keeping their own company. For there is no
220   justice in the eyes of men; a man who has done them no harm may be hated on sight before they have formed a true assessment of his nature. And in the case of one who has made his home in a strange city, he must take pains not to alienate the community he has joined. Even the citizen should be criticized if he is a law unto himself and offends his fellows by his lack of finer feeling.

As for myself, this unexpected blow of circumstance has wrecked my confidence. I am finished, my friends, and any pleasure I took in life I now renounce; it's death I want. The man who was the world to me (oh, how I know the truth of this!) has proved to be the foulest of traitors, my own husband!
230   Of all creatures that have life and reason we women are the most miserable of specimens! In the first place, at great expense we must buy a husband, taking a master to play the tyrant with our bodies (this is an injustice that crowns the other one). And here lies the crucial issue for us, whether we get a good man or a bad. For divorce brings disgrace on a woman and in the interval she cannot refuse her husband. Once she finds herself among customs and laws that are unfamiliar, a woman must turn prophet to know what sort
240   of man she will be dealing with as husband – not information gained at home. Now if we manage this task successfully and share our home with a husband who finds marriage a yoke

he bears with ease, our lives are to be envied. But if not, we'd be better off dead.

When a man becomes dissatisfied with married life, he goes outdoors and finds relief for his frustrations. But we are bound to love one partner and look no further. They say we live sheltered lives in the home, free from danger, while they wield their spears in battle – what fools they are! I would rather   250
face the enemy three times over than bear a child once.

However, we are not in the same position, you and I. You have your city here and the homes where your fathers have lived; you enjoy life's pleasures and the companionship of those you love. But what of me? Abandoned, homeless, I am a cruel husband's plaything, the plunder he brought back from a foreign land, with no mother to turn to, no brother or kinsman to rescue me from this sea of troubles and give me shelter. And so there is one small kindness I ask of you, if I devise some ways and means of making my husband pay   260
for this suffering of mine: your silence.[5] Women are timid creatures for the most part, cowards when it comes to fighting and at the sight of steel; but wrong a woman in love and nothing on earth has a heart more murderous.

CHORUS-LEADER: I will do as you ask, Medea; it is just that you should take revenge upon your husband. Your grief at what has happened to you causes me no surprise. But here I see Creon, ruler of this land, approaching. He brings news of   270
fresh decisions.

[*Enter* CREON.]

CREON: You there, Medea, with your sullen looks and angry feelings against your husband, I order you to leave this land and become an exile, taking with you your two sons, and to lose no time! I am sole arbiter of this decree and shall not return to my palace until I banish you beyond this country's boundaries.

MEDEA: Oh, I am ruined, utterly ruined! Oh, misery! My enemies are running up full sail and there is no easy place for me to reach and escape from ruin. I will put the question in   280
spite of all the abuse I am suffering: why, Creon, are you sending me away from this land?

CREON: I fear you – there is no need of prevarication here – in case you do some irreparable harm to my daughter. Any number of things make me afraid of this. You are a sorceress and a woman who is no stranger to dark knowledge. Your husband's desire for you is gone and the loss vexes you. I hear that you are making threats, so my informants tell me, to do some harm to the three of us, my daughter, her new husband and myself who gave away the bride. And so I will protect myself against this before anything happens to me. Better for me to be hateful now in your eyes than to be talked round by you and regret it bitterly in the future.

290

MEDEA: Ah, this is hard to bear! This is not the first time but one of many, Creon, that my reputation has hurt me and caused me serious harm. Any man of good sense should never have his children taught to be unusually clever. For, apart from being good for nothing, into the bargain they invite the envy and hostility of their fellow citizens. Present fools with clever new ideas and they will think you useless and a born fool yourself. And those with a reputation for fine intelligence will regard you with hatred, if the city judges you are their superior. I myself have fallen victim to this misfortune. Because I have special knowledge, some view me with resentment, others again with distaste.

300

This knowledge that is mine has limits. Never mind, you find me frightening. What unpleasantness do you fear may happen to you? Have no fear of me, Creon; my circumstances at present do not encourage me to offend against kings! After all, in what way have you done me wrong? You gave your daughter in marriage to the man of your choice. No, my hatred is reserved for my husband. You had sound reasons for doing what you did, I have no doubt. So now I do not grudge you the successful outcome of your plan. Make your marriage and heaven's blessings on your house! But allow me to live in this land. I will not speak out, though I have been wronged, and will yield the victory to stronger opponents.

310

CREON: Your words are soothing to the ear but I have a terrible misgiving that in your heart you are hatching some evil plan. This makes me trust you even less than previously. A woman who is hot-tempered, and likewise a man, is easier to guard against than one who is clever and controls her tongue. No, away with you, and this very moment! Enough of your talk! This decision is fixed and all your skill with words will not keep you in our company when you are my enemy. 320

MEDEA: No, I beg you most humbly, in the name of your newly wedded daughter!

CREON: You are wasting words; you would never persuade me.

MEDEA: What? Do you mean to drive me out and show no respect for my prayers?

CREON: I do; am I to show you more love than my own family?

MEDEA: O Colchis, my dear homeland! How I think of you now!

CREON: There you are right; only my children win more love from me than my country.

MEDEA: Ah, the loves of mortal men! What a boundless source of woe! 330

CREON: That would depend, I imagine, on the circumstances of each case.

MEDEA: Zeus, I pray that you do not forget who has caused these sufferings!

CREON: On your way, foolish woman, and rid me of my troubles.

MEDEA: You have troubles, but have I not met with troubles myself?

CREON: In a moment you will feel the rough hands of my servants as they bundle you out.

MEDEA [*sinking to her knees and seizing* CREON *by the hand*]: Oh no, Creon, not that, I beg you!

CREON: It seems you are determined to cause trouble, woman.

MEDEA: I will go into exile; it was not that I begged from you.

CREON: What does this new show of resistance mean? Let go my hand!

MEDEA: Allow me to stay for just this one day. Let me think about my going into exile and a start in life for my children, now that their father sees fit to make no plans for their future. Show them some pity! You are also a father of children; my little ones should stir some kind thoughts in you. I do not care 340 what happens to me if I go into exile; it's my children, my poor, suffering children I weep for.

CREON [*disengaging his hand*]: I am no tyrant in my heart but a king; yet in showing respect to petitioners I have too often
350   invited disaster. And now, too, woman, I see my own error but, for all that, your wish will be granted. But this I command you: if the light the god sends tomorrow sees you and your children within the boundaries of this land, you shall be put to death. This is my word and it shall prove true.

[*Exit* CREON.]

CHORUS-LEADER: Oh, the pity of it! Poor lady, wretched in your sorrows, where will you ever turn? Who will now show
360   you hospitality? What house, which land will save you from these troubles? Oh, a god has launched you on a sea of troubles, Medea, setting your course where no course lies.

MEDEA: [*now back on her feet and composed*] Troubles indeed, wherever I look; there's no denying it. But my present situation is by no means terrible – don't think that! They still have trials to face, these newly-weds, and, as for the one who made the match, his troubles will not be slight. Do you imagine I would ever have stooped to flattery of this man without having some profit, some scheme in mind? Would I
370   have wasted breath on him or touched him with these hands? Never! But he is so advanced in folly that, when he might have thwarted my plans by banishing me from Corinth, he has allowed me to stay for this day, the day on which I will make corpses of three of my enemies, father, daughter and husband – my husband!

I have no shortage of deadly routes to follow that will lead them to their deaths; I don't know which one I should try first, my friends. Shall I set fire to the bridal chamber or steal
380   into the palace to the place where their bed is spread and thrust a sharpened sword through their hearts? There is one difficulty I must face: if I am caught entering their house and plotting, I will be killed and give my enemies a chance to laugh at me. The best way is the direct one, in which I am particularly expert, using poisons to overcome them.

Very well; there they are, dead. What city will open its

doors to me? Who will show me hospitality and grant me
protection by providing a country where I cannot be harmed,
a home where I would enjoy security? Impossible! I will delay
for just a short while and, if I find someone to support me   390
without fail, I'll use cunning and secrecy to carry out this
bloody deed. But if I am foiled by circumstance and driven
out, I will show my resolution to all: I'll take a sword in my
own hands and kill them, even though I am to die for it. Not
one of them will live to boast of vexing my heart – this I
swear by the mistress I revere above all others, my chosen
accomplice, Hecate, who dwells above the hearth deep within
my home. Pain and sorrow I will give them for this marriage,
pain for this union and this exile they have forced on me!   400
Come, Medea, make full use of your knowledge, plan and
plot! On to the dreadful deed! Now is your courage put to
the test! Do you see how you are treated? Are you to be
laughed at by this Jason and his Sisyphean wedding,[6] you
whose noble father is the Sun? You have the knowledge;
what's more we are women, quite helpless in doing good but
surpassing any master craftsman in working evil.

CHORUS [*Strophe*]: Uphill flow the waters of sacred rivers;   410
nature and all things are overturned. Men make deceitful
plans and the pledges they swear in the name of the gods no
longer stand firm. As for the manner of our lives, the stories
will change it from a foul to a fair name; recompense is coming
for the female sex. No more shall we women endure the   420
burden of ill-repute.

[*Antistrophe:*] The songs sung by poets of early days shall
cease to harp on our faithlessness. For Phoebus, Lord of
Poetry, did not put in our minds the lyre's inspired minstrelsy;
else would I have made my song ring out against the sex of
men. The rolling ages have much to tell of our side, much, as   430
well, of men's.[7]

[*Strophe:*] From your father's home you sailed with madness
in your heart, threading the twin rocks of the great sea; but
now you dwell in a foreign land, poor lady, with no husband
to warm your marriage bed, and are driven without rights
into exile.

[*Antistrophe:*] Vanished is the binding spell of oaths and
440   reverence abides no more in all the length of Greece but has
taken wing to the skies. You have no father's home, unhappy lady, to offer haven from your troubles, and another
queen has triumphed over your bed and holds sway in your
home.

[*As the* CHORUS *finishes its song,* JASON *enters and addresses*
MEDEA.]

JASON: This is only one of numerous times I have observed how
incurable an evil is a surly temper. You had the opportunity to
have this country and this house as your home by submitting
graciously to the will of those in power, but no: you speak
450   your foolish mind and for this exile is to be your reward. Now
as far as I'm concerned this matters little; please continue to
tell the world about 'that arch-criminal, Jason'. But as regards
what you have said against the royal house, count yourself
lucky that banishment alone is your punishment. As they
seethed with indignation, I tried repeatedly to calm their
feelings of anger, arguing for your continued stay. But you
would not back down from your stupid attitude, your constant abuse of the royals. This is why Corinth cannot be a
home for you now. None the less, in spite of all this, I have
460   not disowned my family and here I am; I am looking to your
future, my lady, to prevent your being driven out together
with our children, either penniless or in need of anything else:
many are the troubles that exile carries in its wake. You may
feel hatred for me, but I could never wish you anything but
good.

MEDEA: You unspeakable wretch – my tongue can utter no
worse abuse against your spinelessness – have you come to
face me, has my worst enemy come? This is no feat of arms
470   or audacious stroke, to subject one's own family to ill-
treatment and then to look them in the face, but the malady
that plagues mankind more than any other: shamelessness.
Yet I thank you for your visit; my heart will gain some relief
once I have told you what I think of you and, further, my
words will make painful listening for you.

    I shall start my tale from the very beginning. You owe your

life to me, as they all know, those brave men of Greece who boarded the *Argo* as your shipmates, when you were sent to master with the yoke the bulls that breathed fire and to sow the field of death.[8] And there was the serpent that kept 480 sleepless watch over the golden fleece, enfolding it within its sinuous coils – this creature's death I caused and so lifted up the torch that lit your way out of peril. I betrayed my own father, my own family to come here with you to Iolcus under Pelion, showing more eagerness than sense. Pelias, too, I killed by the most painful of deaths, at the hands of his own daughters, bringing destruction on his entire house.

All this I have done for you and yet you have betrayed me, you unfeeling monster; you have taken a new wife, though we have children of our own. For if you still had no sons, it 490 would be something I could forgive, this desire you have for a new bride. Gone is the trust to be placed in oaths; I cannot discover if you think that the gods you swore by then have lost their sovereignty or that new laws these days are prescribed for men, since you know well the value of your oaths to me. Ah, my poor hand, that you so many times would take in yours, my poor knees so earnestly clasped in entreaty, and all, all for this, you man of stone! My hopes are dashed!

Come, I will confide in you as if I had your love (and yet 500 what benefit do I imagine I will gain from you? Still, I will do it, for my questions will expose more clearly your lack of principle). Where am I to turn now? To my father's house that I betrayed together with my homeland when I came here? Or to Pelias' wretched daughters? A fine welcome to their home would they give me, the woman who caused their father's death! No, this is how things stand: my own family at home now have cause to hate me, while, to please you, I have become hated by the very people who should have had kindness from me, not harm.

And so, for all this you have made me the envy of many a Greek woman. Yes, a remarkable husband I have in you (may 510 the gods help me!), a true heart if ever there was one, seeing that I am to be cast into exile from this land, without a friend to help me, I and my children, partners in isolation! A splendid reproach this to the new bridegroom, that your children and I who saved you should wander as beggars! O Zeus, why is it you have given men clear ways of testing whether gold is counterfeit but, when it comes to men, the body carries no stamp of nature for distinguishing bad from good?

520 CHORUS-LEADER: Terrible is the anger and almost beyond cure, when strife severs those whom love once joined.

JASON: It seems I must prove myself a capable speaker indeed, my lady, and, like a seasoned helmsman, I must trim the edges of my sail to run before the tempest of your noisy protestations. My own view, since you put such a heavy emphasis on your favours to me, is that only one person, human or divine, lent success to my voyage, and that was the Cyprian. Now, you do possess a shrewd mind; but it would

530 be invidious to recount how Love with his inescapable arrows compelled you to save my life. Butввеth is is not a point I will count too strictly; where you did give assistance it was of some benefit.

But in fact in saving me you gained more than you gave, as I shall tell. In the first place, instead of an uncivilized country your dwelling is now the land of Greece, where you have come to know justice and the use of law, instead of being subject to force. Your special gifts became known to all Greeks

540 and won you renown. If you had been living at the furthest ends of the earth, your name would be quite unknown. I should not wish either for gold in my house or the skill to sing a song lovelier than any Orpheus sang, if these gifts were not accompanied by a famous name.

This and this alone have I said on the subject of my labours; after all, this verbal encounter was not of my choosing. But as regards the criticisms you made of my marriage to the princess, I shall demonstrate that in so doing I have shown wisdom, yes, and prudence, and further that I have acted like

550 a true friend to you and to my children.
[MEDEA reacts angrily.]

No, calm down! When I came here from the land of Iolcus, weighted down as I was by countless insoluble problems, what happier stroke of luck could I have met than this, to win the hand of a king's daughter, I, a man with no country of his own?

It was not because I had lost my desire for you – the thought that torments you – and had fallen hopelessly in love with a new bride, or even that I was eager to rival fathers with many sons. For I have a sufficient number of sons and am well content with them.[9] No, my motives were different; above all I wanted us to live comfortably and not go without anything, for I know that an impoverished friend is shunned, given a wide berth by everyone he knows. I also wanted to raise my sons in a manner worthy of my house and, by producing brothers for my sons by you, to put them on an equal footing and so, by joining our two families into one, to ensure my prosperity. 560

For what need have you of children? But it is to my advantage to assist my existing ones by means of children yet unborn. Surely I have planned well? Even you would grant this, if you were not so embittered by jealousy. The fact is that you women have reached the point where you think your happiness is complete when love smiles on you but, should some misfortune mar that love, you take all that is good and beautiful in life and turn it into grounds for bitter hatred. There should have been some other means for mankind to reproduce itself, without the need of a female sex; this would rid the world of all its troubles. 570

CHORUS-LEADER: Jason, you have set out your arguments skilfully and plausibly; it is my view, however, though I may surprise you with these words, that you have betrayed your wife and are behaving unjustly.[10]

MEDEA: How much I differ from many people! For in my eyes the criminal with a gift for speaking deserves the worst of punishments. So confident is he in his tongue's ability to dress his foul thoughts in fair words, there is nothing he dares not do. But he is not as clever as all that, and neither are you. Spare me your courteous looks and polished words now! For one word will floor you. If you were a man of honour, you should have won my consent to this new marriage instead of keeping it a secret from your own family. 580

JASON: Oh yes, you would be supporting this proposal whole-
heartedly, I imagine, if I had told you about the marriage,
590   when you can't bring yourself even now to abandon the anger
that sears your heart!

MEDEA: This was not your motive for saying nothing; it was
marriage to a foreigner that you felt would detract from that
great name of yours as old age drew near.

JASON: Be assured of this right now, no woman's charms are
the cause of this royal match I have made; no, as I said before
now, my intention was to make you safe and to father princes
who would be kindred to my own sons and so provide security
for our family.

MEDEA: I only hope I may never enjoy a life of prosperity that
brings pain or a happiness that would torment my heart.

600   JASON: Change your prayer and you will prove wiser, believe
me. Pray that good things may never distress you and that
you never think yourself deserted by fortune when she is your
friend.

MEDEA: Continue with your insults; you have a place of refuge,
but I am to turn my back on Corinth with none to share
my fate.

JASON: This was of your own choosing; do not put the blame
on anyone else.

MEDEA: And what was it I did? I took you for my husband, did
I, and then betrayed you?

JASON: You uttered unholy curses against the royal house.

MEDEA: In fact I *am* now a curse to your house as well!

JASON: I will not debate the rest of this business with you. But
610   if you want to accept any sum of money from me to help you
or our children on the journey from here, just say; I am ready
to provide it with ungrudging hand and to send tokens of
introduction to those who owe me favours and will open their
homes to you. If you refuse this offer you are mad, my lady;
give up this anger and you will find things more to your
advantage.

MEDEA: I would not on any terms resort to friends of yours or
accept anything from you; make me no such offer; gifts from
wicked people bring only harm.

JASON: Well, anyway, I call the gods to witness that I am willing
to do anything I can for both you and the children. But you   620
are indifferent to these advantages and out of stubbornness
you reject those who wish you well. This is why your pain is
all the greater.

[*He turns away and makes swiftly for the doors.*]

MEDEA: Go away! You are overcome by desire for your new-
won bride and are wasting valuable time here outside the
house. Don't disappoint her!

[JASON *is now out of earshot.*]

It may well turn out (and may the gods agree) that you are
entering upon a marriage you will have cause to lament!

CHORUS [*Strophe*]: When passions come upon men in strength
beyond due measure, their gift is neither one of glory nor of
greatness. But if the Cyprian tempers her visit, no other god-   630
dess is so gracious. Oh never, my lady, may you fire at me
from your golden bow the unerring arrow you have poisoned
with desire!

[*Antistrophe:*] May I know the blessing of a heart that is
not passion's slave; no fairer gift can the gods bestow. But
may the dread Cyprian never inflict upon me quarrelsome
moods and insatiable strife, firing my heart with love for   640
a stranger; may she rather show respect for marriages
where peace reigns and judge with a shrewd eye the loves
of women.

[*Strophe:*] O land of my birth, O my home, never, never may
I know exile, living that helpless, wearisome life that is the
most piteous of sorrows! Sooner may death, death, lay me   650
low, finished with this life. To be denied one's native land is
a misery beyond all others.

[*Antistrophe:*] My eyes have seen it; this is no tale heard from
others that I can reflect upon. You have no city, no friend to
show you pity when you have suffered suffering's worst.
Untouched by grace or favour may he die, the man who   660
cannot honour his loved ones, by opening a heart that har-
bours no guile! Never shall he be friend of mine.

[*Enter* AEGEUS,[11] *the elderly king of Athens, who is passing
through Corinth on his way from Delphi to Trozen.*]

AEGEUS: Medea, I wish you joy. No one knows a finer prelude than this in addressing friends.

MEDEA: And my greetings to you, Aegeus, son of Pandion the wise. Where have you been that you should visit this land?

AEGEUS: I have come from the ancient seat of Phoebus' oracle.

MEDEA: Why this pilgrimage to the earth's prophetic navel?[12]

AEGEUS: Children; to ask how I might father offspring . . .

670 MEDEA: What? You mean that you have been childless for all these years?

AEGEUS: I have no children because some god has willed it so.

MEDEA: Do you have a wife or have you never married?

AEGEUS: I am indeed a married man.

MEDEA: And what was it Apollo said to you about children?

AEGEUS: Words too wise for human intelligence to fathom.

MEDEA: Is it right that I should know the god's response?

AEGEUS: Most certainly, indeed a shrewd mind is what is needed.

MEDEA: Well, what was his oracle? Tell me, if it is something I may hear.

AEGEUS: That I should not undo the wineskin's jutting neck . . .[13]

680 MEDEA: Until doing what or coming to which country?

AEGEUS: Until I had come once more to my hearth and home.

MEDEA: And what is your purpose in making the voyage to this land?

AEGEUS: There is a man, Pittheus, who rules the land of Trozen.

MEDEA: Yes, Pelops' son, they say, a most god-fearing man.

AEGEUS: He is the one I wish to consult about this saying of the god.

MEDEA: Certainly he is a man of wisdom who has experience of such matters.

AEGEUS: Yes, and I value none of my allies more highly than him.

MEDEA [with emphasis]: Well, I wish you success! I trust you gain all your heart desires!

AEGEUS [looking at her more closely]: But why do you look so pale and wasted?

MEDEA: Aegeus, no woman has a husband as vile as mine!

AEGEUS: What are you saying? Tell me plainly what is troubling your heart.

MEDEA: I am being wronged by Jason, though I have done him no wrong.

AEGEUS: What has he done? Tell me more plainly.

MEDEA: He has taken a new wife and given her authority over me in his home.

AEGEUS: Can he really have dared to do something that shameful?

MEDEA: Make no mistake about it; he loved me once but now I stand for nothing.

AEGEUS: Has he fallen in love? Does he no longer find you attractive?

MEDEA: Oh yes, passionately in love! Loyalty to loved ones is not his way!

AEGEUS: Good riddance, then, if he's a bad lot as you say.

MEDEA: Marriage to a royal bride – that's the prize he set his heart on.

AEGEUS: Who gives his daughter to him? Tell me the full story!

MEDEA: Creon, who rules this land of Corinth.

AEGEUS: Now I see why you are distressed, my lady. You have my sympathy.

MEDEA: I am ruined. And what is more I am banished from the country.

AEGEUS: By whom? This is yet another fresh trouble you tell me.

MEDEA: Creon is driving me into exile from the land of Corinth.

AEGEUS: And Jason allows this? I hardly approve of that.

MEDEA: He says he objects but he is prepared to tolerate it. [*As before with* CREON, *she assumes a posture of helplessness in front of him.*] Oh, I appeal to you by this beard of yours,[14] by your knees, I make myself your suppliant; pity me, pity this luckless woman and do not look on when I am banished without a friend but receive me in your country and at the hearth of your home! Then may the gods fulfil your desire for children and prosperity accompany you to the grave! You do not know what a piece of luck you have found in me. I will

put a stop to your childlessness and give you the power to
father sons.[15] Such are the charms I know.

AEGEUS: There are many reasons why I am ready to oblige
720   you in this request, my lady: chiefly the gods and then your
assurance to me of the birth of children. For in this matter I
confess myself completely helpless. This is what I propose: if
you come to Athens, I shall try to give you my country's
protection as is within my rights. But you must manage your
departure from this land on your own. If you come to my
home of your own accord, you shall stay there safe from harm
and under no circumstances will I give you up to anyone. I do
730   not want to incur guilt in the eyes of friends.

MEDEA: So be it. But if I should have your assurance on this, I
would be entirely content with your offer.

AEGEUS: Surely you do not doubt my word? What difficulty do
you have?

MEDEA: I do not doubt it. But I have made enemies of Pelias'
family and of Creon. If you were bound by this oath, you
would not abandon me to them when they tried to drag me
from your land. If mere promises made up our agreement and
you had not sworn in the name of the gods, you might perhaps
become their friend and comply with their demands. My
740   position is weak, while they have all the resources a royal
house enjoys.

AEGEUS: You have shown considerable foresight in what you
say. If this is what you think best, I am quite prepared to carry
it out. Indeed this course involves me in less risk: I have an
excuse to present to your enemies and your fortunes are put
on a firmer footing. Prescribe your gods.

MEDEA: Swear by this solid Earth and by the Sun, father of my
own father, not omitting all the race of gods.

AEGEUS: To do or not to do what? Tell me!

MEDEA: For your own part, not to expel me ever from your
750   land, and, if anyone else, an enemy, wishes to take me away,
not to give me up of your own accord while you live.

AEGEUS: I swear by Earth, by the shining light of the Sun and
by all the gods to abide by these your words.

[MEDEA *rises to her feet.*]

MEDEA: I am satisfied. What are you to suffer, if you prove false to this oath?

AEGEUS: The fate awaiting mortals who offend against the gods.[16]

MEDEA: Go on your way with my blessing! For all is well. I shall come to your city with all speed, once I have carried out my intention and achieved my wish.

CHORUS-LEADER: May Maia's royal son, the traveller's guide, bring you to your home and may you gain the prize your 760 heart desires so much, for in my judgement, Aegeus, you have a noble heart.

[*Exit* AEGEUS. MEDEA'*s tone changes completely.*]

MEDEA: Zeus! Justice, child of Zeus! Light of the Sun! Now, my friends, I will triumph gloriously over my enemies! My journey is begun! Now I have hope that my enemies will get their deserts! This man has shown himself a haven to my plans, just when my ship was rolling in heavy seas. To him I shall fasten my stern cable, once I reach the town and citadel 770 of Pallas. Now I will tell you all my plans. Listen to my words; they won't be spoken lightly. I shall send one of my servants requesting that Jason visit me. When he comes, I shall use honeyed words, saying that this royal marriage he has betrayed me to make is for the best, yes, and well thought out. I will ask for my children to stay, not with the thought 780 of leaving them in the land of my enemies, but so that I may kill the king's daughter by means of trickery. I will send them, you see, with presents in their hands: a finely woven dress and a coronet of beaten gold. And if she takes this finery and puts it on her, she shall perish horribly, as shall anyone else who touches the girl. Such are the poisons with which I shall anoint the gifts.

But now I dismiss this business from my thoughts. It makes 790 me groan to think what deed I must do next. For I shall kill my own children;[17] no one shall take them from me. I will wreak havoc on all Jason's house and then quit this land, to escape the charge of murdering my beloved children, after daring to do a deed that is abominable indeed. You see, my friends, to suffer the mockery of my enemies is something I

800   will not tolerate. The time I went wrong was when I left my
        father's house, persuaded by the words of a Greek, who, with
        the gods' help, will answer to me yet. For never shall he see
        children born of me living in the years ahead, never father a
        child by his new-won bride, since, foul creature, she must
        meet a foul end through my poisons. Let no one think me a
        weak and feeble woman, or one to let things pass, but rather
        one of the other sort, a generous friend but an enemy to be
810   feared. It is people like that who achieve true fame in life.

CHORUS-LEADER: Since you have confided this scheme to me,
        I tell you, from a heart that wishes you well yet would not
        break mankind's laws, do not do this thing.

MEDEA: There is no other way. I can understand your saying
        this, however; you have not suffered the treatment I have.

CHORUS-LEADER: But to kill your very own children – will you
        have the heart for that, lady?

MEDEA: Yes; it is by doing this that I shall hurt my husband
        most.

CHORUS-LEADER: But no woman would then know greater
        misery.

MEDEA: So be it! Anything you may say now is wasted. [*Turning
        to the* NURSE, *who has been a silent presence on stage since*
820   MEDEA'*s entry*:] Come! Go and fetch Jason here! In all matters
        of trust it is you to whom I turn. Say nothing of my plans if
        truly you are a loyal servant and a woman.

CHORUS:[18] [*Strophe*]: Happy have they been from earliest
        days, the stock of Erechtheus,[19] and sons of the blessed gods,
        sprung from their sacred land untouched by foeman's spear
        and nurtured on the arts most glorious, ever moving with
830   delicate step through the brilliant air, where once, they say,
        the Pierian maids, the Muses nine, created golden-haired
        Harmony.

        [*Antistrophe*:] And on Cephisus' bank, they tell, the Cyprian
        drew water from that fair-flowing stream to sprinkle on the
840   land, breathing upon it the winds' breezes, soft and odorous;
        and ever she wears, flung on her hair, a garland of sweet-
        smelling roses and ever sends the Loves to sit by Wisdom's
        side, inspiring with that goddess all manner of excellence.

[*Strophe*:] How, then, shall the city of sacred streams or the land so hospitable to friends give you a home, the killer of your children, the unholy one who would live among them? Consider what it is to strike your children down, consider whose blood it is you mean to spill. No, at your feet, by every means, in every way we beg you not to murder your children! [*Antistrophe*:] Where will you find the boldness for such a deed? And in the fearful act, as you bring death upon your children, how will you prepare hand and heart? How will you look upon your children and in the act of slaying them refrain from weeping? When your children fall down to beg for mercy, you will not be able to dip your hand in blood with a heart that does not falter.

[*Enter* JASON.]

JASON: Here I am at your bidding. You may think of me as an enemy, but I would not deny you this right; I will listen. What new request do you wish to make of me, my lady?

MEDEA: Jason, I ask your forgiveness for what I said earlier. It is reasonable that you should be tolerant of my moods; we two have many memories of love once shared. I had words with myself and did not spare my own feelings: 'What a perverse creature I am! Why do I madly resent those who have my interests at heart? Why do I view as enemies the rulers of the land and my husband who is doing what is best for me in marrying a princess and fathering brothers for my children? Shall I not give up my anger? What is the matter with me? Are the gods not generous? Do I not have children? Have I forgotten that I am in exile and in need of friends?'

When I reflected on this, I realized the full extent of my folly and the futility of my anger. So now you have my thanks; indeed, I consider you showed good judgement in making this new match for us. I have been the foolish one; I should have shared in these plans of yours, helping to bring them to fruition, standing beside the nuptial bed and happily seeing to the needs of your bride. But we are what nature made us, I will not say creatures of wickedness, but women. You ought not to imitate our shortcomings or seek to vie with us in childish behaviour. I ask for your favour and admit to a lack of sense earlier; I have now come to a better understanding of my situation.

[*The* CHILDREN *now enter with the* TUTOR.]

Children, children, come here, leave the house! Come out and give us your greeting! Join me in saying goodbye to your father and share with your mother her change of heart – not hatred now for those who loved us but love! For we have made peace, we two, and bitterness has gone. Take hold of my right hand! [*As memory of* JASON'*s treachery stirs in her again:*] Ah! It came upon me there, the thought of sorrows hidden from us now! Oh, children, in all your years to come will you greet your mother like this with loving arms outstretched? What a wretched creature I am, how quick to shed tears and full of fear! These tender eyes fill with tears to think my quarrel with your father is finally over!

CHORUS-LEADER: Fresh tears spring from these eyes of mine as well. I pray that this trouble may not proceed to greater lengths than now.

JASON: I approve of this attitude, my lady, and do not blame you for what you said before. It is natural for womenfolk to feel anger against a husband when he deals in contraband love. Your heart has changed for the better and now at last you have come to see the superior way of thinking. This is how a sensible woman should behave. As for you, children, your father has shown himself no fool in working to achieve – the gods willing – your perfect safety. You shall yet be foremost in this land of Corinth, I fancy, you and your brothers together. Grow to manhood only; your father and whatever friends he has in heaven will see to the rest. May I see you reared in proper fashion and grown to man's estate to triumph over my enemies! [*Noticing that* MEDEA *has again broken down:*] What is this, lady? Why these fresh tears moistening your eyes? Why do you turn away a pale cheek? Are you not pleased to hear me say these words?

MEDEA: It is nothing; I was thinking about these children.

JASON: No more fears now; I will settle this business well.

MEDEA: I will do as you say; I will take you at your word. A woman is a soft creature, made for weeping.

JASON [*giving way to exasperation*]: Why all these sighs over the children now? It is too much!

MEDEA: I gave them birth. When you prayed for a long life for them, I felt a pang of pity at the thought that this might not happen. But I have touched on only some of the reasons for your coming to talk to me; the rest I will come to now. Since it is the royal will that I be banished from Corinth (and I am well aware this is the best course for me, not to continue living here as an embarrassment to you and the king, with people thinking I am bitterly opposed to the royal family), I will leave this land for exile; but to ensure that your hands guide our children's upbringing, ask Creon to waive banishment for them.

JASON: I do not know if I am likely to persuade him but I must try.

MEDEA: In that case tell your wife to beg her father not to banish them.

JASON: Yes, that I'll do; I expect I'll win her round all right, if she's a woman like all the rest!

MEDEA: I, too, shall give you my support in this task. I will send her in the hands of my children gifts more lovely, I know, by far than any in the world today. A servant must fetch the finery here without delay. She will count her blessings not singly but beyond telling when she gains as husband such a hero as yourself and becomes the owner of the finery that Helios, my father's father, bequeathed once to his offspring.
[*A* SERVANT *enters with gifts and presents them to* MEDEA, *who then turns to the children:*]
Take these bridal gifts in your hands, children, and carry them to the princess. Present them to the lucky bride! Once she has accepted them, she will find they are not to be despised.

JASON: Have you lost your senses, madam? Why do you give away gifts such as these? Do you suppose the royal house has a shortage of clothes or gold? Keep them for yourself, don't give them away! If I count for anything in my wife's eyes, she will prefer me to wealth, I have no doubt.

MEDEA: Oh, please humour me! Gifts win over the gods themselves, they say; gold carries more weight with mortals than

any number of words. Her star now shines, her sails swell with divine favour, she is young and a queen! To save my children from exile, I would give my life, not merely gold! Come, children, go into that wealthy house with the gift of this
970   finery and humbly beg your father's new wife, my mistress; entreat her to let you stay in Corinth. What is essential is that she receives these gifts into her own hands. Off with you now, lose no time! I pray you are successful and bring your mother good tidings of the prize she longs to gain!

[JASON *now leaves with the* CHILDREN.]

CHORUS [*Strophe*]: Now no more have I hopes that the children will live, no more; already they are going to embrace a bloody death. The bride will receive, she will receive, poor girl, the circlet of gold that will bind her to destruction. With her
980   own hands will she set on her blonde hair the ornament of death.

[*Antistrophe:*] The charm and divine brilliance of gowns and coronet wrought in gold will persuade her to put them on; soon she will dress for her wedding in the company of the dead. Such is the trap, the mortal doom she will fall into, poor lady; she shall not escape destruction.

990   [*Strophe:*] And you, poor fool, bridegroom of sorrow, making marriages with royalty, all-unknowing you are bringing destruction on your children's lives and a hateful death on your wife. Wretched man, you are indeed deceived in your destiny!

[*Antistrophe:*] But I grieve now for your anguish, pitiful mother of sons, who will shed your children's blood to avenge
1000   your bridal bed, forsaken lawlessly by your husband so that he might have another to share his house and bed.

[*The* TUTOR *now enters with the* CHILDREN.]

TUTOR: Mistress, they're spared, you must know! No banishment for these children now! And your gifts are in the hands of the royal bride, joyfully received! As far as she's concerned, your little ones are under no threat. But what's this? Why do you stand in such distress when fortune is smiling on you?

MEDEA: Oh, misery!

TUTOR: This sounds a note that jars with the news I've brought.

MEDEA: Oh, misery, I say, misery!

TUTOR: Can it be that I have delivered terrible news without knowing it? Was I mistaken in thinking my message a happy one? 1010

MEDEA: Your message was such as it was; I have no fault to find with you.

TUTOR: Then why these downcast looks, these tears you weep?

MEDEA: I have no choice, old man, none at all. This is what the gods and I devised, I and my foolish heart.

TUTOR: Have no fear; your children shall surely have you restored.

MEDEA: I shall give others a resting place before then, the gods pity me!

TUTOR: You are not alone in being separated from your children. One that is mortal must bear adversity with a patient heart.

MEDEA: And so I shall. Go inside the house and prepare their daily food for the children. 1020

[*Exit the* TUTOR, MEDEA *turns to address her* CHILDREN.]

O children, children, you have a city and a home where, leaving me to my misery, you will live for ever without a mother; but my fate is exile, to go to another country before I can take any pleasure in you and witness your happiness, before I see the water brought to you on the day you take your brides or deck your marriage beds or raise on high the wedding torches.

   Oh, this stubborn heart of mine! What misery it has cost me! It was all for nothing, then, children, that I reared you, all for nothing that I struggled and knew the agony of labour, 1030 suffering needlessly those stabbing pains when you were born? There was a time, oh yes, when, fool that I was, I had great hopes in you, that you would care for me in old age and, when I died, would dress me for the grave with tender, loving hands, a thing all men envy. But now that thought and its sweet comfort are no more. Robbed of your company, I shall endure a life that brings me pain and sorrow. And you, you will look no more at your mother with those eyes I love, once you have passed on to another form of life.

1040   Oh no, no! Why do you fix your eyes on me, children? Why
smile at me with that last smile? Ah, the pain! What shall I
do? My heart dissolves, ladies, when I see the shining faces of
my children! I could not do it! Goodbye to those plans I
made! I will take my children away from Corinth with me. In
bringing suffering on them to cause their father pain, why
should I bring twice as much suffering on myself? No, I shall
not do it. Goodbye to my plans.

And yet what is the matter with me? Do I want to become
1050   a laughing-stock by letting my enemies off scot-free? I must
find it in me to do this thing. To think I could have been so
weak! Did I actually let myself be influenced by such cowardly
thoughts? Off with you now, children, into the house! If
anyone would harm my sacrifice by his presence, I give him
warning now. I shall not weaken my hand![20]

Ah, stop, my heart, do not do this deed! Let them be, poor
fool, spare your children! When they are there living with us
they will bring you joy. No, by those vengeful spirits that
1060   dwell in Hades' realm, it shall never be! I will not leave my
children to the mockery of my enemies. In any case the deed
is done; she will not escape. Already the coronet is upon her
head and in her dress she begins to die, the royal bride, make
no mistake! Enough of that; I am now to tread a road of bitter
pain and to send these children on one more painful still. I
wish to speak to them.

1070   Give me your hands, children, give your mother your hands
to kiss! O hands I love so much, dear, dear lips, my children,
my pretty ones with your faces so noble! All happiness be
yours, but not here! You have lost this world, thanks to your
father. O how I love to hug them! The softness of their skin,
the sweetness of their breath, my darling ones! Away, inside
with you! I cannot look at you any more; my sorrows overwhelm me.

[*The* CHILDREN *disappear into the house.*]

I am well aware how terrible a crime I am about to commit,
but my passion is master of my reason, passion that causes
1080   the greatest suffering in the world.

CHORUS: Many times ere now I have entertained thoughts

more subtle and engaged in arguments more weighty than the
female sex should pursue. We also have a Muse, you see, who
accompanies us and tutors us in wisdom, not all of us but a
handful you might find among many who are not strangers
to the Muse. And I declare that, in the matter of happiness,   1090
those mortals who have produced children are less fortunate
than those who have no experience at all of parenthood. The
childless, who have failed to attain children, because they are
uncertain whether they are in the end a blessing or a torment
to mankind, are spared many trials. As for those who do
possess in their homes young offspring that they cherish, I see
them worn away each passing hour by anxiety, first as to how   1100
they are to rear them properly and from what resources they
are to leave them the means to live; further to this, it is hidden
from them whether good children or bad will be the reward
for their efforts.

One trouble, the last now of all that plague the world of men,
I will describe. Suppose these children have won a sufficient
livelihood and reached manhood and proved honest. Then,
should fate so ordain, look, Death has made the journey to the   1110
kingdom below, taking with him the bodies of your children.
What profit is it, then, to mankind, that the gods should cast
upon them, to crown their other woes, this bitterest sorrow,
all for the love of sons?

MEDEA: My friends, I have been waiting all this time for something to happen, watching how things will develop in the
palace. And now I see one of Jason's servants here on his way
out of doors. He's breathing hard; that shows he has a tale of   1120
strange suffering to tell.[21]

MESSENGER: Medea, flee, flee! Take whatever you can escape
in – sea vessel or land carriage!

MEDEA: What has happened that I should flee?

MESSENGER: The princess is newly dead, she and Creon, her
father, killed by your poisons.

MEDEA: Now there's a welcome piece of news! From this day
on I'll count you among my benefactors and friends!

MESSENGER: What are you saying? Are you thinking straight,
my lady? Are you sane? You have desecrated a king's home   1130

and now delight in hearing the tale! Have you no fear of the consequences?

MEDEA: I, too, have a reply I might make to what you have said. But don't be in too much haste, friend; tell your story! How did they perish? You would make me twice as happy if they died in agony!

MESSENGER: When those two sons of yours had left with their father and made their way into the bride's home, we servants who had sympathized with you in your troubles were pleased. At once every tongue in the palace was describing how you and your husband had mended your quarrel of earlier days. One of us was kissing the children's hands, another their golden heads. As for me, such was my delight I followed the children right into the ladies' quarters. The mistress who now wins our reverence in place of you did not at first notice your two children but kept her eyes lovingly on Jason. But then at their entrance she showed her revulsion, covering her features with a veil and turning away a white cheek. Your husband tried to dispel the young woman's anger and resentment with these words: 'Do not regard my family as your enemies. Do stop feeling angry and look at them once more. Please consider worthy of your love all those who enjoy your husband's love. Accept their gifts and entreat your father to spare my sons the penalty of exile, for my sake.'

Now, when she saw the finery, she could not restrain herself, but agreed to everything her husband said. Before your children and their father were any distance from the house, she had taken the elaborate dress and put it on. The golden coronet she placed upon her curls and began to arrange her hair in the gleaming mirror, casting smiles the while at her lifeless reflection. And then, rising from her seat, she walked through the rooms, stepping delicately with feet so white as she revelled in her gifts, and time and again stopping to stare back down at her ankles.

But then we were exposed to a horrific sight. The colour left her face and, with limbs trembling, she lurched backwards towards the throne and collapsed on to it, barely stopping herself from falling on the ground. At this an old servant

woman, thinking, I suppose, that Pan[22] or some other deity
was attacking her wits, raised the cry honouring the god, until
she saw white foam trickling over her lips, her eyes rolling
and protruding, and a bloodless pallor invading her flesh.
Then, to counter her earlier cry, she uttered a loud scream of
lamentation. At once one servant rushed into Creon's palace,
another to the girl's new husband to tell what had happened
to his bride.

Every room in the palace echoed to the sound of constant   1180
running. A fast runner, in his stride, would have turned the
stadium bend and be closing on the finishing line by the time
the poor girl broke her silence and woke from her trance with
a terrible cry of pain. For she was being assailed by a double
torment. The golden coronet resting on her head released a
wondrous stream of devouring fire, while the fine dress that
she wore, the gift from your children, began to consume the
wretched girl's white flesh. Up she leapt from the throne, all
aflame, and took to her heels, tossing her head and hair this   1190
way and that in her desire to be rid of the crown. But the gold
kept its fastening and would not move, while each time she
shook her head, the flame burned twice as fiercely. She sank
to the ground, crushed by her affliction, barely recognizable
except to a parent's eye. For her eyes had lost their normal
look, her features their healthy bloom, blood congealed with
fire was dripping from the top of her head and, as the poison's
jaws worked away unseen, the flesh melted away from her   1200
bones like resin from a pine-tree – a sight to stop the heart.
She was dead, but not one of us was brave enough to lay a
hand on her; her fate was a lesson we had all learned.

Then suddenly her father entered the room, unaware, poor
man, of what had happened. Flinging himself on her corpse
he cried out at once in pain and, folding her in his arms, he
kissed her and spoke these words: 'My girl, my poor girl,
which god has brought you to this heartless end? Who has
stolen you from me, an old man myself, ready for the grave?
Oh, if only I could share your death, my child!' When he had   1210
ceased his weeping and wailing, he tried to raise his aged
frame but he stuck to her fine dress, as ivy clings to laurel

branches. His struggles appalled us. Try as he might to lift up
a knee, she clung to him and each time he used force to
extricate himself, he tore the withered flesh from his own
bones. At last the wretched man could strive no more against
his awful predicament; he gasped and breathed his last.
1220 Together they lie in death, old man and young daughter.

I will say nothing now of what lies in store for you; you
will discover for yourself that you cannot evade punishment.
As for the life of man, I think and have often thought it is a
shadow. I would not hesitate to say that those who pass for
thinkers on this earth, for men of subtle reasoning, are guilty
of being the greatest fools. For no one in this life of ours
knows happiness. When fortune's tide flows towards him,
1230 one man may surpass another in prosperity, but you should
not call him happy.

[*The* MESSENGER *leaves.*]

CHORUS-LEADER: This day it seems heaven has rained many
blows justly on the head of Jason.

MEDEA: My friends, I have decided to act and at once. I will kill
the children and then quit this land. I will not delay and so
deliver them to other hands to spill their blood more eagerly.
1240 They must be killed; there is no other way. And since they
must, I will take their life, I who gave them life. Come, my
heart, put on your armour! We must not hesitate to do this
deed, this terrible yet necessary deed! Come, wretched hand
of mine, grip the sword, grip it! On to the starting line! A
painful race awaits you now! No time now for cowardice or
thinking of your children, how much you love them, how you
brought them into this world. No, for one day, one fleeting
day, forget your children; there will be the rest of your life for
weeping. For though you will put them to the sword, you
1250 loved them well. Oh, I am a woman born to sorrow![23]

[MEDEA *turns and goes into the house.*]

CHORUS [*Strophe*]: O Earth, O Sun whose rays illumine all,
look down, look upon that deadly woman before she lays
bloody hands upon her children, slaying her own flesh and
blood! For they are yours, sprung from your golden race, and
it is a fearful thing that human hands should spill the blood

of a god. No, brightness born of Zeus, restrain her, hold her
back, drive her from the house, the wretched woman whom
fiends have turned into a murderous Fury![24]   1260

[*Antistrophe*:] Gone for nothing is the toil you spent on your
children; for nothing, it seems, lady, you bore these boys you
love, after threading your way through the dark Clashing
Rocks so feared by travellers! Unhappy woman, why do you
surrender to this anger that crushes your heart, why this lust
for blood? For kindred blood polluting the ground weighs
heavy upon mortals; the murderers are paid in just measure
by the sorrows that heaven wills upon their houses.   1270

ONE OF THE CHILDREN [*from inside the house*]: Oh, help!

CHORUS [*Strophe*]: Do you hear it, do you hear it, the cry of
the children? Oh, you wretched, accursed woman!

FIRST CHILD: Oh no! What can I do? Where can I escape my
mother's hands?

SECOND CHILD: I don't know, dearest brother! We are to die!

CHORUS: Should I enter the house?[25] Yes, I will save the children
from slaughter!

FIRST CHILD: Yes! For heaven's sake, save us! We need your
help!

SECOND CHILD: Yes, we stand already in the shadow of the
sword!

CHORUS: Wretched woman, so you are made of rock or of iron,
poised to kill the fruit of your womb, these children, with   1280
your own hands!

[*Antistrophe*:] One woman, only one, I have heard, in earlier
times did violence to her own children: Ino,[26] whom the gods
had robbed of her senses, when she was driven from her home
into a life of wandering by the wife of Zeus. Unhappy girl,
prompted by the blood she foully shed, she stepped over a
cliff that bordered on the sea and, plunging into the waves,
perished, sharing the fate of her two sons. What further horror   1290
could match this? Oh, how many the troubles caused by the
loves of women! How many sorrows you have brought on
mankind before now!

[JASON *rushes on stage in great agitation*.]

JASON: You women standing here beside the house, is she in

this house, that arch-criminal, Medea, or has she fled from Corinth? For she must either hide herself below the earth or soar on wings into the vault of heaven if she is to escape the vengeance of the royal house. Does she suppose she can shed the blood of this land's king, and of his daughter, and then escape scot-free herself from this house? But she doesn't make me anxious so much as the children. She will be paid in kind by the victims of her misdeeds, but I fear for my children[27] and am here to save them from any harm the king's relatives may intend them should they seek to avenge their mother's impious act of murder.

CHORUS-LEADER: Jason, you are to be pitied; you have no idea of the depth of your misfortune. These words of yours would then never have been uttered.

JASON: What is your meaning? Perhaps she has it in mind to kill me as well, is that it?

CHORUS-LEADER: Your children are dead by the hands of their mother.

JASON: Oh no! What will you say next? You have destroyed me, lady!

CHORUS-LEADER: Your children's lives are at an end and you must recognize this.

JASON: Where did she kill them? Inside the house or out of doors?

CHORUS-LEADER: Open the doors and you will see your murdered children.

JASON: Quick, you servants, remove the bars, undo the fastenings![28] I want to see this double catastrophe!

[At this point MEDEA suddenly appears above the stage in a chariot drawn by dragons. Visible also to the audience are the corpses of her children.]

MEDEA: Why are you shaking the doors and removing their bars in your desire to see the dead ones and the one who made them so – myself? Save your labour! If you have need of me, tell me what you want; never will you lay hands on me, though. Such is the chariot that the Sun, my father's father, has given me, to keep me safe from enemy hands.

JASON: You abomination, what woman can earn more hatred

than you, from the gods, from me, from the whole human race? You had the heart to plunge a sword into your children, you, their mother, and have robbed me of life as well as sons! This you have done, this monstrous deed you have dared commit, and still you look upon the sun and earth? I curse you! Now I see it clear but what a fool I was before, when I brought you from that house of yours in a barbarous land to a home in Greece, a deadly passenger who had betrayed your father and the country that reared you. The spirit of vengeance for your crimes has been sent by the gods to punish me.[29] When you boarded my fine ship *Argo*, had you not first shed your own brother's blood in the home you shared? That was how your career began. And when I had taken you to wife and you had given me sons, you destroyed them because I chose to leave your bed. Not a woman in Greece today would ever have dared such a thing[30] and I passed them all over to marry you, a union that brought me hatred and danger, taking to myself not a woman but a lioness, with a nature more savage than Tuscan Scylla's. But enough of this; were I to heap insults on your head, I would not touch your conscience, so engrained is your audacity. 1330

1340

Away with you, artist in the unspeakable, children-killer! Now I must bemoan my fate; no joy for me in the marriage lately made, no words of greeting from the sons I fathered and raised up; they were alive but now are lost to me. 1350

MEDEA: I would have spoken at some length in reply to these words, were it not that father Zeus knew what kind of treatment you have had from me and I from you. It was not for you or your princess to trample on my love and live a life of pleasure, laughing at me, and not for Creon who made this match of yours to cast me out of this land without regretting it. So call me lioness, yes, if you wish to, for I have my claws in your heart as you deserve. 1360

JASON: The pain is yours to feel as well; you share in this suffering.

MEDEA: Let me tell you one thing: my pain is cancelled now that any mockery of yours is silenced.

JASON: O children, what a wicked mother you had!

MEDEA: O my sons, how your father's weakness caused your deaths!

JASON: Yet it was no right hand of mine that dealt them ruin!

MEDEA: No, it was your lustful heart and that new marriage of yours.

JASON: What? You decided to kill them because I loved another?

MEDEA: Do you think this a minor annoyance to a woman?

JASON: Yes, if she is sensible; but to you it is all that is evil.

1370 MEDEA: These children live no more; I say this to wound your heart!

JASON: They live (oh, the pain of it!) to bring dire curses on your head!

MEDEA: The gods know who began this quarrel.

JASON: What they know is the rottenness of your heart.

MEDEA: Yes, hate me! But I grow weary of your tiresome whining.

JASON: And I of yours; I welcome the moment of our parting!

MEDEA: Well then, what am I to do? I, too, long for this!

JASON: Allow me to bury my dead and weep over them.

MEDEA: Never! I will bury them with these hands, taking them to the sanctuary of Hera of the Cape.[31] I will not have them
1380   subjected to mockery by one of my enemies violating their tombs. In this land of Sisyphus I will establish a solemn festival with ritual observances to atone for this impious bloodshed in years to come. For myself, I shall go to Erechtheus' land, to share the home of Aegeus, son of Pandion. And you, as is right, a coward at heart, shall meet a coward's end, struck on the head by part of your *Argo*, so witnessing a bitter end to marrying me.

JASON: May you be struck down by our children's avenging
1390   curse and Justice who punishes murder!

MEDEA: What god, what spirit listens to you, the breaker of oaths, the deceiver of hosts?

JASON: Oh, this is agony! You contemptible creature, killer of children!

MEDEA: Go into your house and bury your wife.

JASON: I go, bereft of my two children.

MEDEA: You do not know lamentation yet; wait until you are old.

JASON: O children, my dear, dear children!

MEDEA: Dear to their mother, yes, but not to you!

JASON: And then you killed them?

MEDEA: Yes, to cause you pain.

JASON: Ah, pity me, I long to clasp them, to kiss the dear lips   1400
of my children!

MEDEA: Now you have words for them, now a loving welcome,
but then you thrust them away.

JASON: In heaven's name let me touch my children's soft skin!

MEDEA: It cannot be; your words are uttered in vain.

JASON: Zeus, do you hear how I am rejected, what injury she
does me, this abomination, this lioness who takes the lives of
children? But with all my power, with all my strength I do
lament and call upon the gods, asking them to witness how,   1410
with my children's blood on your hands, you prevent me from
touching them or giving their bodies burial. I wish I had never
fathered them to see them later destroyed by you!

[MEDEA *now disappears from view, taking with her the
bodies of her* CHILDREN.]

CHORUS:[32] Many are the things Zeus on Olympus has in his
keeping and many things do the gods accomplish beyond
men's hopes. What men expect does not happen; for the
unexpected, heaven finds a way. And so it has turned out here
today.

THE CHILDREN OF
HERACLES

Preface to *The Children of Heracles*

This play is less well known than the other three in this volume, and also treats a mythological episode which is much less familiar to the average reader than, for example, the stories of Troy or the Argonautic expedition. It may therefore be useful to provide a brief summary before making any further comments.

During his lifetime, the great hero Heracles was for a long time enslaved to the Argive king Eurystheus, in whose service he performed his famous labours. When this play begins, Heracles is long dead, but his young children, together with his mother Alcmene and his nephew Iolaus (by now an old man), are still being persecuted by the tyrannical Eurystheus. Although they seek refuge in many different cities, the Argive king always catches up with them and threatens the hospitable cities with war unless they drive out the refugees. In this play they have found their way to Athens, where it seems that they will be safe; but despite the goodwill of the Athenian king Demophon (son of Theseus), the Argives put pressure on the Athenians to expel them; and a prophecy warns Demophon that they will lose the imminent conflict unless a virgin dies as a sacrificial victim. One of Heracles' daughters, who is not identified in the play, but in other accounts was called Macaria, undertakes to die for the good of the others. In the ensuing battle the Athenians are victorious, reinforced by the forces of Heracles' son Hyllus, and unexpectedly aided by the strength of Iolaus, who is miraculously rejuvenated. In the closing scene, the captive Eurystheus is brought on and denounced by the vengeful Alcmene, who is eager to destroy her enemy, though the Athenians have spared him. Finally, Eurystheus prophesies as he prepares to die: his body will remain in Attic soil, and will protect the Athenians in times to come, though remaining bitterly opposed to the line of Heracles. In other words, he is to become a 'hero' in the religious sense, a dead man who receives religious offerings, and who, though less than a god, has special powers to bring good or ill upon the living. There is some damage to our texts of the end of the play, but most recent discussions conclude that only a few lines have been lost.

This is in many ways a harder play than most for the modern audience: despite some striking scenes, we do not find here characters with whom we can readily sympathize, and the situation may seem artificial, the religious atmosphere archaic. The patriotic treatment of Athens as a place of refuge, with her people ready to defend those in need, doubtless appealed to the original audience, but may seem merely self-congratulatory to us. Nevertheless, this means that the play tells us more about the Athenian conception of their own mythical past, and of the special qualities of their country, than plays which focus on the misfortunes and crimes of Thebes, or on the exploits of a non-Athenian hero. Like the funeral speech of Pericles in Thucydides' *History*, *The Children of Heracles* offers the Athenians an idealized picture of themselves, remote but doubtless uplifting in time of war. It has even been suggested that the reference in Eurystheus' final speech to the invasion of Attica by 'these children's descendants' (1034ff.) may allude to the invasions by the Spartans and their allies during the period when Euripides was writing; the general prophecy could include a particular contemporary allusion.

In any case, in this play Athenian generosity is manifest, and involves no sacrifice or transgression by the city itself: it is Macaria who must die for victory, and it is Alcmene who will exact revenge. In later dramas there is more room for disagreement about the rights and wrongs, and for concern at the consequences of war: it might reasonably be argued that the *Suppliant Women*, a play with a rather similar plot, paints a bleaker picture of the cost of war; and several of Euripides' later works suggest a degree of disillusionment with rational or democratic decision-making.

The play also allows us to see something of the tragedians' stock-in-trade, for in Greek tragedy, as in Shakespeare (and indeed in Homer), there are certain 'typical scenes' or 'story-patterns' which the dramatist may use to structure his plot. Several tragedies can be classed together as 'suppliant-plays': in these, the convention is that the helpless suppliants flee across Greece, find a possible refuge and must make an effort to win hospitality there. When the pursuers arrive, conflict of some sort ensues, and often suffering for the protector; but the rights of the suppliant will normally be vindicated. The medieval custom of seeking sanctuary on holy ground is an obvious parallel. This pattern forms the basis of Aeschylus' *Eumenides* and of Sophocles' *Oedipus at Colonus*, amongst others. Naturally Athens is often the place of refuge, but not always: the *Suppliant Women* of Aeschylus has the refugees seeking a home in Argos. Although the myths were many and various, the dramatists naturally turned often to legends and situations which offered particular opportunities for powerful speeches or emotional appeals. Another recurring feature which we find especially in Euripides is the noble self-sacrifice of a young man or woman, exemplified by Macaria in this play, by Creon's son Menoeceus in the *Phoenician Women*, and by Iphigenia (after initial reluctance) in the *Iphigenia at Aulis*: in each case the victim is formally slain for the good of the community. The death of Alcestis plays a variation on this theme: there, the death is for an individual's benefit, and is in any case reversed.

Unlike the *Medea* and the *Hippolytus*, *The Children of Heracles* seems to ask no hard questions about the gods. The play dramatizes a reversal of fortunes: from being powerless and persecuted the family of Heracles rise to a position of security and strength; Athenian virtue and piety serve to bring this about. Earlier in the play Alcmene had expressed doubts about Zeus' concern for her (718–19), but these comments are brief and bitter, belied by events. If there are darker notes struck at the end of the play, these arise from human .passions (Alcmene's thirst for revenge): the gods have played their part, and their concern for the Heraclids is shown not only through the military victory but through the accompanying miracle of rejuvenation for Iolaus.

Greek drama, unlike modern theatre or cinema, never attempted to put battle-scenes or large crowds on stage. Consequently, in this play decisive incidents, such as the Athenian assembly, the questioning of the oracles, the sacrifice and the battle, are all described at second-hand. Rather than dismissing this practice as a sign of inferior drama, we should learn to appreciate what Euripides does give us: powerful emotions, hard-hitting rhetorical contests and unexpected twists in the plot (the need for sacrifice, the arrival of Hyllus, the determination of Iolaus to enter battle, the appearance of Eurystheus, a captive yet defiant). *The Children of Heracles* is not as terrifying a play as the *Medea*, but it is fully worthy of Euripides in its ingenuity of plot and the vigour of its language.

Characters

IOLAUS, *loyal old friend of Heracles*
HERALD, *servant of Eurystheus*
CHORUS *of old men of Marathon*
DEMOPHON, *king of Athens*
ACAMAS, *brother of Demophon*
MAIDEN, *daughter of Heracles*
SERVANT *of Hyllus, eldest son of Heracles*
ALCMENE, *mother of Heracles*
MESSENGER
EURYSTHEUS, *king of Argos*
A group of young children, the sons of Heracles

[*The scene is the altar of the god Zeus at Marathon. Seated on the steps are the young sons of the hero Heracles, now dead, and their protector,* IOLAUS, *nephew of the hero and himself now an old man.*]

IOLAUS: For many years now this is what I have observed: one man is just to his neighbours, another thinks solely of his own profit and, useless to his fellow citizens, shows himself intractable in business dealings and loyal only to himself. It's experience has taught me this lesson. I had the chance to spend my days untroubled in Argos but out of respect for my own conscience and loyalty to kinsmen I alone shared in most of the labours of Heracles while he was among us. [*He raises his arms protectively over the silent children.*] And now that he has his home in the sky, I have taken his children here   10
under my wing, giving them the protection I stand in need of myself.

When their father had left the earth, Eurystheus' first wish was to kill us. We fled, forfeiting our city but saving our lives. We wander, exiles, from one city to another, driven each time across the frontier. For, to crown our other sufferings, Eurystheus has seen fit to inflict this outrage upon us: wherever he learns we have settled he sends heralds, demanding   20
that we be extradited and denied asylum, asserting that it is no trifling matter to make a friend or foe of Argos and pointing out how powerful a king he is. Now, when they see the weakness of my position and the tender years of the children, deprived of a father, they yield to the authority of the stronger party and deny us access to their land.

My decision has been to share the children's exile, to know
the misery that they know; I cannot bring myself to betray
them and so invite some man's barbed words: 'Look at how
30   Iolaus helps his kinsman's children, now that their father is
dead!' Since every part of Greece is barred to us, we have
come to Marathon and its three surrounding towns and here
at the altars of the gods we sit as suppliants,[1] dependent on
their aid. This land, they say, is governed by Theseus' two
sons, who received it by lot as kinsmen of Pandion and are
related to these children. This is why we have made this
journey to the boundaries of famous Athens. Two people of
40   advanced years are in charge of this flight: I am looking
after these lads, a task that weighs heavily on my mind,
while Alcmene keeps safe in this temple the daughters of
her son, guarding them with protecting arms; shame pre-
vents us from exposing young girls to public view by letting
them sit here on the altar steps. Hyllus and his older
brothers are searching the land for some place where we can
build a fortification to serve as our home, should we be
ejected forcibly from Marathon. [*He suddenly catches sight
of Eurystheus'* HERALD *approaching and starts beckoning
furiously to the children.*] Children, children, over here! Grab
my clothes! I see him there, Eurystheus' herald, making for
50   us, the man who hounds us and turns us into fugitives, denied
shelter in every land. [*He addresses the* HERALD *directly:*]
You loathsome creature, how I wish you would die, you and
the man who sent you, to pay for all those times that mouth
of yours has delivered its wicked tidings to their father as
well!

HERALD: No doubt you think you've found a fine place of
sanctuary here to rest and a city that will call your enemies
her own – what folly! The man does not exist who will prefer
the useless power you have to that wielded by Eurystheus.
On your way! Why do you make this trouble? You must leave
60   this place for Argos, where the penalty of death by stoning
awaits you.

IOLAUS: We shall not; this altar of the god will give us protection enough, and the land where we have come is subordinate to none.

HERALD [*with menace*]: Do you mean to create difficulties for me?

IOLAUS: You shall never take me or these children by force and lead us off!

HERALD [*seizing two of the children*]: You'll learn; it looks as if your powers of prophecy in this case leave a lot to be desired.

IOLAUS: No! You'll never succeed, not while I live!

HERALD: Get out of here! Whether you like it or not, I shall treat them as Eurystheus' property, as indeed they are, and carry them off.[2]

IOLAUS: O men of Athens,[3] dwellers in this land from earliest days,[4] give us your help! We are suppliants of Zeus of the 70 Agora,[5] yet violence is being used on us and our holy branches are defiled, disgracing your city and dishonouring the gods! [*In the accompanying struggle* IOLAUS *is knocked to the ground. The* CHORUS *now enters at speed. They are old men of Marathon, similar in age to* IOLAUS.]

CHORUS: What is this? Why the cry for help near to the altar? What trouble shall we see next?

[*Strophe*:] Look at him there, stretched out on the ground, the helpless old man! My poor friend, who was it caused you to fall so miserably on the ground like this?

IOLAUS: The man before you, sirs. He is treating your gods with contempt, seeking to drag me by force from the steps of Zeus' altar.

CHORUS: What is your homeland, old friend? What brings you 80 here to the folk who inhabit the Four Towns? Did you take ship from over the strait, leaving behind the shore of Euboea?

IOLAUS: Mine is no islander's life, friends; we have come to your land from Mycenae.[6]

CHORUS: And by what name did the people of Mycenae call you, old fellow?

IOLAUS: I imagine you have heard of Heracles' helper and comrade, Iolaus. My name is not unknown to men.

90   CHORUS: We know it well from long ago. But whose children
       are they, these young lads you have in your care? Tell us.

      IOLAUS: They are the sons of Heracles, my friends, and have
       come here to throw themselves on Athens' mercy and on
       yours.

      CHORUS [*Antistrophe*]: What is it that you need? Tell us, do
       you want to discuss something with our people?

      IOLAUS: We ask not to be handed over or to be dragged off to
       Argos in defiance of your country's gods.

      HERALD: But this will not be tolerated by your masters; you
100   belong to them and yet they find you here.

      CHORUS: It is right to show respect to the gods' suppliants, sir,
       wrong that they should be forced by violence to abandon
       their shrines. Justice is a holy maid; she will forbid this.

      HERALD: Then send them away from your land. They belong
       to Eurystheus. I will then refrain from any violence.

      CHORUS: It is an offence against the gods for a city to turn away
       strangers who beg for help as suppliants.

      HERALD: It's also a good thing to keep one's feet clear of trouble
110   and to accept good advice when offered.[7]

      CHORUS: Should you not have spoken first to the ruler of
       this land and shown respect for its independence before you
       ventured on this course, seeking to drag away strangers in
       open defiance of the gods?

      HERALD: Who is king of this land and city?

      CHORUS: Demophon, son of Theseus, child of a noble father.

      HERALD: Then it is with him that this case would best be argued;
       further talking is pointless.

       [*The* KING *now enters hurriedly, accompanied by* ACAMAS,
       with their attendants.]

      CHORUS: But here he comes in person, in haste, and Acamas,
       his brother, to hear this dispute.

120   DEMOPHON: Since you outstripped us younger men, for all
       your years, in answering the cry for help from this altar
       of Zeus, tell me, what has happened to make this crowd
       gather?

      CHORUS: These children who sit here as suppliants, my lord,
       with their wreaths hung around the altar as you see, are the

sons of Heracles. This man is their father's loyal friend and
helper, Iolaus.

DEMOPHON: Why these cries for help, then?

CHORUS [*pointing to the* HERALD]: This man was trying to take
them away from the altar here by force and made them cry
for help. Then he tripped up the old man, a pitiful sight that
made me weep.

DEMOPHON: Well, the clothes he wears, the shape of his cloak   130
are a Greek's, but he is behaving like a barbarian. [*Addressing
the* HERALD *directly:*] It's time for you to answer my questions
and let's have no delay! What brings you here? What land
have you come from?

HERALD: Argos is my home, to answer your question. My
purpose in coming and my master's name I will tell you now.
King Eurystheus sends me here from Mycenae to fetch these
people. And I have come, sir, with many a valid point to make
in speech and action alike. I, an Argive myself, am taking off
as my prisoners these Argives, runaways from my land and   140
sentenced to death by Argive law. As citizens of that city we
are entitled to enforce judgments against our own folk. We
have come to the altars of many other people and taken our
stand on the self-same arguments without anyone daring to
bring troubles on his own head. No, they came here, either
recognizing some folly in you, or else prepared to hazard
everything on one desperate throw, to win or lose. They
would hardly expect you, provided you're in your right   150
senses, when they have trodden up and down the length of
Greece, to be the only one to shed foolish tears of pity at their
misfortunes.

Come, weigh the advantages on either side: whether you
grant them a home in your land or let us take them away;
where will your interest lie? Here are the kinds of benefits we
can bring you: the fighting-force of Argos and all Eurystheus'
might – these you gain for Athens. But if, through paying
attention to their tearful appeals, you grow tender-hearted,
then the matter becomes one of armed conflict. You must not
suppose we will give them up without trial of the spear. And   160
what pretexts will you offer to explain your being at war with

Argos? What territory have we taken from you? Have you been cheated by us in any way? What allies will you be defending? For whose sake will they have given their lives in battle, those Athenians you will have to bury? Abuse from your fellow citizens will be your reward, if, to oblige an old relic, a living corpse, so to speak, and these children, you propose to get into such deep water! You will say this gesture

170 will give you grounds for hope,[8] if nothing else; that scarcely matches up to what we offer you now. When these boys reach manhood, if this is what gives you confidence, they'll make poor opposition for Argive men-at-arms! Before that day comes, there's plenty of time for you to be crushed in war.

No, take my advice: make no concession but simply let me take what is mine and then enjoy the friendship of Mycenae; do not fall into your customary trap of siding with the weak when strength is yours for the choosing.[9]

CHORUS-LEADER: No one can judge a case or discriminate in
180 argument until he has heard clearly what both sides have to say.

IOLAUS: My royal lord, in your land I enjoy the right to speak and to listen in turn, without any man intervening to cast me out, as happened in other states in the past. Between this man and us there is no common ground. Now that we are exiles from our own country, cut off henceforth from Argos by the decision of their votes, how can he justify calling us Mycenaeans and making us his prisoners, when it was they who drove us from that land? Argives we are no more. [*To*
190 *the* HERALD:] Or do you claim that anyone exiled from Argos should be banished from all Greece? Well, Athens' doors are not barred; her people will not let any fear of Argos make them drive from their land the sons of Heracles. You may have succeeded in driving these children from Trachis or some Achaean hill-town, relying, as you did, not on any principle of justice but on the same kind of boastful claims for Argos as you now make, and ignoring their status as suppliants at the altar. But things are different here. If you succeed and they decide in favour of your arguments, then I no longer recognize Athens as a free state. But the spirit and quality of

her people are things I do know. Death will not deter them, for in the eyes of brave men life counts for less than loss of honour. 200

As far as Athens is concerned, these words are enough; praise that goes beyond the mark creates ill-feeling and well I know how often I have been angered by extravagant compliments. But I want also to tell you that, as ruler of this land, you have no choice but to protect these boys.

Pittheus was Pelops' son and the father of Aethra, who gave birth to your father, Theseus. Now I will trace back for you the family of these youngsters: Heracles was son of Zeus and 210 Alcmene and she was born to Pelops' daughter; sons, then, of cousins were these lads' father and your own. Their bloodline, Demophon, is, therefore, close to yours.[10] But family ties apart, let me tell you the obligation that requires you to befriend these boys. I tell you that once I sailed with their father as his shield-bearer to fetch for Theseus the girdle that cost so many lives; and from the murky recesses of Hades he brought your father back safe to this world.[11] All Greece can testify to this. In return for that these boys ask this of you: do 220 not give them up or deny them the sanctuary of Athens, mocking your own country's gods by letting others drag them away! [*The children extend their arms in appeal to* DEMOPHON.] This act would bring disgrace on you, disgrace, too, on your city, if homeless suppliants, your own kin – oh, what they have suffered! look at them, look! – were dragged away by violent hands. Oh, I beg you most humbly, these hands I clasp together are my suppliant boughs,[12] do not refuse to take under your protection the sons of Heracles! Show yourself to be their kinsman and friend, their father, 230 brother, master even; any fate is better than becoming Argive property!

CHORUS-LEADER: My lord, this tale of woe makes me pity them. Never have I seen nobility so crushed by circumstance. The sons of so great a father do not merit such misfortune.

DEMOPHON: In three ways, Iolaus, my conscience compels me not to reject your appeal. There is, firstly, Zeus, at whose altar you sit, surrounded by these young fledglings. There is

240   also the tie of blood and the old debt that requires they should
      have from me the kindness I had from their father. Third
      comes my own good name and here I must take special
      thought. If I allow a stranger's hands to despoil this altar by
      force, men will think I am living in a country that is not free
      and betraying suppliants through fear of Argives. Hanging
      would appal me less than this! No, I may wish you had arrived
      in happier circumstances but rest assured: no one will wrest
      you or these young ones from this altar. [*Turning to the*
250   HERALD:] And you, sir, return to Argos and tell Eurystheus
      this. Tell him, besides, that if he brings an action against these
      strangers in our courts, he shall meet with justice.[13] But never
      will you take them away by force.

HERALD: Not if it is a just action and my arguments win the day?

DEMOPHON: Where is the justice in leading off suppliants
      against their will?

HERALD: Then the disgrace in this would be mine; your name
      is untarnished.

DEMOPHON: Hardly, if I allow you to drag them off.

HERALD: You need only send them beyond your borders and
      we will take charge of them then.

DEMOPHON: What a fool you are, presuming to outwit a god![14]

HERALD: It seems your country is the place where criminals
      should run for help.

260   DEMOPHON: All men alike find sanctuary where gods have
      their dwelling.

HERALD: I doubt if Mycenae's citizens will share these sen-
      timents.

DEMOPHON: Do I lack sovereignty, then, in my own land?

HERALD: Not if you behave sensibly and let no harm come to
      Argos' people.

DEMOPHON: Then Argos be harmed! I will not offend against
      the gods.

HERALD: It is not my wish that you engage in war with Argives.

DEMOPHON: Nor is it mine; but I will not abandon these
      children.

HERALD: Yet they are mine and I will take them away from
      here.

DEMOPHON: Then you will find your return to Argos a difficult
one.

HERALD: I'll find that out right now when I try.

[*He attempts to seize the children.* DEMOPHON *raises his staff
to prevent him.*]

DEMOPHON: Lay a finger on them and you'll regret it at once!   270

CHORUS-LEADER: No, sir, in heaven's name, don't dare to
strike a herald!

DEMOPHON: I shall, unless the herald learns to know his place!

CHORUS-LEADER [*to the* HERALD]: Go on your way! And you,
my lord, do not touch him!

HERALD: I am going; one man offers feeble opposition in a
fight. But I will return with Ares[15] at my back, all of Argos'
spearsmen mailed in bronze. A force of ten thousand men
waits for me, their shields at the ready, and my royal master,
Eurystheus, to lead them in person. He is waiting on the edge
of the land where Alcathous ruled,[16] expecting word from
here. When he hears of your outrageous conduct, he will
appear with the sun's fury against you and your people,   280
against your land and its crops. How useless they would be,
all those fighting men we have in Argos, if we fail to make
you pay for this!

DEMOPHON: Go and hang yourself! This Argos of yours does
not make *me* afraid! [*The* HERALD *leaves with* DEMOPHON'*s
words ringing in his ears.*] You intended to bring shame on
me by dragging these children away from here, but it was not
to be! This city of mine is not subject to Argives but free.

CHORUS: It is time to take thought before the Argives' army
draws near to our borders; Mycenae's men-at-arms are keen   290
for the fray and after this their appetite for war will be still
sharper than before. It is the custom of heralds to exaggerate
events, yes, twofold in the telling. Imagine the tale he will
unfold to his royal master: 'My treatment was outrageous!
My life hung in the balance!'

IOLAUS: The finest gift a child can have is a noble and virtuous
father; for nobility of birth weathers adversity more strongly
than common blood. We had plumbed misfortune's depths   300
but in these men we have found friends and kinsmen, the only

townsfolk throughout the length and breadth of Greece to champion these youngsters. Give them your right hands, children, give them, and you, sirs, do likewise to them and come close! My boys, we have put our friends to the test; and if
310   ever you do return to your homeland, if ever you inherit your father's house and privileges, think of these men as your saviours and friends for evermore. Never raise your spears in hatred against this land – this you must remember – but think of Athens as your dearest of all friends. They are worth your reverence; they saved us from the mighty land and army of the Argives, shouldering the burden of their enmity, and overlooked our state as homeless beggars, neither giving us up nor driving us from their land. In life or death, when
320   that hour comes, I will sing your praises, my young friend, extolling you at Theseus' side and filling his heart with joy, as I describe how kindly you welcomed and protected the children of Heracles, how nobly you maintain your father's good name throughout Greece, how you have shown yourself no disgrace to your father's noble stock. Not many men are like this; you would find one man in a thousand, perhaps, who could stand comparison with his father.

CHORUS: This land has always wanted to support the weak if
330   justice is on their side. That is why it has endured troubles past numbering for those it has befriended, and now, too, I see this contest of strength drawing near.

DEMOPHON: You have spoken well, old friend, and I am confident that these boys will fulfil your wishes; they will not forget their debt of gratitude. I will muster my citizens and give them their battle stations to meet the Mycenaeans' army with a strong force. First I will despatch scouts to meet the danger of a surprise attack (no Argive is slow to answer the battle-cry)
340   and I will gather the prophets together and perform sacrifices. As for you, leave the altar of Zeus and go into the palace, taking these boys with you. You will have servants to look after your needs, though I am away. Go inside, old friend.

IOLAUS: I will not leave the altar. We will remain here and offer our suppliant prayers for the city's success. When you have completed this trial in triumph, we will withdraw to your palace. The gods who favour us with their support, my lord, are a match for those of Argos.[17] Their champion is Hera, wife of Zeus, but on our side we have Athena. And this, I 350 maintain, contributes to success, having the support of stronger gods. Defeat is something Pallas will not accept.

[DEMOPHON *leaves the stage*.]

CHORUS [*Strophe*]: You may utter your loud boasts, stranger coming from Argos, but no more attention do you get from other men. Your rantings will cause no fear in my heart. I pray that Athens the great, city of lovely dancing-grounds, may escape this fate! You are a fool, as is Argos' tyrant lord, 360 the son of Sthenelus.

[*Antistrophe*:] You come to a city of other men, one not inferior to Argos, and, stranger though you are, try to drag away by force homeless suppliants of the gods who have come to my land. You make no concession to our king and have nothing else to say in justification. What right-minded men anywhere could sanction this? 370

[*Epode*:] My desire is for peace. To you, misguided king, I say that, if you come to this city, you will find that experience belies expectation. You are not alone in possessing swords or shields encased in bronze. You may thirst for war but do not, I pray, ravage with your spear the city where the Graces have their happy home.[18] Hold your hand! 380

[DEMOPHON *re-enters with head lowered*.]

IOLAUS: My son, you come with anxiety in your eyes. What does this mean? Some new manoeuvre by the enemy to tell of? Do they hold back or are they here? What intelligence have you received? You will certainly not say that the herald was lying to us. That king has enjoyed good fortune in the past and he will take the field against you, I have no doubt, his heart swollen with arrogance against Athens. But Zeus chastises those whose pride of heart knows no bounds.

DEMOPHON: They are here, the Argive army and Eurystheus, their king. My own eyes have seen them. A man who claims 390 true expertise in generalship should not study the enemy through the eyes of messengers. Now, as yet he has not sent his troops down here into the plain but prefers to keep watch from his position on a rocky brow, judging (I give you guesswork here) how best to bring his men down from there to our borders and then establish a secure foothold in our territory.

Meanwhile all my own preparations are well made. Athens is armed, the victims for the knife stand ready to fall before the customary gods and the city reeks with sacrifices made by priests.[19] I have gathered together in one place all the chanters of oracles and questioned them on secret lore, both what they have divulged and what withheld from men.

In other matters many differences exist in the oracles, but there is one clear judgement on which all agree: they order me to sacrifice to the daughter of Demeter a virgin girl whose father is of noble blood; this will make our enemy turn and flee and bring my city out of danger. Now, you have seen for yourself the strength of my commitment to you; but I will not kill a daughter of mine or compel any Athenian father to this act against his will. What man, if given the choice, would be so insane as to surrender his beloved children? This very moment my people are to be seen meeting in angry groups, some saying I was right to protect suppliant strangers, others accusing me of folly. If I do carry out this action, then civil war descends on Athens. Think, then, on this, and help me devise a plan for saving you and this land together, without my incurring the disapproval of my people. I do not rule them as some eastern despot his subjects; I must act justly to be treated justly.

CHORUS-LEADER: Surely this cannot be: strangers request our help and Athens is eager to comply but the gods say no?

IOLAUS: Children, we are like sailors who have escaped the savage fury of the storm and found dry land within their grasp only to have the winds sweep them from the coastline back to sea again. So we, thinking ourselves saved when we had now gained the shore, are thrust away from this land. It is hard! O cruel hope, why did you fill my heart with joy then, when you had no thought of realizing your favours? I cannot find fault with this man's actions, of course, if he is not prepared to sacrifice an Athenian child, and even our present situation raises no complaint from me. If it is the gods' will that I suffer in this way, this does not lessen my gratitude to you.

But you, children, what am I to do with you? Where are we to turn? What god has been denied the tribute of our 440 suppliant garlands? What country have we not gone to in search of protection? We shall die, children, yes, we shall be given up. And for myself, I do not care if I must die, unless in dying I give some pleasure to my enemies; it is you I weep for, children, you I pity, and Alcmene, your father's aged mother. Poor lady, what little joy for your long years on earth! What misery for me, too – so many hard tasks completed and all for nothing! It was fated, then, fated that we should fall into an enemy's hands and end our days in shame and wretchedness! 450 [*Turning suddenly to* DEMOPHON:] There is yet a way they may be saved; not all hope is lost. You must help me do something. Hand me over to the Argives in their place, my lord. This removes you from danger and I will ensure the children's safety. I have no need to cling to my life; let it go. It would please Eurystheus particularly to lay his hands on Heracles' comrade-in-arms and subject him to mockery. The man is without finer feeling. A cultured man should pray to have cultured men as his enemies, not barbarians in temperament. One would then receive full measure of respect and fair 460 treatment.

CHORUS-LEADER: Old friend, do not now lay blame at Athens' door; it might be untrue to allege we had betrayed strangers but as a criticism it would still do us harm.

DEMOPHON: Your proposal shows a noble heart but it is impossible. It is not to seize you that the king leads his army here. What use would an old man's death be to Eurystheus? No, it is these young boys he wishes dead. Young men of noble blood growing to manhood with the memory of outrage done to their father make their enemies afraid. All this he has 470 to guard against. But if there is some other plan you know, one that fits our situation better, reveal it. For myself, the oracles I have heard leave me perplexed and full of fear.

[*A young* MAIDEN *now enters from the temple. She is one of Heracles' daughters.*][20]

MAIDEN: Sirs, do not think me presumptuous for coming out here; this I ask of you first. What most becomes a woman is keeping silent, knowing her place and staying quietly in the home. I came outside when I heard your cries of grief, Iolaus,

480   not appointed to represent the family but, since I was a fit messenger and very much concerned for my brothers here and myself, wishing to learn if some fresh disaster, crowning our old misfortunes, is causing you pain.

IOLAUS: My dear daughter, there is no child of Heracles I can more justly praise than you and so it has always been. Our course, I thought, was set fair but now it has swung back again to desperate straits. [*He gestures towards* DEMOPHON:] This man tells us that the chanters of oracles prescribe that no bull or calf but a virgin of noble blood must be sacrificed

490   to Demeter's daughter, if we and Athens are to survive. This has reduced us to helplessness. He says he will not sacrifice his own children or anyone else's. His message for me is not expressed clearly but it is clear enough: unless we devise some solution to this problem, we must find some other land; his wish is to keep this country safe.

MAIDEN: This condition, then, binds us as regards our safety?

IOLAUS: It does; though we must also be successful in the rest.

500   MAIDEN: Then fear no more Argive spears wielded in anger. I am myself ready to die, good old man, and to take my stand at the sacrifice; I need no order. For what will I say, if Athens sees fit to risk great danger on our behalf, while we who have burdened others with our troubles shrink from meeting death when we might have given them life? It is unthinkable! We would invite mockery besides, if we who sat here as suppliants of the gods, uttering cries of woe, showed ourselves to be

510   cowards, we the children sprung from such a father as ours. Where is such behaviour seen among honourable men? It would, I think, be a finer thing if this city were captured (and heaven forbid that!), while I should fall into the enemy's hands and, for all my father's noble birth, suffer ignominy before facing death that will come to me anyway.

Then am I to be driven from this land to a life of wandering? And will I not feel shame when someone says, 'Why have you come here with your suppliants' branches, you who are so in love with your own lives? Leave our land! Cowards will get no help from us!' Again, suppose these boys lose their lives 520 and I keep mine (many before now have betrayed loved ones this way), not even then am I confident of happiness. For who will want to take for his wife a girl without male kin or to father children by me? Is it not better to die than meet this fate so undeserved? It would be more appropriate for a woman of less distinguished family than myself.

Consider where this body of mine must meet its end. Put garlands on me, if this is your wish; begin the rite. Win victory over your enemies! This life I offer willingly, with no 530 reluctance; I freely promise to die for these, my brothers, and myself. Through not loving my own life I have made the finest discovery: how to die and not forfeit one's good name.

CHORUS-LEADER: I am amazed. Words defeat me when I hear the magnanimity of this young woman who is willing to die for her brothers. Who in the world could speak or act more nobly than this?

IOLAUS: My dear child, you are your father's true-born daughter without doubt! You show the god-like spirit of Heracles 540 living on in his offspring! My pride when I hear you speak matches the sorrow I feel at what you must suffer. But let me tell you a fairer way for this to be done. [*Turning to servants:*] You must summon here all this girl's sisters and they should then draw lots to decide who is to die for her family. It is not right that you should die before lots have been drawn.

MAIDEN: I will not let my death depend on such a whim. That way my life is taken, not given. No more of that, old man. No, if you accept this offer, if you wish my wholehearted support, this life of mine I give for these boys but give freely, 550 not under compulsion.

IOLAUS: O my dear girl! These words are nobler yet than those you spoke before, though they were unsurpassed. Each word you utter shows more courage, more generosity of spirit than the last. I do not, of course, prescribe or forbid your death. Yet you will help your brothers live if you die.

MAIDEN: This is wise. You must not fear pollution from this death of mine. No, since I go to face the terrible knife, let me give my life freely, if I am daughter to the man I claim as my
560   father. Attend me there, good old man! I want your arms to catch me when I die and wrap my body in my dress.

IOLAUS: I could not stand by and watch your death.

MAIDEN: Then ask the king to arrange that women, not men, are holding me as I die.

DEMOPHON: You have my word, you brave, unhappy girl! Indeed my reputation would suffer for many reasons if your passing did not meet with all the proper marks of respect, but
570   chiefly because of your own fearlessness and for justice's sake. Of all women I have set eyes on you are the most courageous. If there are any last words you wish to speak to these boys and the old man, say them now, before you take your leave. [*Exit.*]

MAIDEN [*embracing* IOLAUS]: Goodbye, old friend, good-bye![21] Please be the teacher of these boys and raise them to be like you, shrewd in every case, no more than that; this will serve them well. Try with all your heart to keep them safe from death. We are your children and your hands reared us. You see me now offering up the blossom of my marriage
580   hopes as I proceed to give my life for them. And you, my brothers, assembled here before me, all happiness be yours! I pray that you enjoy all the blessings that will now be denied to my life. Honour this old man and my father's mother inside the temple here, old Alcmene; honour, too, these our Athenian friends. And if the day ever comes when the gods grant you release from your sufferings and safe passage to your homeland, do not forget the one who saved you or your obligation to give her burial! A glorious end is but my due; I
590   did not fail you in the hour of need but gave my life that our family might survive. This is my treasure, this will be my return instead of children and surrendering my virginity – if there is any life below the earth.[22] I hope there is not! For if we mortals on the verge of death will not escape even there

the thoughts that torment us, I do not know where one is to turn. Is death not regarded as the greatest cure for suffering?

IOLAUS: There is no woman, none on this earth, to match you in courage. Be assured, in death as in life you will have from us undying tribute of honour. And now goodbye! Piety forbids that I speak ill of the goddess who has claim on your life, Demeter's daughter. [*The* DAUGHTER OF HERACLES *now leaves.*] Oh, boys, this is the end of me! Such pain in my heart, my legs can barely support me![23] Take hold of me, children, cover my head with my cloak and set me down on a chair! This day's doings bring me no joy but it means our deaths if the oracle is not fulfilled. That is a still greater calamity; yet what suffering is here! [*He collapses on the ground.*]

CHORUS [*Strophe*]: No man, I say, enjoys happiness or endures sorrow in this life except by heaven's will; nor does the same house always stand firm in fortune's favour, but different fates attend it, one after the other. One man is dashed from high to low estate; another, without honour, fate makes prosperous. What is ordained no man may escape; no subtlety of thought will enable him to keep it at bay. Whoever strives to do this will spend his days in idle and unending toil.

[*Antistrophe:*] So, Iolaus, do not lie prostrate or torment your heart with excess of pain but submit to heaven's will. In dying for her brothers and country this unhappy girl wins renown as her share in death; the name she will inherit from men will be one of glory. It is through trials and tribulations that virtue's crown is won. This action of hers is worthy of her father, worthy of her birth. Whatever reverence you feel for nobility when they die, I share it with you.

[*Enter a* SERVANT *of Hyllus, Heracles' eldest son.*]

SERVANT: Children, good day to you. Where is old Iolaus? Has your grandmother left her place of sanctuary here?

IOLAUS: Here I am, so far as you can say I'm here.

SERVANT [*suddenly noticing him on the ground*]: Why are you lying there? Why the downcast looks?

IOLAUS: I am in the grip of sorrow at the fate of this family.

SERVANT: Get up; lift up your head.

IOLAUS: I am an old man; my strength is finished.

SERVANT: But I am here with news of great joy for you.

IOLAUS: Who are you? Where was it we met? I don't remember.

SERVANT: I work for Hyllus; don't you recognize me when you look at me?

640 IOLAUS: O my good friend, does this mean you are here to save us from harm?

SERVANT: Aye, just that; what's more, this day's fortune has caused the sun to shine on you.

IOLAUS [*moving in excitement to the door of the temple and calling* ALCMENE]: Alcmene, mother of a great hero, come out and listen to this man's words; they'll give you joy! All this while you've been worrying over the children's return, wasting away with the fear they may not come back.

[ALCMENE *enters in a state of confusion.*]

ALCMENE: What does it mean, Iolaus, this shouting that fills the whole temple? It's not some herald from Argos here again, is it, treating you with violence? My strength may be feeble,

650 stranger, but this you should know: there is no way you will take these children while I yet live! Why, if you do, I no longer wish to be known as the mother of Heracles. Lay a hand on them and you'll have the pair of us to deal with, two old folk – little honour for you there!

IOLAUS: No need for alarm, madam. Don't be afraid. It is no herald from Argos, no unwelcome news we have here.

ALCMENE: Then why did you raise a hue and cry to make me think the worst?

IOLAUS: To make you leave the temple and come out here.

ALCMENE: I know nothing of that. Well, who is this fellow?

IOLAUS: He brings word that your son's son has come.

660 ALCMENE: O welcome, friend, with this message of yours! But if he has crossed over into this land, why isn't he here? Where is he now? What can have happened to prevent him from appearing here at your side to fill my heart with joy?

SERVANT: He is making camp and marshalling the troops he has brought.

ALCMENE: What you say now no longer concerns us.[24]

IOLAUS: It does; it is our place now to ask questions.

SERVANT: What is it you wish to learn of recent events?

IOLAUS: What size of allied force does he bring with him?

SERVANT: Many men; I can't tell you the actual number.

IOLAUS: The Athenian commanders know, I imagine.   670

SERVANT: They know all right; he is now on the left wing of their force.

IOLAUS: What? They're armed already, waiting for the order?

SERVANT: Yes, and the beasts for sacrifice have been brought up well in front of the lines.

IOLAUS: Just how much ground is there between them and the Argive spears?

SERVANT: Enough to give a plain view of their commander.

IOLAUS: What is he doing? Seeing to the disposition of the enemy ranks, no doubt?

SERVANT: That was our guess; the words eluded our ears. Anyway, I'm on my way; I wouldn't like my master to cross swords with the enemy without me in my proper place at his side.

IOLAUS: And I'll come along with you; we are of one mind in   680 this, wanting to help our friends by standing shoulder to shoulder, as it is right we should.

SERVANT: That was a foolish thing for someone like you to say. It hardly becomes you.

IOLAUS: And the same goes for failing to share the labours of battle with my friends.

SERVANT: The strength you had once, sir, is yours no more.

IOLAUS: I'll take them on just the same, not one man less of them!

SERVANT: The weight you put in the scale will hardly tip the balance for your friends.   690

IOLAUS: Not one of my enemies will be able to look me in the eye.

SERVANT: It isn't looks that wound in battle but a sturdy arm.

IOLAUS: Can I, too, not strike through a shield?

SERVANT: You may strike, but before you struck home you'd fall over yourself.

IOLAUS: Don't try to keep me from action. I'm all set to fight.

SERVANT: Fighting is something you're incapable of; the will is there, no doubt.

IOLAUS: I'm not staying here; be sure of that, whatever you say next.

SERVANT: How do you mean to appear as a man-at-arms without any armour?

IOLAUS: There's armour inside the temple here, taken in battle;[25] that's what I'll use. I'll return it, if I'm spared; if I'm not, the god won't ask for it back. Go inside, take down a suit of infantryman's armour from the pegs and bring it to me here double quick! This is a shameful turn of events, that some should fight while others stand back out of cowardice; it is making a housewife out of me!

[*The* SERVANT *goes into the temple, shaking his head.*]

CHORUS: Your spirit has not been subdued by time; it flourishes, though your strength is gone. Why do you labour in vain at a task that will bring harm to you and little benefit to our city? Resist what your heart tells you and have regard for your years; do not attempt what is impossible. Youth once gone is a prize you will never capture again.

ALCMENE [*now breaking her silence in exasperation*]: You're out of your wits, proposing to leave me here defenceless with my grandchildren – why?

IOLAUS: Fighting is the business of men; your office is to look after these children.

ALCMENE: And what if you are killed? How will I survive?

IOLAUS: You will be cared for by your son's children, those of them who are spared.

ALCMENE: But if, heaven forbid, something does happen to them, what then?

IOLAUS: These new friends will not betray you; have no fear!

ALCMENE: Yes, this is all that gives me hope; I've nothing else to sustain me.

IOLAUS: And Zeus has regard for your sufferings, I have no doubt.

ALCMENE: Ah, Zeus! I will not speak ill of him but none knows better than he if he gives me the respect he owes me.

[*The* SERVANT *comes out of the temple with armour.*][26]

SERVANT: Here you are now, look: armour, a whole set of it! Cover yourself in this and lose no time! The battle is at hand

and Ares reserves his deepest hate for the sluggard! If it's the armour's weight that alarms you, set out unarmed for now and put all the gear on once you've reached the lines. I'll carry it meanwhile.

IOLAUS: Good idea. Bring the armour and have it ready for me to use. But put a spear in my hand and support me by the left elbow as you guide my steps.

SERVANT: Must I take the warrior in hand, then, and lead him like a boy to school?

IOLAUS: I must not stumble as I make the journey for good luck's sake.[27]   730

SERVANT: If only this stomach for the fight were matched by strength!

IOLAUS: Let's get on – if I miss the battle it will be the end of me.

SERVANT: You're the one who's holding us up, not I; you're deluding yourself with this effort.

IOLAUS: Look how well I'm setting the pace – don't you see?

SERVANT: What I see is speed more imagined than real.

IOLAUS: You'll change your tune once you see me there . . .

SERVANT: And what deeds will I witness? I hope fortune may be smiling on you!

IOLAUS: . . . striking home through some enemy's shield!

SERVANT: If we ever arrive in time; that's my worry.

[IOLAUS *and the* SERVANT *have by now almost made their exit. The old man suddenly disengages himself and turns back to make a final speech.*]

IOLAUS: O my trusty arm, if only you could lend me now the   740
help you gave when you sacked Sparta at Heracles' side – oh, you were young and strong then, how well I remember![28]
How I would make Eurystheus turn and run! He has not the heart to face the spears' onset. Wealth has in it a feature that misleads the onlooker: the assumption of courage; for we suppose the prosperous man is wise in all things.

[IOLAUS *leaves with the* SERVANT. ALCMENE *remains.*]

CHORUS[29] [*Strophe*]: O Earth, and Moon that shines the night long, O you radiant beams sent by the god to light our mortal   750
world, deliver your message to me! Proclaim it loud in the

heavens, to the throne where sits our sovereign lord,[30] and in the dwelling of grey-eyed Athena. In defence of the land of our forefathers, of the homes where we give welcome to suppliants, we are ready to cut through the danger with grey steel.

760

[*Antistrophe:*] That a city as prosperous as Mycenae, so celebrated for the valour of its warriors, should harbour ill-will against our land, this is a fearful thing; but disgrace follows, citizens, if we hand over suppliant strangers at the bidding of Argos. Zeus is our ally, we have no fear, Zeus justly bestows his favour on us; never will we think gods less powerful than men.

770

[*Strophe:*] Lady divine,[31] as yours is this land's soil and city, as you are its mother, mistress and protectress, direct elsewhere the one who flouts justice by leading here from Argos his spear-shaking host! Our deeds merit better than this – to be driven from our own homes!

[*Antistrophe:*] For in your honour the unceasing rite of sacrifice is richly paid, while the music of boys' voices and dancers

780

with their songs keep in memory the waning day of the month. And on the windy hill shouts of joy ring out as girls' feet move the night long in rhythmic dance.

[*Enter a* MESSENGER.]

MESSENGER: Madam, I bring you news that will not take long to hear and will fill you with joy: we have defeated the enemy and a trophy is being set up with full armour taken from your foes.

ALCMENE: Dearest of men, this day has raised your fortunes;

790

this message has won you your freedom. There is one misgiving from which you do not yet set me free: the fear I have that my loved ones may not be alive.

MESSENGER: But they are and there's not a man in the whole army who doesn't sing their praises!

ALCMENE: And the old man, Iolaus, is he safe? Tell me!

MESSENGER: Most certainly; in fact, his contribution to the victory was outstanding, thanks to the gods.

ALCMENE: What's that? You don't mean he managed to achieve anything in the battle?

MESSENGER: He's an old man no more – changed back to a young man again!

ALCMENE: That's miraculous news! But first I want to hear you tell how our friends so happily won the day.

MESSENGER: All this I'll make clear to you in a single speech. When we had taken up our positions, armed lines of warriors 800 extended fully and facing one another, Hyllus stepped down from his four-horse chariot and took up a position midway between the two lines of spears. Then he spoke: 'You who have brought your army here from Argos, why should we not let this land and Mycenae return to the ways of peace? You will render no disservice to Mycenae in taking from her a single life. Come, then, fight with me man to man.[32] Kill me and you may take and lead away the children of Heracles; die at my hands and you must surrender to me enjoyment of my father's ancestral privileges and house.'   810

The troops thought he had spoken well. They approved his plan to prevent the conflict and the courage he had shown. But Eurystheus would not be shamed into combat with that young hero, not by the men who heard the challenge or by the craven spirit he was displaying as a commander of soldiers. No, he was an utter coward. And did a man of this stamp come to make slaves of Heracles' children?

Now Hyllus withdrew back into our ranks and the priests, realizing that there was to be no agreement reached by single 820 combat, commenced the sacrificing. There was no shirking of the task; at once they started to slit the oxen's throats, spilling their blood to win the gods' favour. Some men began to mount chariots, others to move their bodies close together behind their shields. The Athenian king was giving orders to his soldiers, reminding them of what was expected of men of good stock: 'Fellow citizens, now is the hour to defend the soil that gave you birth and nurture!' The other, in turn, was entreating his allies not to bring shame upon Argos and Mycenae.

When the shrill note sounded out from the Tuscan trumpet, 830 giving the signal for the two sides to close in battle, can you imagine the thunderous din of clashing shields, of voices

raised in a babel of screams and groans? At first the Argive
spearsmen broke our ranks with the pressure of their advance
but then they in turn gave ground. The battle now grew fierce
as men fought face to face with legs interlocked and casualties
began to rise. Shouts of encouragement vied with one another:
'Men of Athens!' 'You who farm the land of Argos – keep
840   your city free from disgrace!' Then straining every sinew and
labouring hard and long, we at last turned those Argive
spearsmen in flight. It was then that old Iolaus saw Hyllus
setting off at speed, and, stretching out his hand, begged him
to give him a place in his chariot. He seized hold of the reins
and set off in pursuit of Eurystheus' team. What happened
next I could only tell from others' description, as I witnessed
no more than this.

As he sped past the holy hill of Athena Pallenis, divine
850   maiden, he saw Eurystheus' chariot and prayed to Hebe and
Zeus that, for a single day, he might recover his youth and
take revenge upon his enemies. Now you are privileged to
hear of a miracle.[33] Over the horses' yoke two stars appeared
that concealed the chariot in a murky cloud. Those experienced in such matters said they were your son and Hebe. But
from that dense gloom stepped Iolaus, displaying the sturdy
arms of a young athlete. At the cliffs of Sciron, like the hero
860   he is, he captured Eurystheus' chariot and team. He bound
his wrists with firm ropes and returns, leading as his glorious
victory-prize the captain-general so favoured once by fortune.
This fate of Eurystheus proclaims to all mankind a lesson of
utmost clarity: envy no man his apparent prosperity until you
see him in his grave; fortune can desert him in a single day.

CHORUS-LEADER: O Zeus, turner of the battle-tide, now I may
look upon a day that is liberated from a terrible fear!

ALCMENE: Zeus, after many a day you took note of my suffer-
870   ings; but for what you have done here you have my gratitude.
Before this day I did not think my son enjoyed a place among
the gods but now I know for certain that he does.[34] [*Stretching
her arms out to the children:*] Children, now you will be free
of your troubles, now free of Eurystheus who will come to a
sorry end! Now you will see your father's city and inherit his

landed estates, now offer sacrifice to your ancestral gods, all that you were denied when as wandering outcasts you lived a life of wretchedness. [*Turning to the* MESSENGER:] But what cunning thought lies behind Iolaus' decision to spare Eurystheus' life? Speak! There is nothing clever, in my judgement, in failing to exact revenge when your enemy is in your grasp.

MESSENGER: It was out of respect for you; he wanted you to feast your eyes on Eurystheus in the hour of your victory, when he had become yours to do with as you pleased. Mind you, Eurystheus put up a fight; it took an effort to make him bow his neck to what must be. He had no wish to come before you and take his punishment. [*Taking his leave:*] Accept my good wishes, madam, and be kind enough to remember what you said at the start of my speech, that you would make me a free man. In such a case as this a lady like your worship should honour her promises.

CHORUS [*Strophe*]: A pleasant thing to me is dancing,[35] when the flute's clear notes charm the ear and songs are heard; pleasant, too, is Aphrodite when in gracious vein; and to see prosperity smile on friends hitherto unblessed, that, too, is cause for joy. Manifold is the offspring of Fate, giver of fulfilment, and of Time, son of Creation.

[*Antistrophe:*] You have a righteous path, Athens; never must you lose hold of this, and that means honouring the gods. The man who denies this rides close to madness, as these proofs make plain. To each age the gods send their message that none can doubt, time and again curbing the arrogance of wicked men.

[*Strophe:*] Your son has passed into heaven, old mother. I shun the tale that he descended to Hades' halls, his body wasted in the awful flame of the fire;[36] in the palace of gold he lies in Hebe's lovely arms. Hymenaeus,[37] two children of Zeus were honoured by you, daughter and son.

[*Antistrophe:*] Many a time men's lives are bound up with one another; these boys' father, men say, once received Athena's help and now they have been saved by the city and people of that goddess; she cut short the insolent pride of that man whose violent spirit turned away from justice. May I

always be free from such arrogance and insatiable ambition!
[*The* SERVANT *again enters. He is followed by* EURYSTHEUS
bound as a prisoner.]

SERVANT: My lady, your own eyes will tell you but I'll say it
just the same. Here we come, bringing this man, Eurystheus,
930 before you, a sight you didn't expect to see and no less a
surprise for him. He boasted he would never fall into your
hands when he began his march from Mycenae, battle-
hardened spearsmen behind him, to sack the city of Athens,
his heart swelling with unrighteous pride. But the god cast his
vote otherwise and caused a reversal of fortune.

Hyllus and the noble Iolaus were raising a statue in honour
of Zeus the Giver of Victory to mark the day of triumph but
they told me to bring this man to you, wishing to give you
940 joy. To see an enemy's prosperity transformed to misery, that
is true pleasure.[38]

ALCMENE [*turning on* EURYSTHEUS]: You loathsome creature,
is this you here? Has Justice caught you in her net at last?
Now first of all turn your face towards me and have the nerve
to look your enemies in the eye; for now you are the conquered
and conqueror no more. Are you the man – I wish to know –
who saw fit in his wickedness to heap indignities on my son,
950 wherever he may be, sending him off with orders to destroy
hydras and lions? I will not speak of the other horrors you
devised for him; the tale would be long in the telling. There is
no insult you spared him, none; you even made him descend
alive to Hades. But these cruelties did not satisfy your effrontery; from every part of Greece you hounded us, these children
and myself, though we sat as the gods' suppliants, some of us
elderly, some still children.

Then you came here and found a city of free men, men you
could not intimidate. Now you must die a coward's death.
And yet you will be truly thankful for it: so numerous are
960 your offences you ought to taste death many times over.

SERVANT: The law will not permit this; you may not put this
man to death.

ALCMENE: Then was it for nothing that we took him prisoner
from the battle? What law stands in the way of his death?

SERVANT: The rulers of this land are opposed to it.

ALCMENE: Are they, indeed? Do they find it dishonourable to kill their enemies?

SERVANT: They do, if the enemy has been taken alive in battle.[39]

ALCMENE: Did Hyllus subscribe to these sentiments?

SERVANT: It is hardly right that he should go against Athenian wishes.

ALCMENE: It is right, however, that this man should forfeit his life and never again see the sunlight.

SERVANT: Wrong was done to him then for the first time when   970
he was denied a death in battle.

ALCMENE: Is it no longer right that a man should suffer punishment?

SERVANT: You will find no one here ready to end his life.

ALCMENE: I shall do it; and yet I can say that I am 'someone'.

SERVANT: You will not lack criticism, believe me, if you do this.

ALCMENE: Athens is a city I love; no one will deny me this. But now that this man has fallen into my hands, no one on earth will take him from me. So let them criticize me, all who want to, calling me 'impudent' and 'that woman who is more   980
arrogant than a woman should be'; this is a business I mean to see through.

CHORUS-LEADER: It is a fearful thing, my lady, I know full well, the hatred for this man that possesses you, and yet I can understand it.

EURYSTHEUS: Rest assured, madam, you will get no flattery from me, not a single word of pleading for my life, if it means I must be thought a coward.[40] This bitter quarrel of ours was not something I entered lightly. I knew I was your cousin by birth and so kinsman to Heracles, your son. But Hera – it made no difference whether I wished it or not, as she is a goddess – forced me to endure this sickness and so I became   990
your son's enemy. Knowing this was a contest I would have to fight out to the end, I set myself to devise one dangerous trial after another. I would share my thoughts with each passing night and found her hours a fertile mate in my desire to scatter and destroy my enemies and live the rest of my days without fear. For I knew your son to be no ordinary man but

one of true heroic stamp. He may have been my enemy but I recognize his worth; I can give him only praise.

1000   Once rid of him, exposed as I was to the hatred of these children and conscious of an inherited enemy, was I not right to leave no stone unturned as I resorted to executions, expulsions and scheming? These were the means to make my position secure. Now, if you found yourself in my predicament, would you not react by persecuting the angry lion-cubs, your enemy's offspring? Oh no, you would have shown tolerance and allowed them a home in Argos! This strains credulity, I think.

    Well, now that I have escaped death in battle, despite my
1010 best efforts, the laws of Greece impose pollution, if I am killed, on the one who spills my blood. Athens has shown her restraint in sparing me; she honours the gods far more than she respects your hatred of me. You have had your say and heard my response; from this day, if I die, you must call me by two names: the victim whose blood demands vengeance and the hero of noble heart.[41] This, then, is what I feel: I do not wish for death but to quit life would cause me no pain.

CHORUS-LEADER: I would offer a little advice, Alcmene: let this man go; it is the will of Athens.

1020 ALCMENE: What if he dies and I still accede to the city's wishes?

CHORUS-LEADER: That would be the ideal solution. How can this be achieved?

ALCMENE: It is an easy lesson to teach: I will kill him then hand over his corpse to the friends who come for him. As far as his person is concerned, I will not go against Athens' wishes and he by his death will give me the revenge I seek.

EURYSTHEUS: Then kill me; I do not ask for mercy. But as for the people of this city, who spared my life and were ashamed to kill a captive, I mean to present them with a gift: an ancient oracle of Loxias[42] that will confer on them in days to come
1030 blessings greater than you now imagine. When I am dead you will bury me where fate prescribes,[43] before the shrine of Pallene's holy Maid.[44] There will I lie under your soil, a guest in perpetual residence, extending goodwill to you and protection to your city but bitterly opposed to these children's

descendants, whenever in betrayal of this day's kindness they march in strength against your land.[45] Such is the nature of these strangers whose lives you have saved today.

Why, then, knowing what I do, did I come here in defiance of the god's oracle? I thought that Hera was more powerful than any oracle and would not betray me. Do not permit   1040 libations or blood of sacrifice to drip on my tomb. I will make their homecoming a sorry one to pay for this. The benefit you will gain from me will be twofold: in my death I will confer blessings on you but injury on them.

ALCMENE [*turning angrily to the Athenians*]: Well, why are you wasting time, after hearing words like these? If it is to bring salvation for your city and your children's children, kill the man! He points out the safest course. He is an enemy and yet he benefits you by his death. [*To servants, standing by:*] You men, take him away and kill him! Then his body is to be   1050 thrown to the dogs. [*Rounding finally on* EURYSTHEUS *himself:*] Don't expect you will ever live to drive me from my father's land again!

CHORUS:[46] This meets my approval. [*To servants:*] On your way, men! No guilt shall fall on the king's head from actions of ours.

HIPPOLYTUS

Preface to *Hippolytus*

In the *Women at the Thesmophoria* of 411 BC, Aristophanes makes the angry Athenian women complain that Euripides 'has deliberately chosen stories where there are bad women, producing Melanippes and Phaedras, but never a Penelope' (546–7), and throughout that play he is satirically treated as a persistent critic of the female sex. We have already seen that this account is inadequate: in the *Alcestis* he presents an unambiguously 'virtuous' woman, and in the *Medea* he creates a complex character who performs a terrible deed but cannot be simply dismissed as a monster of villainy. The complications in the portrayal of Phaedra are of a different kind and arise partly from the fact that Euripides had already covered this ground before, in an earlier *Hippolytus*, now lost. Ancient scholars, who knew both plays, distinguished them as *Hippolytus veiled* and *Hippolytus bearer of the garland*. The latter is the play that we have; the title refers to his offering to Artemis mentioned by Hippolytus when he first appears on stage (73–83).

The reconstruction of lost dramas, even when, as with Euripides' first *Hippolytus*, some short quotations and critical comments do survive, is a hazardous and speculative business. What seems certain is that in the earlier *Hippolytus* Phaedra was a conventional 'bad woman', who made sexual overtures to the honourable Hippolytus, was rejected and denounced him to her husband Theseus: Hippolytus died for his supposed crime and Phaedra killed herself. This type of story can be paralleled elsewhere in Greek myth and indeed in the Bible (Genesis 39, Joseph and Potiphar's wife). In the surviving play Euripides handles the same material, the outcome is the same (death for both Phaedra and Hippolytus), but the motives and psychology are much more interesting and ambiguous. Perhaps Euripides was piqued at the negative reception his earlier play had received, perhaps he was stimulated by the production of a play by Sophocles (also lost) on the same theme, or perhaps he was simply determined to do something new with a well-known legend. At any rate, his efforts were rewarded: the tetralogy including the extant *Hippolytus* won first prize.

Although the play is called *Hippolytus*, and his death at the end of the play overshadows that of Phaedra, the interest of the spectator is divided between the two: Hippolytus makes a brief appearance in the opening scenes, but the first half is dominated by Phaedra's agonies of love and indecision, the second by the more masculine conflict of father and son. Many will find Phaedra's dilemma more sympathetic: initially firm in her resistance to the overwhelming power of Aphrodite, she intends to starve herself to death and die with her shameful love unsuspected. It is not Phaedra who brings about the catastrophe, but her well-meaning Nurse, who cannot understand Phaedra's nobility: by her interference she first induces Phaedra to reveal her secret, then betrays it to Hippolytus. By contrast, the young man's foolish arrogance towards Aphrodite, his vicious denunciation of all women, and his tactless handling of his father are likely to reduce any audience's sympathy. Although the early scene in which he prays to Artemis is touching and beautiful in its religious devotion, his later speeches seem to show him in a less attractive light, and many critics have written disapprovingly of his puritan (or even pathological) psychology. It is easy to go too far in condemning Hippolytus: despite his furious response to the Nurse's misguided overtures, he does keep Phaedra's secret in the face of extreme provocation, refusing to break his oath. His most notorious line (622), in which he claims that only his tongue, not his heart, is bound by that oath, does not represent his considered attitude. By contrast, Phaedra, however sympathetic, not only fails in her original resolve (but can a mortal hope to defy a goddess's power?) but also unjustly libels Hippolytus – partly to preserve her own reputation, but also to take revenge for his insults to her and her sex (728–31).

Neither character is wholly admirable, but in the last analysis Hippolytus' self-destructive integrity may be thought preferable to Phaedra's morally ambiguous pride in her own good name.

Theseus, the most famous hero of Athenian mythology, has fathered Hippolytus in one of his many sexual liaisons. It is significant that Hippolytus' mother was an Amazon queen, one of a race committed to hunting and antagonism to men. His hostility to women, his devotion to a virgin goddess and huntress, his uneasy relationship with his father, who does not really understand him, and his self-consciousness about his status as a bastard (1083; 1455), all cohere in a convincing psychological picture: as often, Euripides shows himself astonishingly modern in his understanding of human emotions, attitudes and reactions. By contrast, Theseus is a man of action, impatient with his son's self-conscious purity and peculiar ways (948–57). Confident that he knows the truth, he curses his son without waiting to hear his case. The scene in which they confront each other, more than most Euripidean conflict-scenes, has the flavour of a courtroom, with much talk of oaths, witnesses and the like; but the crucial piece of testimony cannot be brought out, and the verdict and sentence have been uttered before the trial begins. Theseus' rashness in accepting his wife's word untested, without appealing to prophets or oracles, is condemned later by Artemis (1321–4; cf. 1055–6); as so often in tragedy, Theseus discovers the truth too late.

The two opposing divinities, Aphrodite and Artemis, goddesses of passion and chastity, preside over the play: they were surely represented by statues on stage, and are referred to by the characters throughout, often with unconscious ironies (e.g. 87; 361; 522–3; 725). The appearance of the deities as characters, in prologue and final scene, differentiates it from the *Medea*, where the destructive forces at work are human in origin, though daemonic in scale. The fact that Euripides has here given his human characters such vivid personalities, and portrayed their reactions so realistically, has tempted many critics to regard the divinities as dispensable, and to explain the action in terms of human psychology. But this interpretation must be wrong: we need the supernatural dimension for Theseus' curse to work

(the bull from the sea is no mere tidal wave); even more important, the revelation of Hippolytus' innocence can only convince
Theseus if it comes from an unquestionable divine source. The
gods in Euripides are real for the purposes of the drama, even if
they work on what they find in the minds of their human victims
(thus Phaedra's family has a history of dangerous and immoral
sexuality, to which she refers at 337ff.).

If the gods are truly like this, vengefully striking down those
who dishonour them, does this make for a negative, pessimistic
picture of human life? Certainly it seems cold comfort that
Artemis will continue the conflict by destroying Aphrodite's
favourite Adonis (1420–22). But we should remember that this
is tragedy, high drama, treating the actions and sufferings of
mythical figures from the remote past: in this genre we can
expect suffering and disaster. Moreover, tragic myth tends to
deal with extreme situations, dilemmas which allow no painless
resolution, whereas in everyday life the audience would rarely
if ever be confronted with choices of this kind. The normal
Athenian would have no difficulty in worshipping both Artemis
and Aphrodite in their proper place: it is not Hippolytus' chastity
but his bad-mouthing of Aphrodite that is punished. Nevertheless, with all qualifications made, the Euripidean portrayal of
divinity regularly raises worrying questions, in this play high-
lighted by the servant who vainly advises Hippolytus to mend
his manners towards Aphrodite. When the young man has left
the stage, the servant begs Aphrodite to forgive this hot-
headedness: 'pretend not to hear him. Gods should be wiser
than men' (119–20). But are they? The nature of divine wisdom
is a subject which recurs persistently in the work of Euripides.

The *Hippolytus* is a less starkly tragic play than the *Medea*,
though hardly less powerful. In particular, the disaster is somewhat alleviated because Hippolytus lives long enough to forgive
his father, at Artemis' bidding: father and son are reconciled in
the closing lines. Moreover, Hippolytus' untimely death will be
commemorated in ritual: unmarried girls will cut their locks in
his honour before proceeding to the wedding that he never had
(1423ff.). The claims of Artemis and Aphrodite are symbolically
reconciled through cult. By contrast there is little concern for

the unfortunate Phaedra at the end of the play: as a result of Artemis' revelations her much-treasured reputation is tarnished (though at 1301 she is allowed some degree of nobility), and posterity must assign her once more to the ranks of bad women.

Characters

APHRODITE, *goddess of love*
HIPPOLYTUS, *a son of Theseus and devotee of Artemis*
CHORUS *of huntsmen, followers of Hippolytus*
SERVANT *of Hippolytus*
CHORUS *of women of Trozen*
PHAEDRA'S NURSE
PHAEDRA, *wife of Theseus and stepmother of Hippolytus*
THESEUS, *king of Athens*
MESSENGER
ARTEMIS, *goddess of hunting and chastity*

[*The scene is outside the royal palace in Trozen*[1] *with, centre stage, the wide doorway of the palace with double leaves. Two statues are visible, one of Aphrodite, the other of Artemis.* APHRODITE *appears above the stage-building and begins her soliloquy.*]

APHRODITE: I am the goddess called Cypris. In heaven and earth alike my name and power are renowned. All who live between the Great Sea[2] and the boundaries of Atlas, all who see the sun's light, are my subjects. If they show a proper respect for my power I give them due status, but overthrow any who harbour arrogant thoughts towards me. For even the race of gods has this trait: they enjoy being honoured by men. I'll show the truth of these words soon enough.

Theseus' child, Hippolytus, the boy he fathered by the Amazon[3] and gave to Pittheus[4] the pure of heart to raise, is the only one among the citizens of this land of Trozen to call me the foulest of divinities.[5] He scorns the bed of love, rejecting wedlock, and pays tribute to Phoebus' sister, to Artemis, daughter of Zeus – she is his queen of heaven. He never leaves her side – a chaste union this – and through the green forest he and his swift hounds strip the earth of game to hunt, mortal man and goddess in ill-matched partnership. I do not grudge them these pastimes; why should I? But for his crimes against me I'll have my revenge on Hippolytus this day. My plans have been well advanced for some time now and little further effort is required.

When he went once from Pittheus' home to the land of Pandion[6] to witness and participate in the holy mysteries

there, his father's royal bride, Phaedra, saw him, and my
scheming caused a terrible longing to seize her heart. Before
she came here to Trozen, there, beside the very rock of Pallas,
30   she founded a temple to Cypris,[7] to look out over the land
and mark her love for one across the sea. And in the future
men shall speak of this shrine as established for the goddess
in memory of Hippolytus. But now that Theseus has left the
land of Cecrops, his hands polluted by Pallantid blood,[8] and,
submitting to a year's atonement in exile, has sailed to this
land with his wife, now the wretched woman, groaning and
reduced to madness by love's cruel jabs, is dying without
40   speaking a word. Not a soul in her household shares the secret
of her sickness.

But this love of hers must have a different end. I will reveal
the affair to Theseus;[9] it shall not stay in the dark. And this
young man who makes war on me shall be killed, through his
own father's curses, by the gift Poseidon, king of the sea, gave
to Theseus – that he might three times call upon the god's aid
and have his prayer fulfilled. To the lady Phaedra I grant a
death that saves her honour, yet she must die. For I will not
50   let the thought of her suffering rob me of the satisfaction of
seeing my enemies punished.

Enough. I see him approaching, Theseus' son Hippolytus,
his hunting energies spent for the day. I'll quit this place. And
at his heels they bay, his pack of trusty followers, honouring
in their songs Artemis the divine. For he does not know that
Hades' gates lie open and that this day's light he sees shall be
his last.

[*Exit* APHRODITE. HIPPOLYTUS *enters with a band of huntsmen, his servants, and, at some distance, an old* SERVANT, *a
palace retainer. They gather at Artemis' statue and sing her a
brief hymn.*]

HIPPOLYTUS: Follow, follow on and sing the praise of Zeus'
60   child, heavenly Artemis, our protectress!

HIPPOLYTUS AND FOLLOWERS: Sovereign lady, lady most
holy, offspring of Zeus, all hail, Artemis, daughter of Leto
and of Zeus, fairest by far of virgin maids, who in the broad
heavens dwell in your noble father's halls, the richly golden

house of Zeus! All hail, fair lady, fairest of the fair on   70
Olympus!

HIPPOLYTUS: Mistress, for you I bring this garland I have
woven. I fashioned it from flowers in a virgin meadow where
no shepherd dares to let his flock graze and the ploughshare
has not yet come. It is a pure meadow and the bee passes
over it in the spring. Reverence[10] tends it with river water for
all who have gained self-discipline in everything they do –
no mortal man their tutor but nature alone; its flowers are   80
for them to gather, while the wicked are prohibited. Dear
mistress, permit a devoted hand to set this garland on your
golden hair. For I am the only mortal who has this privilege;
I am at your side, I talk with you and am answered, hearing
your voice but not seeing your face. Oh, may I end life's race
as I have begun!

[*His offering and prayer made,* HIPPOLYTUS *remains before
Artemis' statue in an attitude of silent reverence. The old*
SERVANT *moves forward and addresses him.*]

SERVANT: My lord – after all, it's gods should be called our
'masters' – if I advised you well, would you listen?[11]

HIPPOLYTUS: Of course; I'd be a fool not to.   90

SERVANT: Well, you know the general rule among mankind?

HIPPOLYTUS: No, I don't. Just what's this question about?

SERVANT: I mean the way that pride and unfriendliness to others
is not tolerated.

HIPPOLYTUS: Quite right too; show me anyone who likes proud
people.

SERVANT: Is it an attractive quality, being good at talking to
people?

HIPPOLYTUS: Very much so; it costs little effort and can bring
benefits as well.

SERVANT: What about gods? Do you think it's the same with
them?

HIPPOLYTUS: Yes, if we behave on earth as they do in heaven.

SERVANT: Then why don't you pay your respects to a proud
goddess?

HIPPOLYTUS: Which one do you mean? Careful! Watch that   100
tongue of yours!

SERVANT: This one standing here at your doors, the Cyprian.

HIPPOLYTUS: I keep my distance when I greet her; I am pure.

SERVANT: But she's a proud one, she is. Mortals greatly honour her.

HIPPOLYTUS: No god worshipped by night wins my respect.

SERVANT: Gods must have their worship, boy.

HIPPOLYTUS: Likes and dislikes will differ in men as in gods.

SERVANT: Good luck to you, then, and all the sense you need!

HIPPOLYTUS: Inside, men! Into the house and see to some food!
110   After hunting a full table is a real pleasure. And there are my
horses to be rubbed down. Once I've eaten my fill I'll take
them for a drive and give them the workout they deserve. As
for your Cyprian, she's not mine – good riddance!

[*Exit* HIPPOLYTUS *with band of huntsmen into the palace.*]

SERVANT: Well, I'll make my prayers to your statue, Lady
Cypris, speaking as a slave should. For we shouldn't imitate
young folk when this is what's in their heads. Forgiveness is
what we need. If someone in the heat of youth says foolish
things about you, pretend not to hear him. Gods should be
120   wiser than men.

[*Exit* SERVANT *and enter the* CHORUS, *fifteen young married
women of Trozen.*]

CHORUS [*Strophe*]: A rock there is, dripping water from Ocean
(so men say), and from its face it sends a gushing stream
whose waters bathe the proffered pitchers. There it was a
friend of mine was washing crimson robes in the flowing
spring and spreading them on a rock warmed by the sun.
130   From her I first heard tell of my lady;

[*Antistrophe:*] how she wastes away on a bed of sickness and
keeps to the palace, her blonde head shaded by fine-spun
veils. This is the third day, I hear, that she had let no food
pass her lips and kept her body pure of Demeter's grain. Some
unspoken trouble prompts her to bring her craft to rest on
140   death's unhappy strand.

[*Strophe:*] Are you possessed, sweet lady?[12] Do you wander
in the grip of Pan or Hecate? Is it the holy Corybantes who
haunt you or the Mountain Mother? Or can it be Dictynna,
mistress of wild things, you have offended? Her sacred rites

or offerings neglected – is that the sin that withers you so?
Over the salt lake too she ranges and the sandy spit amid the   150
sea's eddies.

[*Antistrophe:*] Or can it be that your husband, noble prince
of Erechtheid blood, finds comfort in his home with another,
in a union that is secret from your bed? Or has some sailor,
putting out from Crete, voyaged to the port where seamen
find most ready welcome, bringing news for the queen of
some sorrow that chains her anguished soul to her bed?   160

[*Epode:*] A miserable, wearying helplessness too often
accompanies the irritable constitution of women before the
pains of labour, making our wits go astray. Through my
womb once this breeze blew strong. But on the heavenly one
I cried, the archeress who eases labour, Artemis, and always
– gods be thanked! – she comes to my side, the answer to all
prayers.

CHORUS-LEADER: Ah, here before the doors is her old Nurse,   170
bringing her out of the palace. But the cloud of melancholy
thickens on her brows. My heart longs to know what the
cause is, what it is has wasted the queen's body and drained
it of colour.

[*As the* CHORUS *chant these lines, the palace doors open and*
PHAEDRA'S NURSE *emerges, followed by her mistress, who*
lies on a bed carried by serving women.]

NURSE[13] [*to* PHAEDRA]: How horrible life is with its sickness
and troubles![14] I just don't know what to do with you, I really
don't. Here is sunlight, look! Here's fresh air and brightness;
you can lie on your sickbed outdoors now. 'I want to go   180
outside!' was all we heard from you then but in no time it'll
be, 'Take me to my bedroom at once!' You're up one minute,
down the next; nothing pleases you. You're never happy with
what's in front of you; you're more interested in what you
lack. I'd rather be a patient than a nurse; the one's a simple
matter, the other means worry and sore hands. It's nothing
but pain, this life of ours; we're born to suffer and there's no
end to it. If anything more precious than life does exist, it's   190
wrapped in darkness, hidden behind clouds. We're fools in
love – it's plain enough – clinging to this glitter here on earth

because we don't know any other life and haven't seen what lies below. It's stories sweep us along, silly stories.

PHAEDRA: Lift my body, hold up my head. I have lost control
200   of my limbs. Take hold of my hands and slender arms, maid-servants. This net is heavy that holds my hair. Remove it, let my hair fall over my shoulders.

NURSE: Don't fret, my girl, stop tiring yourself out with all this movement. You'll find your illness easier to bear if you stay calm and show a noble spirit. Everyone on earth suffers – it's the way life is.

PHAEDRA: Ah, if only I might take a draught of pure water
210   from a fresh spring and rest on the ground under poplars in some lush meadow![15]

NURSE: What are you saying, child? You musn't speak like this for anyone to hear, wild words that ride on madness.

PHAEDRA: Take me to the mountains! To the forest I'll go, among the pines, where hounds run their prey to ground, fastening upon the spotted deer. O you gods, I beg you! How I long to cheer on my hounds, to hold a barbed spear of
220   Thessaly in my hand, to lift it high and hurl it past my shining hair!

NURSE: Why are you so worried about these things, you poor dear? What's all this about hounds and hunting? Why are you in love with running springs? Right here, alongside the city walls, is a watered slope – that's the place for you to drink!

PHAEDRA: Artemis, mistress of the salt mere and the exercise
230   grounds where horses gallop hard, I wish I were in your sanctuary, breaking in colts of Venetia!

NURSE: More madness! Why are you babbling like this? Just now you were off to the mountains, all on fire for the hunt, but now it's horses you're after beside the waveless sands. It needs all of a prophet's skill to learn which god pulls you on the rein and drives your wits astray, my girl.

PHAEDRA: Oh, pity me! What have I done? Where have I
240   wandered from true reason's path? Madness came upon me, a god dulled my mind and I fell. Oh, I am in misery, misery! Nurse dear, cover my head once more; I am ashamed

of what I have said. Cover it! Tears fall from my eyes; a look
of shame is plain to see there. To keep control of my senses is
agony; yet this madness repels me; no, to die aware of nothing
is best.

NURSE: There, I'm covering it. But tell me, when shall death   250
pull his veil over my body? A long life has taught me a great
deal. We mortals should limit any love we feel for each
other; it shouldn't pierce us through and through. The heart's
affections shouldn't weigh us down; we should find them easy
to cast off or to tighten. It's a heavy load when one heart
suffers pain for two, as I share this woman's torment. A life   260
of strict, unswerving conduct more often leads to failure, they
say, than to happiness, and is no friend to health. Excess,
then, wins no praise from me. 'Know when to stop' – that's
my life's rule, and the wise will say I'm right.

CHORUS-LEADER: Old woman, we can see for ourselves the
miserable state our queen is in but there's nothing to tell us
what her illness is. You are Phaedra's nurse and she trusts
you; please tell us what we want to learn.   270

NURSE: I'm in the dark for all my questions; she won't say.

CHORUS-LEADER: Not even how these troubles started?

NURSE: You're no further forward there either; she's not saying
a word about any of it.

CHORUS-LEADER: Oh, how weak and haggard she looks!

NURSE: And wouldn't you if this was your third day without
food?

CHORUS-LEADER: Is she out of her mind or trying to kill herself?

NURSE: Kill herself, you say? Well, her refusal of food is certainly
likely to remove her from life.

CHORUS-LEADER: I simply can't believe her husband puts up
with this.

NURSE: She keeps him in the dark – pretends there's nothing
wrong with her!

CHORUS-LEADER: But can't he tell from looking at her face?   280

NURSE: No, he's out of the country, as it happens.

CHORUS-LEADER: But can't you force her to say what's causing
this senseless behaviour and making her ill?

NURSE: I've tried everything; it's no good. Mind you, I won't

let things rest even now, so you can see with your own eyes
and tell others if I'm the type to desert a mistress in trouble.
[To PHAEDRA:] Come on, my pet, let's both forget what
290   we've said. Don't be so hard on me. Let's have no more of
these frowns and stubborn thoughts. There were times then I
could have been more understanding; well, I'll change and
find better things to say. If it's some trouble you can't mention
makes you ill, look, these people here are women who can
help you find a cure. But if men can be told your ailment, out
with it and we'll consult doctors. Well? Still nothing to say?
Either correct me if what I've said is wrong or agree with
what is right; but you mustn't sit there dumb, child! Say
300   something! Look at me! [PHAEDRA *does not react*.] Oh, what
can I do, ladies? This is a hopeless task, hopeless! We're no
closer than we were before. My words fell on deaf ears then
and still she won't listen. [To PHAEDRA, *again*:] But let me
tell you this, and then you can be as stubborn as the sea itself:
if you die, you'll have betrayed your own children – no share
for them in their father's estate – no, by that horse-riding
Amazon queen! She produced a son to lord it over your
children, a bastard who thinks of himself as true-born, you
310   know him well, Hippolytus . . .

PHAEDRA [*suddenly erect*]: Oh no!

NURSE: Am I getting through to you now?

PHAEDRA: You're destroying me, Nurse dear! I beg you, in the
gods' name, don't speak of this man again!

NURSE: You see? You're sane all right but just the same you're
not prepared to help your children or save your life.

PHAEDRA: I love my children! A different storm drives me on
to the rocks.

NURSE: I take it your hands are clean of blood, my girl?

PHAEDRA: My hands, yes, but my heart is defiled.

NURSE: Some harmful spell, perhaps, from someone who hates
you?

PHAEDRA: One I love is my destroyer – not of his choice or
mine.

320   NURSE: Theseus – has he wronged you in some way?

PHAEDRA: Oh no, and may I never be seen wronging him!

NURSE: Then what is it, this frightening thing that makes you want to die?

PHAEDRA: Leave me to do wrong; it's not you I offend against.

NURSE [*falling at* PHAEDRA's *feet and clasping her hand tightly*]: Never, if I can help it! If I do fail, the fault will be yours.

PHAEDRA: What are you doing? Forcing me by seizing hold of my hand?[16]

NURSE: Yes, and your knees as well; I'll never let go!

PHAEDRA: Oh, you poor soul, it will be terrible for you if you learn this, terrible!

NURSE: And just what could be more terrible for me than failing to win your confidence?

PHAEDRA: It will be the death of you! Yet I will be honoured for my action.

NURSE: What? And still you mean to keep it a secret, when   330
what I'm asking of you is for your own good?

PHAEDRA: Yes! My state is shameful, but out of it I plan to bring good.

NURSE: Well then, talking about it will bring you all the more honour, surely?

PHAEDRA: Oh, go away, in heaven's name! Let go my hand!

NURSE: Never, until you give me the gift you owe me!

PHAEDRA: You shall have it; I must respect your hand as a suppliant.

NURSE [*relaxing her grip*]: Now I'll stop pressing you; it's your turn to talk.

PHAEDRA: O Mother, my poor Mother, what a terrible passion seized you![17]

NURSE: The one she had for the bull, child? Is this your meaning?

PHAEDRA: And you, too, Sister, loved to your cost by Dionysus![18]

NURSE: What's the matter with you, girl? Slandering your own   340
family now?

PHAEDRA: I am the third in line: their ruin has become mine – pity me!

NURSE: I'm astonished. Whatever will she say next?

PHAEDRA: Then it was, not in recent days, that my sorrows began.

NURSE: I still don't know any more of what I want to hear.

PHAEDRA: Ah, if only you could say for me what I must say!

NURSE: Am I a prophet, then? Do I know for sure what no one sees?

PHAEDRA: What does it mean when they say people are . . . in love?

NURSE: Oh, joy, my girl, so sweet and yet so bitter, too.

PHAEDRA: That last will be the taste on my tongue, then.

350 NURSE: What's that? You're in love, my girl? Who on earth is he?

PHAEDRA: Whoever would he be? It is that one, the Amazon's . . .

NURSE: Hippolytus, you mean?

PHAEDRA: You spoke that name, not I.

NURSE: No! No! What will you say next, girl? You've finished me! [*Turning to the* CHORUS:] Ladies, it's unbearable! I won't live on now! I hate the sight of day, hate its light! I'll throw myself down, jump clear to my death! Farewell! I'm dying, as good as dead! For good and faithful wives have sinful desires – it's not their own wish but still they have them. She's no goddess, then, the Cyprian, but something greater – call it 360 what you will – bringing ruin on this woman, on me and on this house.

[*Her energies spent, she flings herself down in despair and the* CHORUS-LEADER *sings a short lament.*]

CHORUS-LEADER: Did you hear, ah, did you catch the sufferings – monstrous, pitiful – that the queen was crying out? [*Turning to* PHAEDRA:] For myself, dear lady, I would sooner die than ever reach your state of mind. [*Groaning aloud:*] Oh, the pity of it! What sorrows you have, poor lady! How men must feed on sorrows! You are ruined, you have exposed your ghastly secret to the light! What do they have in store 370 for you, all the hours of this day? A change for ill shall come upon this house. No more is it unclear where it sinks and sets, the star of fortune sent you by the Cyprian, luckless child of Crete.

[PHAEDRA *has risen from her bed and advanced towards the* CHORUS, *whom she now addresses.*]

PHAEDRA: Ladies of Trozen,[19] who live on this furthest head-
land of the Peloponnese, already in the long hours of the
night I have given thought to human lives that end in ruin.
And my view is that it's not the way they think that makes
them go wrong, for they are intelligent enough in most cases.
No, this is how we should look at it: we know what is right
and understand it, but we don't put it into practice, some out   380
of laziness, others by letting some other pleasure come first,
and life has many pleasures – long hours of conversation, and
time to do nothing (precious moments that can lead us astray)
and a sense of shame. This takes two forms, one beneficial,
the other a burden on families. If we had no doubts about
each case, there would not be two of them with the same
name.[20]

Since these are my thoughts on the matter, no magic charm
would have power to change them for the worse or force me   390
to contradict myself. I will tell you, too, the path my mind
took.[21] When I first felt love's dart, I tried to find the best way
to endure the wound. This, then, was how I began: I said
nothing about this illness, kept it secret. For there's no trusting
the tongue; it knows how to tell other people when their
thinking's wrong but creates havoc when it speaks for itself.
My second course was to win the battle by using self-
discipline; this was how I planned to live through this madness
decently. Thirdly, since I was failing to defeat the Cyprian by   400
these means, I decided to die, the best course – no one will
deny it – I could have devised. For just as I wouldn't want
my right actions to go unnoticed, I wouldn't want my sins
witnessed by the world.

As for the act and the illness, I knew they brought disgrace
on me and, again, I was well aware of being a woman,
something hated by all men. Whatever woman first set about
playing the adulteress, may all the world's curses fall upon
her shameless head! It was in well-born families that this evil   410
first infected womankind; when noble ladies sanction acts
of shame in their own lives, the low-born will think their
behaviour respectable, mark my words! And I despise them,
women who preach faithfulness to husbands but dare the

worst behind their backs. [*She turns to face Aphrodite's statue by the palace doors.*] Oh, my royal lady, sea-born Cypris, how can they share their husbands' beds and meet their eyes without shuddering at the thought of the darkness and roof beams, accomplices in their acts, voicing what they witnessed!

420   It's this, you see, my friends, just this that is killing me, so that I may never be caught disgracing my husband or the children I brought into the world. No, it is freedom I want for them, the freedom to speak their minds and flourish as citizens of glorious Athens,[22] their good name untarnished on their mother's part. For a man becomes a slave, however bold he is in spirit, on the day he learns the crimes his mother or father has committed. It's this and this alone, they say, that helps you win life's race: having a just and honest mind. The wicked are exposed, sooner or later, when Time reflects them

430   in his mirror, as a young woman sees her own features. May I never be seen in their number!

CHORUS-LEADER: Ah, what a fine thing it is to have self-discipline in all circumstances! How true that the fruit it bears in this life is a good reputation!

NURSE: My lady, I got a terrible fright for a moment, when I heard just then about your trouble. But now I realize I was being silly. It's funny how often our second thoughts are wiser. There's nothing out of the ordinary in what's happened to you; it can all be explained: it's the goddess' anger has landed on your head. You're in love; what's so strange about

440   that? So is half the world. And then, because of love, are you going to end your life? A poor lookout for all lovers, eh, today and tomorrow, if it's going to cost them their lives! She's more than a body can bear, the Cyprian, when she comes in full flood – gentle enough in coming after anyone who yields to her but any she finds above himself and arrogant she takes and gives him a shocking time, believe me. Through the heavens she roams, the Cyprian; she's there in the waves of the sea and all things take their life from her. It's she who has

450   love's seed in her hand and scatters it and all of us on earth are her offspring.

Then there are all those with books written in times past,

who spend their lives in reading – they know how Zeus once
wanted Semele for his bride; they know how once love made
radiant Dawn snatch Cephalus up to join the gods.[23] And yet
they have their homes in heaven and do not shun the company
of the gods; they are content, I think, to accept their fate.
Won't you put up with yours? Your father should have fixed
special terms when you were conceived or found other gods   460
as masters, if these laws of theirs don't suit you! How many
men, do you think, thoroughly sensible men, prefer to turn a
blind eye when they see their wives misbehaving? How many
fathers help their lovesick sons get the girl they want? It's
plain good sense, you see, to sweep any dirt under the carpet
– ask anyone! We shouldn't bend over backwards to make
our lives perfect. Would a builder strive for precision in
making the roof for a house? In any case, now that you are in
such dangerous waters, how do you propose to swim clear?   470
No, you are not a god: if the good you have outweighs the
bad, you can count yourself lucky.

　　Dear child, let's have no more of this stubbornness; stop
showing such pride! For pride it is, pure and simple, wishing
to set yourself above the gods. Find the strength to continue
with your love! It is a god's will. If you're ill, then find a good
way to defeat your illness. Charms exist and spells with power
to bewitch; a remedy for this illness will come to light. We are
women, after all, and will find a way; it would be a long wait   480
to rely on a man.

CHORUS-LEADER: Phaedra, this woman's advice is more help-
　　ful in meeting your present trouble, but I take your side. Yet
　　this praise will please you less than her words and grate more
　　on your ear.

PHAEDRA: This is what destroys well-established cities and
　　homes on this earth: fine words, too well spoken! Words
　　should be spoken to create a good name, not to please the
　　ear.

NURSE: Oh, stop preaching! It's not high-sounding words you   490
　　need, it's the man. We mustn't beat about the bush any longer;
　　let's speak the truth about you, no pretence! If your life were
　　not in such danger and you were a woman in control of

herself, I would never egg you on like this to get you into bed
with your man; but our backs are against the wall now: your
life's at stake and who would grudge me this?

PHAEDRA: What an appalling thing to say! Close your mouth!
I never want to hear such vile talk from you again!

500 NURSE: Vile it may be but better for you than your lofty morals.
Better to do the deed and stay alive than bask in your good
name and die.

PHAEDRA: Oh no, I beg you – your words are clever but vile –
stop there! Desire has tilled my heart as well as any field, and
if you argue so well for what is wrong, I shall be consumed in
what I am trying to shun.

NURSE: Well, if that's how you feel . . . [Pausing:] You shouldn't
be in love at all; but as you are, do what I say; it's the next
best way of obliging me. In the house I have a charm that is a
510 spell for love – it only came into my mind this moment – it
will rid you of this sickness and do no harm to your wits or
your reputation, provided you don't turn coward. But we
need to get some token from him, the one you long for, a lock
of hair, or something from his clothes, and then join the two
– token and spell – for a happy result.

PHAEDRA: This charm – is it an ointment or a potion?

NURSE: I don't know;[24] a cure is what you should be after, my
girl, not answers to questions.

PHAEDRA: Oh, you may prove too clever for me, that's my fear!

NURSE: You'd fear anything, that's your trouble! What's your
worry?

520 PHAEDRA: That you may pass any of this on to Theseus' son.

NURSE: Leave it to me, my girl; I'll take good care over this.
[Pausing in front of Aphrodite's statue:] Only help me, my
royal lady, sea-born Cypris, and be my accomplice! What
other things I have in mind need only be told to friends inside.
[The NURSE goes into the palace.]

CHORUS [Strophe]: Eros, Eros, you who distil your drops of
longing on the eyes of lovers and fill with sweet joy the hearts
of those you set out to conquer, never, I pray, show yourself
530 in anger to me or come beyond due measure! For neither shaft

of fire nor beam of the stars is stronger than Aphrodite's dart shot from the hands of Eros, son of Zeus.

[*Antistrophe:*] In vain does the land of Greece kill bull after bull in sacrifice by Alpheus' stream, in vain at Phoebus' Pythian shrine, if Eros, monarch of men, who holds the keys to Aphrodite's chambers of desire, fails to receive our worship, 540 the god who devastates mortals when he comes and hurls them through every misfortune.

[*Strophe:*] The girl of Oechalia[25] was virgin once, a filly still unyoked, to men and marriage a stranger; but put in harness and taken from Eurytus' home, like a running nymph or wor- 550 shipper of Bacchus, amid blood and smoke, in a marriage sealed by slaughter, she was given to Alcmene's son – the Cyprian's work, all. O wretched bride!

[*Antistrophe:*] O sacred wall of Thebes, O mouth of Dirce's spring, you could confirm the manner of the Cyprian's coming. For to the flaming thunderbolt she gave in marriage the girl who was to bear twice-born Bacchus and laid her to 560 sleep with death for bridegroom.[26] Terror is in her breath and none escapes it; like a bee she flits where she will.

[PHAEDRA *has moved close to the palace doors where she stands listening to voices inside.*]

PHAEDRA: Silence, women! This is the end for me!

CHORUS-LEADER: What is it in the house that frightens you, Phaedra?

PHAEDRA: Quiet! Let me hear what they're saying inside!

CHORUS-LEADER: I'll stop. But this isn't a happy start to things.

PHAEDRA: Oh no! Not that, no! What must I suffer? Oh, 570 misery!

CHORUS-LEADER: What misery? Why are you screaming like this? Tell us, lady, what words rush on your mind and make you afraid?

PHAEDRA: I'm as good as dead! Come, stand here by the doors and hear the shouting that fills the house!

CHORUS-LEADER: You're at the door;[27] you are the one to pass on any message from the house. Tell us, tell us, what awful 580 thing has happened?

PHAEDRA: He's shouting, the son of the riding Amazon, Hippolytus, pouring curses and abuse on my servant!

CHORUS-LEADER: I hear a voice but it's not clear. The sound
carries well enough where the cry came to you through the
door.

PHAEDRA: It's clear enough now, all right; 'whore's maid' he
590   calls her, 'betrayer of her master's bed'.

CHORUS-LEADER: Oh, this is monstrous! You are betrayed,
dear lady! How can I help you out of this? Your secret is
known to all and you are ruined – oh, it's unbearable –
betrayed by a friend!

PHAEDRA: In telling of my troubles she has destroyed me; she
tried to cure my sickness and acted lovingly but fatally.

CHORUS-LEADER: What now? What will you do? Your position
is hopeless!

PHAEDRA: I know one thing only: I must die at once; there is
600   no other cure for this anguish I feel.

[HIPPOLYTUS *rushes on stage followed by the* NURSE.
PHAEDRA *cowers at the side.*]

HIPPOLYTUS: O mother earth! Open sunlight! What words I
have heard – foul, unspeakable!

NURSE: Be quiet, boy, stop shouting, before someone hears you.

HIPPOLYTUS: Quiet? Be quiet, after hearing such terrible
things?

NURSE: Please! I beg you, by this fine right arm of yours!

HIPPOLYTUS: Ugh! Don't touch me! Take your hands off my
clothes!

NURSE: Oh, I clasp your knees and beg you,[28] don't ruin me,
please!

HIPPOLYTUS: How can I, if, as you say, you have said nothing
wrong?

NURSE: Those words were not for all ears, my boy, certainly
not!

610   HIPPOLYTUS: Fine words are all the finer said in public.

NURSE: My boy, the oath you gave me, you'll never break that?

HIPPOLYTUS: It was my tongue that swore, not my heart.[29]

NURSE: Child, what do you mean to do? Ruin one who is near
to you?

the bigger - enemy of virtue is
virtue itself: discuss.

HIPPOLYTUS: Near me? Get out of here! A criminal near to
  me? The idea!

NURSE: Find it in you to forgive, my son; it's human to err.

HIPPOLYTUS [*ignoring her*]: O Zeus,[30] why did you allow
  women to live in the light of the sun and plague mankind
  with their counterfeit looks? If you wished to propagate the
  race of men, it wasn't from women you should have provided
  this; no, men ought to enter your temples and there pur-   620
  chase children at a valuation, each at its appropriate price,
  depositing in exchange bronze or iron or weight of gold, and
  then live in freedom in their homes without women.[31]

  Here's your proof that woman is a dangerous pest: her
  father, who gave her life and raised her up, puts down a
  dowry for her and sends her to another home to rid himself of
  his trouble. The husband, taking into his house this poisonous   630
  creature, has never known such happiness; he decks his idol
  with jewellery, fair gifts for such foulness, and, poor fool,
  takes pains to purchase one fashionable dress after another,
  exhausting the family fortune. Being married to a nonentity
  gives a man the least trouble and yet there's no good comes
  of having a woman enshrined at home in her stupidity. Clever-
  ness in women I detest; I never want her darkening my door,   640
  the woman with more intelligence than a woman should have.
  For the Cyprian breeds evil more often in clever women; the
  helpless ones are saved from promiscuous urges by their lack
  of brains.

  No servant should ever come into contact with a woman;
  dumb and savage beasts should keep them company and then
  they could not speak to any servant or have one speak to
  them in reply. But as it is they sit at home and think up wicked
  schemes in their wicked hearts, while their servants carry
  them to the outside world. [*To the* NURSE:] This you have   650
  done with me, you old witch, coming to persuade me to enter
  my father's bed and enjoy what I may not. I'll wash this filth
  away with spring water, flushing my ears. How could I stoop
  to this, when just hearing such words makes me feel polluted?
  Let me tell you, woman, only my reverence for the gods keeps
  you from harm; had you not taken me off guard and made

misogynist

religious

me swear an oath in their name, I would never have stopped
myself from telling my father this. But as things are, I shall
660   leave the palace until Theseus returns; I won't utter a word.
But when my father does come, I will come back and note
how you, yes, and your mistress,[32] meet his eye.

I curse you all! Never will I have my fill of hating women,
even though they say I never cease to speak of them. Do they
ever cease from sinning? Let someone teach them to control
their desires or leave me to trample them underfoot for ever!
[HIPPOLYTUS *rushes off stage.* PHAEDRA *sings a short
lament.*]

PHAEDRA: How wretched, how ill-starred is the fate of woman-
670   kind! What means, what words have we now to untie the
knot that words have tied, once we have tripped and fallen?
I have got my deserts. O earth and daylight, where can I
escape from what has happened to me? How can I hide my
sorrow, my friends? What god or man would appear to help
me, to sit at my side or assist me in this criminal act? This
suffering I have is bringing me ever nearer to my death – it is
a hard crossing! No woman knows misery such as mine!

680   CHORUS-LEADER: I pity you truly. It is all over; your servant's
schemes have failed, my lady, and disaster has struck.

PHAEDRA [*turning on the* NURSE]: You vile old witch! Destroyer
of your friends! Look at what you have done to me! May
Zeus, my father's father, blast you with his lightning and
destroy you root and branch! Did I not tell you (did I not
foresee what was in your mind?) to say nothing of what now
smears my name with shame? But you could not hold your
tongue and so no longer shall I die with honour.[33] No! New
plans are what I need now. This man, roused to fury, will
690   denounce me to his father for your crimes; he will tell old
Pittheus what has happened and fill the whole land with his
tale of shame! Damn you and all well-meaning fools who seek
to benefit their friends against their will by dishonourable
means!

NURSE: My lady, you can blame me for what I've done wrong
all right; your sense of hurt has teeth and stops you thinking
straight; but, if you'll hear me out, I can say some things in

my defence. I brought you up; I'm fond of you; when I looked
for a cure for your sickness what I found was something I had
no wish to find. Now, had I been successful, who would not
have called me one of the wise? It's success or failure makes
us seem wise or foolish.

PHAEDRA: Do you really think this is a fair and sufficient way
to deal with me, to wound me and then try to win me round
with words?

NURSE: We're talking too much; I should have exercised some
self-control. But there's a way to escape with your life even at
this stage, my child.

PHAEDRA: Enough! Not a word more! It was bad advice you
gave me before and what you attempted was wicked. Get out
of my sight! Think about your own affairs now; I will take
proper care of mine.

[*Again the* NURSE *goes into the palace but this time haltingly,
shaking her head.* PHAEDRA *turns and addresses the*
CHORUS.]

And you, noble daughters of Trozen, grant this favour I ask:
bury in silence what you have heard here.

CHORUS-LEADER: By holy Artemis, daughter of Zeus, I swear
never to reveal any of your sufferings to the daylight.[34]

PHAEDRA: I am grateful for that. There is one further thing I
am going to say: I have found a way out of this trouble of
mine; it will allow my sons to live with heads held high and
bring me benefit in meeting this cruel throw of the dice. For
never will I bring shame on my Cretan home or look Theseus
in the eye after this dishonour if only one person's life is the
price.

CHORUS-LEADER: What is it you intend? What terrible thing
that you cannot undo?

PHAEDRA: To die; but how will be for me to decide.

CHORUS-LEADER: You mustn't speak such words!

PHAEDRA: Your task is to give me good advice. [*Turning to
Aphrodite's statue:*] And as for the Cyprian, my destroyer, I
will make her glad this day by my death; a cruel love will
bring me low. But in so dying I will prove deadly to another's
life, to teach him not to triumph over my downfall; when he,

700

710

720

730

too, feels this sickness I have known, then he shall learn what restraint is.

[*She turns and slowly enters the palace.*]

CHORUS[35] [*Strophe*]: Oh, to lie concealed in the crevices of some steep rock, where a god might make me a winged bird among the flying flocks! To soar above the sea waves of the Adrian shore and Eridanus' waters, where the sorrowful girls in
740   lament for Phaethon drop into the dark swell the amber-gleaming lustre of their tears!

[*Antistrophe:*] To reach my journey's goal at the apple-sown shore where the Hesperides sing, where the sea-lord of the murky shallows denies further passage to sailors, establishing the sacred boundary of heaven that Atlas holds! There divine springs flow past the bridal bed of Zeus, where
750   holy earth with her bountiful gifts swells the happiness of the gods.

[*Strophe:*] O white-wing'd ship of Crete that carried my royal lady from her wealthy home over the salty depths of the pounding sea, you brought her to a marriage whose profit was sorrow! Ill-omened was the day she flew from Minos'
760   land to glorious Athens, ill-omened again when on Munichus' shore they made fast the twisted cable-ends and stepped on to the mainland.

[*Antistrophe:*] And so it was that Aphrodite sent a fearful sickness of impious passion that crushed her heart. And foundering now beneath her cruel misfortune she will fasten a
770   hanging noose to the beams of her bridal chamber, fitting it around her white neck; bowed with shame at her loathsome fate, she will choose instead the fame of fair repute and rid her heart of its painful longing.

NURSE [*from inside the palace*]: Help! Help! Anyone near the palace, come quickly and help! She's hanging, my mistress, Theseus' wife!

CHORUS-LEADER: Oh no! It's all over! Our royal lady's dead, dead, swinging in the noose she has fastened!

780   NURSE: Get a move on, all of you! Someone fetch a double-edged sword so we can cut through this rope knotted round her neck!

CHORUS-LEADER: What shall we do, friends?[36] Do you think we should go into the palace and free the queen from the tightened noose?

ANOTHER MEMBER OF THE CHORUS: Why? Aren't there young men in there attending on her? It's always risky to meddle like that.

NURSE: She's dead, my poor girl; lay her out and straighten her limbs. How he'll regret leaving her to manage the house, my master!

CHORUS-LEADER: So she's dead, I hear, the wretched woman; already they are laying out her lifeless body, it seems.

[*Enter* THESEUS *with retinue. He wears on his head a garland signifying a favourable response from an oracle.*]

THESEUS: Ladies, do you know the meaning of the shouting in   790
my house? I caught the sound of servants in distress. This is not how my house should greet me on my return from the god; I should find doors thrown wide and words of gracious welcome! Nothing untoward has happened to old Pittheus, has it? He's well on in years, it's true, but still I'd grieve his passing from this house.

CHORUS-LEADER: What has happened to you does not affect the elderly, Theseus; it is the death of the young that gives you pain.

THESEUS: Oh, no! My children, it's not my children robbed of life?

CHORUS-LEADER: They live; this grief will cut you to the quick: 800
their mother's dead.

THESEUS: What are you saying? She's dead, my wife? How did this happen?

CHORUS-LEADER: Strangulation, by the noose she had fastened for herself.

THESEUS: But what caused this to happen? Did grief chill her soul?

CHORUS-LEADER: This is all we know; we, too, have just come to your house, Theseus, to mourn your misfortunes.

THESEUS: Ah, why is my head crowned with this leafy garland when the god has repaid my visit with misery? Open up the doors that bar the entrance, you servants, undo the fastenings

810   that I may see my wife, a sight to wither my eyes, the one whose death is death to me.

      [*The palace doors open and* PHAEDRA'*s corpse is revealed*.][37]

CHORUS-LEADER: Oh, my poor lady! Oh, how I pity you for your sufferings! Your sorrows and actions alike are enough to make havoc of this house. What you dared to do takes my breath away, a violent death by an unholy act, the struggle of your own pitiful hand. Who is it, unhappy lady, has doused your lamp of life?

THESEUS: Oh, what troubles I have! This is the greatest sorrow I have ever known, good folk of Trozen. O misfortune, how
820   heavily you have come upon me and my house, an unseen blight sent by some harmful power. You are the ruination of my life – I cannot live through this. I see before my wretched eyes a sea of woes too vast for me to swim safely to shore; I cannot rise above the waves of this calamity. How can I describe your hideous fate, my love, oh, how can I find the truth? You are like a bird that has vanished from my hand, plunging in swift descent to the realm of darkness. Oh, this is
830   torment! Pity, oh pity what I am suffering! Someone in earlier days has sinned and this is the harvest I now reap from time gone by, sent upon me by the gods.[38]

CHORUS-LEADER: These sorrows have not visited you alone, my king; many another man has lost a noble wife.[39]

THESEUS [*continuing his lament*]: Beneath the earth, I wish I might go to dwell in the gloom beneath the earth, sharing my sorrowful home, a dead man, with the darkness, now that the joy of your company has been taken from me. For you have destroyed more lives than your own. What was it? Where did
840   it come from, my poor lady, the deadly fortune that settled on your heart? Will someone tell me what took place here or does your king foolishly keep under his palace roof a servant rabble? Oh, my love, my love, this breaks my heart! What anguish for the house have I seen, past endurance, past all telling! Oh, I am ruined! My home is deserted, my children motherless. Oh, you have abandoned us, abandoned us, my
850   love, noblest of all women seen by the light of the sun or the starry lustre of the night!

CHORUS-LEADER: I pity you, poor man; a heavy curse has fallen on your house. My eyes brim with tears that pour down at what has befallen you. But I have long been shuddering because of the calamity to follow.

THESEUS: Ah, look! What's this attached to my love's hand – a message that tries to tell me something I don't know? Did she write a letter, poor soul, requesting me to honour our love and our children? Never fear, my poor lady; no woman shall take your place in Theseus' home or his bed. See, here, the imprint of her golden signet brings me her caress, her poor, lifeless greeting! Come, let me undo the thread twisted round the letter and see what it wishes to tell me. 860

CHORUS-LEADER: Oh, no! Here is another disaster, a fresh one, that a god brings on us to take the place of the old. What ill-fortune could strike now after what has happened? It is destroyed, it is no more – oh, the pity of it! – my royal master's house. 870

THESEUS: Ah, can I bear it? A fresh wave of ruin to crash upon me! I cannot endure this, cannot find words for it – oh, what misery!

CHORUS-LEADER: What is it? Say, if I may hear.

THESEUS: The letter – it cries out, cries out horrors! Where can I escape these crushing woes? I am ruined, my life is over, such a refrain, such a refrain have I seen in this writing! I am wretched! 880

CHORUS-LEADER: Ah, these words foretell sorrows to come!

THESEUS: No more shall I hold back in the gates of my mouth the deadly sorrow that pains me as it emerges. Oh, hear me, men of Trozen! Hippolytus has dared to violate my wife, flouting the sacred eye of Zeus.[40] Now, Poseidon, my father, use one of the three curses[41] you promised me once and destroy my son; may he not escape this day, if the curses you gave me are sure! 890

CHORUS-LEADER: My king, take back these words! In heaven's name, pray for this not to happen! Do what I say! You will learn in time that you have made a mistake!

THESEUS: Impossible! I'll do more – I'll banish him from Trozen, so one of two fates shall lay him low: either Poseidon will respect my curses and send him dead to the halls of Hades or, a vagrant in exile, he shall eke out a life of misery on foreign soil.

[HIPPOLYTUS *rushes on stage with his hunting companions*.]

CHORUS-LEADER: Here he is in person, just in time, your son, Hippolytus. Give up this dangerous anger, Theseus my lord, and consider the best course for your family!

HIPPOLYTUS: I heard your shout, Father, and here I am, no time lost. I don't know what distresses you, though, and I'd like to hear from you. Ah, what's this I see – your wife, Father, a corpse? I'm amazed, utterly amazed! Only a moment ago I was leaving her, it's no time since she was looking on this light of day! What has happened to her? [THESEUS *remains silent*.] How did she meet her death? Father, I want to be told, and by you! Nothing? That's no help in a crisis, saying nothing! It's never right to keep friends in the dark in your troubles and I am not just a friend.

THESEUS: Oh, how ineffective mortals are, how prone to error![42] You teach countless skills, devise and discover all things but one you do not know, you have not tracked down – how to teach good sense to those who have none. Why is this?

HIPPOLYTUS: A formidable instructor he would be, the man capable of forcing wisdom on fools! No, Father, this isn't the time for idle speculation; I'm afraid this calamity is making you talk wildly.

THESEUS: Oh, men should have some permanent, reliable gauge for friends, a means of judging their hearts, to tell whose love is genuine and whose feigned; every man should have two voices, the one his natural voice, the other an honest one, so that, if one harboured treachery, it might be refuted by the honest one and we would not be deceived.

HIPPOLYTUS: Can some friend have attacked me, pouring his slander in your ear? Am I blamed by you for no good reason? I'm stunned; your words are so disordered, so wide of the mark, they leave me astonished.

THESEUS: Oh, the mind of man, how far will it go? Will its daring, its effrontery have any limit? If it so expands in the course of a man's lifetime, and each new criminal is to surpass his predecessor, gods will have to graft another land on to the earth, one that will house born enemies of justice and goodness. Look at this man – my own son, he has shamed my bed and now is plainly convicted by this dead woman as the foulest criminal!

Come, let your father see you face to face[43] – your presence contaminates me already. So you're the one who consorts with gods, are you, the man set apart from others, you the man in control of his emotions, untainted by evil? Who would believe your boasts? Where is the fool who thinks the gods stupid on your account? Not this man before you! Oh, yes, preen yourself now, play the exhibitionist with that vegetable diet of yours, take Orpheus for your master and join him in the frenzied dance, bow down before all his worthless scribblings[44] – for you are caught! I charge all men to shun people like this; they try to catch your soul with lofty words and what they are plotting is far from honourable.

She is dead; do you imagine this will acquit you? It's this that convicts you more than anything, you creature of evil! What kind of oaths, what words would outweigh this woman and serve to exonerate you? Will you say she hated you, that bastards and freeborn people are natural enemies? You make her a sorry bargainer in life, if she threw away her most precious possession out of spite to you! Or will you say that men are not promiscuous, while women are naturally so? Young men – I speak from experience – are just as unstable as women whenever the Cyprian stirs up their youthful hearts; but it is to their advantage that they are male.

Oh, why do I bandy words with you like this when here lies her corpse, the most reliable of witnesses? Get out of this land at once and go into exile! Never again set foot in god-built Athens or cross the borders of a land where my spear holds sway! For if after this treatment I allow you the victory, Sinis of the Isthmus will never testify that I killed him but that I am an empty boaster; and the rocks washed by the sea, where Sciron[45] met his end, will say I deal gently with criminals.

CHORUS-LEADER: I know no way to call any man prosperous;
even those in the first rank have their fortunes reversed.

HIPPOLYTUS: Father, the strength and intensity of your mind
is terrible; but though this business lets you make a fine case,
on closer inspection it is not at all fine. I am not clever at
making speeches in front of a crowd; with a few people of my
own age I have more skill. This is natural enough: men who
seem poor speakers among experts are found more eloquent
990   by the mob. However, faced with this situation I have no
alternative but to speak out.[46]

I shall begin my defence at the point where you tried first
to trap me, expecting to crush me and leave me no reply. You
see this daylight and this earth: there lives here not one man
– whether you agree or not – of purer nature than myself. I
know, in the first instance, how to revere the gods and to have
as friends men who attempt no wrong but would be ashamed
to send such evil instructions to acquaintances and to pay
them back with shameful services. I am not one to laugh at
1000   those who keep me company, Father, but one whose friends
will find him constant, whether near or far. And there is one
thing I have never touched – just where you fancy now you have
me caught: to this day I remain a virgin. Of the act of love I
know only what I hear in accounts or see portrayed, for being
virgin in heart, I have no urge even to look at these things.

Well, my indifference to earthly pleasures does not impress
you; so be it; but it is for you to show by what means I became
corrupted. Was it that this woman's beauty was unequalled?
1010   Or did I hope to be master in your house by marrying the
woman who would inherit it? That would have been foolish
of me, no, plain idiotic. Or was it your throne? Do you
imagine a man in his senses finds this an attractive prospect?
Far from it, since this ambition is incompatible with sanity.
My own ambition would be to come first in the Greek Games
but second in the state, enjoying good fortune at all times
with the noble as my friends; for in this position a man can
act and it gives him more than royal privilege to know he is
1020   clear of danger.

There is one point I have yet to make; the rest you have

heard. If I had a witness to establish my true character, if I were pleading my case with this woman still alive, then an examination of the facts would have shown you who the guilty were. But, as it is, I swear by Zeus, guardian of oaths, and by the ground beneath our feet that I never laid hands upon your wife, that I would never have wished it, never have entertained the idea. May I perish with none to remember me, none to preserve my honour or even my name, may my lifeless flesh be rejected by sea and land if my nature is vile.   1030
What terror drove this lady to take her life I do not know; I am forbidden to say anything further. She acted like a chaste wife when chastity was not within her reach, while I, though I possessed it, did not use it well.

CHORUS-LEADER: You have said enough to clear yourself of guilt, adding oaths by the gods, not a pledge to be taken lightly.

THESEUS: Isn't he a born magician, this man, a dealer in spells, so confident of winning me over with his easy temper, treating his father with contempt!   1040

HIPPOLYTUS: That easy temper is what I find incredible in you, Father; if you were my son and I your father, I would not have let your punishment rest with banishment; I'd have seen you dead if you presumed to touch my wife.

THESEUS: How predictable a remark! But you will not die this way, satisfying the principle you have fixed for yourself. No, for a man in misfortune a speedy death is all too easy. You shall wander in exile from your native land and endure a life   1050
of pain on foreign soil.

HIPPOLYTUS: Oh, no! What will you do? Drive me into exile without letting Time testify in my trial?

THESEUS: Yes, beyond the Great Sea and Atlas' boundaries, if I had the power, so loathsome are you in my eyes.

HIPPOLYTUS: You mean to banish me from Trozen without trial, not testing my oath, my assurance of good faith, or what the prophets say?[47]

THESEUS: This letter needs no prophet's insight to condemn you on certain grounds. As for the birds that fly overhead, I couldn't care less about them.

1060 HIPPOLYTUS [*lifting up his eyes*]: O you gods, why do I not unseal my lips, when it is you whom I revere who are destroying me? No, I will not. I would fail utterly to convince those I should and violate for nothing the oaths I swore.

THESEUS: Oh, it will be the death of me, this pious cant of yours! Away with you, out of your father's land, and this instant!

HIPPOLYTUS: Where will I turn in my wretched state? Who will give me kind welcome into his home, when this charge causes my banishment?

THESEUS: Anyone who enjoys welcoming as guests men who violate wives and share their beds as well as their homes.

1070 HIPPOLYTUS: Ah, that hits me hard! This almost reduces me to tears, to be thought as foul as this – and by you!

THESEUS: That was the time for tears and thinking of consequences, when you dared to violate your father's wife.

HIPPOLYTUS: O house, if only you might find speech and testify to the goodness of my heart!

THESEUS: You take refuge in dumb witnesses – clever of you; but the deed needs no voice to brand you as evil.

HIPPOLYTUS: Oh, if only I could stand where you are and look at myself, to weep at the cruelty of my treatment here!

1080 THESEUS: Yes, you always practised self-worship far more than showing a just and pious regard for your father.

HIPPOLYTUS: O Mother, my unhappy Mother! What hatred shrouded my birth! I hope no friend of mine is ever born a bastard!

THESEUS: Drag him away, you servants! Listen to what I tell you! Have I only *now* pronounced him an exile?

HIPPOLYTUS: If one of them lays a finger on me, he'll be sorry! Thrust me out of the land with your own hands, if that's what you want!

THESEUS: And so I shall, if you disobey my words. I feel no pity coming over me at the prospect of your exile.

1090 HIPPOLYTUS: It is settled, then, it seems. What a wretch I am! I know the facts of the case but not how to express them. [*He turns to face Artemis' statue.*] O goddess I love the most, Leto's daughter, my companion in the hunt, at rest and in full

cry, it is indeed exile for me from glorious Athens. Farewell
to that city, then, and Erechtheus' land. Farewell to you, land
of Trozen, and all the happiness you hold for those who grow
to manhood here! This is the last time I will set eyes on you
or speak to you.

Come, my young friends, we've grown up here together,
give me your goodbyes and see me on my way from Trozen.
You'll never see another man more pure of heart, even if my   1100
father disagrees.

[*The stage is left by* HIPPOLYTUS *and* THESEUS.]

HUNTSMEN, FOLLOWERS OF HIPPOLYTUS [*Strophe*]: The
gods' care for us, when it comes to my mind, truly relieves
my sorrow. I have deep within me hopes of understanding,
yet, when I see how fate rewards mortal actions, I am disappointed. For fortunes crowd in on men from every quarter
and their lives are constantly changing, shifting at every   1110
turn.

CHORUS [*Antistrophe*]: May the powers above in answer to my
prayers grant me this fate – a life of good fortune with a heart
untouched by grief. For my thoughts and opinions, may they
not be rigid or at the same time false-coined. May my ways
be flexible and, by adapting them at all times to tomorrow,
may I share in the good fortune tomorrow brings.

HUNTSMEN [*Strophe*]: For my mind is now a troubled pool, my   1120
expectations reversed by what I see: the brightest star of
Grecian Aphaea[48] we have seen, we have seen sent on his way
to another land through his father's anger. O sands of the
city's shore, O wooded mountain slopes where at holy
Dictynna's side he hunted down wild beasts with his swift-   1130
footed hounds!

CHORUS [*Antistrophe*]: No longer will you take the reins behind
your matched Enetic team and fill the track beside the lake
with the steady pounding of their hooves. The song awakened
from the strings of your lyre shall slumber now in your father's
halls. No garlands now to mark where Leto's daughter catches
breath in the thick greenwood. It is finished, the rivalry of   1140
girls for your bridal bed, laid to rest by your exile.

[*Epode:*] And for your misfortune a life of tears will be my lot: unenviable fate. O poor, unhappy mother, what a return for your pains at birth! Ah, the gods, they make me angry! Oh, you Graces, sisters entwined, why do you send him, the poor man, all innocent of this disaster, from his native land, away from his home here?

[*The* HUNTSMEN *leave.*]

CHORUS-LEADER: But here I see a servant of Hippolytus hurrying towards the palace; he's wasting no time and his face has a grim look.

[*Enter* MESSENGER.]

MESSENGER: Ladies, where might I go to find Theseus, ruler of this land? Tell me, if you know. Is he inside the palace?

CHORUS-LEADER: Here he comes in person from within.

[*Enter* THESEUS.]

MESSENGER: Theseus, the news I bring merits your concern and that of the citizens who live in the city of Athens and Trozen's land.

THESEUS: What is it? Not some fresh disaster that has overtaken our two neighbouring cities?

MESSENGER: Hippolytus is no more, as good as, anyway. He still sees the daylight but the scales are poised to fall.

THESEUS: Who is responsible? Did he make an enemy of someone by assaulting his wife as he did his father's?

MESSENGER: His own chariot and team destroyed him, and the curses your own mouth uttered when you prayed about him to your father, the ocean's king.

THESEUS: O you gods! Poseidon, it is true, then, you are my father, answering my prayer as you have! How did he actually meet his death? Tell me! How did the trap of Justice fall and crush him, the man who brought shame on me?

MESSENGER: We were beside the shore where the waves break, combing our horses' manes and shedding tears at the news a man had brought, that Hippolytus would never again set foot in this land, sentenced by you to miserable exile. He came to join us on the shore with the same tearful refrain, and stepping behind him came a vast crowd of friends and people of like age to him. Eventually, when he had stopped lamenting, he said, 'Enough of these foolish tears; my father's orders must

be obeyed. Put my horses in their yoke, lads, and harness
them to the chariot. I no longer belong to this city.'

Then every man stirred himself and, quicker than a man
could say, we had them harnessed and standing ready right
by our master. He grabbed hold of the reins from the chariot
rail, his feet securely in their footstalls. And first he raised his   1190
palms to heaven and made this prayer: 'Zeus, if I am a man
of evil nature, may I die! And may my father come to know
how he dishonours me, either when I am dead or while I yet
see the light!' With this he flicked the switch he had in his
hands over all the horses at the one time. We servants started
to accompany our master above us in his chariot, keeping
close to the bridles, along the road that leads straight to Argos
and Epidauria.

And then we began striking into uninhabited country.
There is a promontory beyond the frontier of this land, facing
what by then has become the Saronic Gulf. There it was that   1200
a rumbling from the earth swelled, like Zeus' thunder, into a
deep roar, terrifying to our ears. The horses lifted up their
heads skyward, pricking up their ears, while we in a real panic
wondered where the sound could be coming from. We looked
out to where the sea broke on the shore and saw an awesome
sight – a wave set fast in the sky, blocking Sciron's coast from
my eye. The Isthmus, too, and Asclepius' rock were hidden
from view. And then, swelling up and spouting thick foam   1210
around as the sea was blown high, it advanced on the shore,
where his four horses stood in harness. And just at the moment
when it broke with a huge surge, the wave sent forth a bull, a
wild and wondrous beast. The whole land was filled with its
bellowing, returning an echo that made us tremble, and to
our staring eyes it seemed a sight beyond endurance.

At once the horses were seized by a blind panic. Their
master, long familiar with their moods, took tight hold of the   1220
reins and pulled, like a sailor on his oar, throwing the weight
of his body back against the straps. But they champed the
harder on their iron bits and swept him on for all his struggling, indifferent to their pilot's hand, to the reins and the
sturdy chariot. Each time he took the helm and tried to steer

a course towards the softer ground, there he would appear in front of them, the bull, to head them off, maddening the team of four with terror. Whenever they rushed, crazed, towards the rocks, he was with them, a silent presence, following close to the handrail of the chariot, until he finally brought it down, dashing its wheels against a rock, and sent it spinning. Then all was in turmoil – axle pins and wheel hubs were leaping in the air, while the poor man himself, caught up in the reins, was dragged along bound fast in an inextricable knot, smashing his head against the rocks and tearing his flesh, as he shouted words terrible to hear: 'Stand fast, my mares, reared in my own stables, don't destroy me! O pitiless curse of my father![49] Who will come to the aid of a man of innocent heart?' There were willing hands in plenty but our legs failed us and we were left behind. He was freed from the leather thongs that held him prisoner – I don't know how – and fell, still breathing for a little while. As for the horses and that monstrous bull that brought such sorrow, they vanished in the rocky earth, I don't know where.

My royal lord, I'm a slave in this house of yours, it's true, but one thing I'll never be able to do and that's believe your son a villain, not even if the whole female sex should hang itself and all the trees on Ida go to make writing material; I know he is a good man.

CHORUS-LEADER: Oh no! A fresh disaster has broken on us; from fate and necessity there is no escape.

THESEUS: Since I feel hate for the man who has suffered this, I took pleasure in this report; but now, out of respect for the gods, yes, and for him, since he is mine, this tale of woe neither pleases nor distresses me.

MESSENGER: What, then? Are we to carry the wretch here? What would you have us do to please you, sir? Give it thought. If you take my advice, you won't be cruel to your son in his misfortune.

THESEUS: Fetch him here. I want to see him before my eyes, the man who denies defiling my bed, and to convict him by my words and the heavy sentence of the gods.

[*Exit the* MESSENGER *to do* THESEUS' *bidding. The* CHORUS *sings its final ode, a short hymn in honour of Aphrodite.*]

CHORUS: Cyprian, you lead captive the unyielding hearts of gods and men, with, at your side, the bright-winged god,   1270
casting his nets on nimble wing. Over the earth Eros flies and across the echoing salt sea. And he casts his spell whenever he lights on some maddened heart, god of the golden-gleaming wings, be it the young of creatures mountain-bred or of the sea, all life that the earth nurtures and the blazing sun sees, or men. All these, all are your subjects, Cyprian, and have   1280
you alone as their sovereign mistress.

[*The goddess* ARTEMIS *appears above the palace and addresses* THESEUS.][50]

ARTEMIS: You, the well-born son of Aegeus, I order you to listen! It is Leto's daughter, Artemis, who speaks. Theseus, you wretch, why do you take pleasure in this, when you have impiously killed your own son, trusting the lying words of your wife though all was not clear? Clear indeed is the ruin you have met! Why do you not hide yourself for shame in the   1290
depths of hell, or take wing to some new home in the skies to escape from this clinging sorrow? For you there can be no place now in the company of good men.

Listen, Theseus, to the true state of your misfortune. It will remedy nothing, it is true, but it will cause you pain. I came here to reveal your son's righteous heart, so that he may die with name untarnished, and your wife's lustful desire – or in   1300
a way her nobility. For the goddess most hated by me and all who love virginity plagued and goaded her into a passionate desire for your son. She tried by strength of mind to master the Cyprian but fell against her will through her nurse's scheming – she it was divulged her mistress' sickness to your son under oath. But he, as was right and proper, rejected her proposal and, god-fearing man, did not retract the pledge he had sworn, not even in the face of your calumny. Phaedra, fearing she might be exposed, wrote a letter of lies and by   1310
trickery destroyed your son – you were persuaded none the less.

THESEUS: Oh no!

ARTEMIS: They wound you, do they, Theseus, these words of mine? Contain yourself; you have louder groans to make when you hear what is to follow. You are aware of the three binding curses you have from your father? One of them you used (how wickedly!) against your son, when an enemy might have felt its force. Your father, then, the sea's lord, wishing you well, gave what he was bound to give, since his word had been given. But you have offended both him and me by your behaviour; you did not wait for proof or advice from prophets, you did not cross-question him, or allow an enquiry over a length of time; no, with improper haste you launched curses at your son and took his life.

THESEUS: Mistress, I pray for death!

ARTEMIS: You have done a terrible thing but nevertheless even you may yet win pardon for this. For it was the Cyprian's will that this took place; she was satisfying her anger. We gods have a law: none seeks to oppose the settled purpose of another; we always stand aside. For, be assured, only my dread of Zeus would have forced me into such a shameful position – doing nothing to save from death the man I love best of all mortals. As for your fault, ignorance first of all exempts you from sin; secondly, by dying your wife made it impossible to test her account and so won over your mind.

On your head this calamity has now broken most of all but I, too, grieve. There is no joy felt in heaven when god-fearing men die; the wicked, however, we destroy, children and house and all.

[HIPPOLYTUS *enters, half walking, half supported by servants.*]

CHORUS-LEADER: Here he comes indeed, the poor man, his youthful flesh and blond head disfigured! O trouble-stricken house! What a double sorrow the gods have fulfilled here, battening on these halls!

HIPPOLYTUS: Ah, pity me, pity me in my wretchedness, disfigured through an unjust father's unjust curses! Oh, misery, I am a thing of pity, ruined! Stabbing pains dart through my

head, spasms leap in my brain. [*To his servants:*] Wait, let me
rest my weary limbs. Ah! Ah! O my fine horses, fed by my
hand, I hate you now, destroyers, killers of your master! Oh
no, no! In heaven's name be gentle, lads, in handling my raw
flesh! Who stands at my side on the right? Lift me gently,   1360
brace yourselves to move me smoothly, the wretch of evil
fortune, accursed, through my father's sinful act. Zeus, Zeus,
do you see this? I, the man of piety, the man who revered the
gods, the man who surpassed all others in not yielding to
passion, am passing to the land of darkness, seeing my death
ahead, my life utterly destroyed. How pointless, all my efforts
to serve my fellow men with acts of piety!

Ah! Ah! It comes on me now, the pain, the pain! Let me   1370
go, for pity's sake – may healing death come to me! Oh,
finish me, I'm hated by the gods, finish me off! I long for a
double-edged sword to split me apart, to lay my life to sleep.
O wretched curse of my father! It is some inherited evil,
stained with blood and issuing from forefathers of old, that
has crossed the boundaries and will not wait but comes upon   1380
me – and why? No guilt is mine for wickedness done. Oh, I
cannot bear it! What shall I say? How can I free this life of
mine from its anguish and find release from pain? Oh, to be
lulled to rest, ill-fated that I am, by Hades' doom, black,
night-dark!

ARTEMIS: Unhappy youth, yoked to so heavy a misfortune!
You have been destroyed by the nobility of your mind.   1390

HIPPOLYTUS [*raising his head*]: Ah! Breath of heavenly fra-
grance! Even in my troubles I knew your presence and felt the
pain in my body ease. The goddess Artemis is here in this
place!

ARTEMIS: She is, poor lad, the god you love beyond all others.

HIPPOLYTUS: Do you see my wretched state, my lady?

ARTEMIS: I see; but I am forbidden to let my eyes shed tears.[51]

HIPPOLYTUS: No longer do you have a companion in the hunt
or one to do you service.

ARTEMIS: No longer, it is true; but you die with my love.

HIPPOLYTUS: No longer one to keep watch over your horses as
they graze or to guard your statues.

1400 ARTEMIS: No; this day was devised by the Cyprian in her shamelessness.

HIPPOLYTUS: Oh, misery! Now I understand what god has brought me to this!

ARTEMIS: She held you to blame over the honour she was denied and was angered by your self-control.

HIPPOLYTUS: A single goddess, she destroyed the three of us, I see it now.

ARTEMIS: Yes, your father, yourself and his wife the third.

HIPPOLYTUS: Then my father's hasty actions make me pity even him.

ARTEMIS: He was deceived by a goddess and her schemes.

HIPPOLYTUS: O my poor father, I pity you for what has passed this day!

THESEUS: I am ruined, my son; all delight in life has gone for me.

HIPPOLYTUS: Your error makes me grieve for you more than myself.

1410 THESEUS: O my child, if only I could be the one to die, not you!

HIPPOLYTUS: What gifts Poseidon sent – cruel gifts for his son to have!

THESEUS: How I wish the words had never passed my lips!

HIPPOLYTUS: How so? You would have killed me at that moment, such anger was upon you.

THESEUS: Yes, the gods had thrown me off balance; my thinking was distorted.

HIPPOLYTUS: Oh, if only mortal men could curse the gods![52]

ARTEMIS: Enough! Not even in the darkness of the earth below shall it go unpunished, this wilful anger of the goddess Cypris that attacks your body; this much I owe to your piety and
1420 righteous heart. With these unerring arrows shot from this hand I will take revenge on another, one of hers, whatever man she loves most on earth.[53] And to you, my stricken friend, in recompense for this suffering I will give highest honours in the city of Trozen. Unmarried girls before their wedding day shall cut their locks in your honour and through the long ages the tribute of their tears shall be yours, shed in deepest sorrow.

When they compose their songs virgin maids shall never fail
to think of you, and Phaedra's passion for you shall not fall   1430
into nameless silence.[54]

As for you, son of old Aegeus, take your son in your arms
and hold him close. You destroyed him but with an innocent
heart. Men can hardly avoid error when the gods inspire it.
And for you, Hippolytus, my counsel is this: do not hate your
father; it was allotted you, this fate that has destroyed you. I
bid you farewell. I am forbidden to look upon the dead or to
defile my sight with life's last breath, the sad end I see drawing
near to you now.[55]

HIPPOLYTUS: Farewell to you, blessed maiden, as you go! How   1440
easily you leave your companion of so many hunts![56] As it is
your wish, I cancel all dispute with my father. In the past as
well I would obey your words.

Ah! Darkness is descending on my eyes now! Hold me,
Father, straighten my body.

THESEUS: Oh, my son, I cannot bear it! I'm cursed, what will
you do to me?

HIPPOLYTUS: My life is over: look, the gates of the dead, I see
them!

THESEUS: Will you leave me here, your blood defiling my hands?

HIPPOLYTUS: Not so; I absolve you of this bloodshed.

THESEUS: What are you saying? You let me go, free of this   1450
blood?

HIPPOLYTUS: Yes; I call to witness Artemis, whose arrows
bring death.

THESEUS: O my beloved boy, what a noble spirit you show to
your father!

HIPPOLYTUS: Farewell to you, Father, a long farewell.

THESEUS: Oh, what a generous soul you have! How truly you
hold the gods dear!

HIPPOLYTUS: Pray for such love from your legitimate sons!

THESEUS: Don't abandon me now, my son! Endure!

HIPPOLYTUS: My endurance is at an end; my life is spent,
Father. Quick – cover my face with my cloak. [He dies.]

THESEUS: O famous boundaries of Aphaea and of Pallas, what
a noble heart you have lost and will never see again! Oh, what   1460

a wretch am I! For many a long day, Cypris, I shall remember this day's spiteful work!

CHORUS: On all citizens together this grief has fallen, foreseen by none. In unbroken lamentation many tears will be shed. The end of great men, heard in song, compels our greater sorrow.

Notes

ALCESTIS

1. *Fates*: according to other authors, Apollo extracted the promise by getting the Fates drunk; perhaps Euripides thought that this would detract from Apollo's dignity in this scene.

2. *pollution*: the gods are immortal, and should not be contaminated with the ugliness of death. Similarly, Artemis leaves Hippolytus before he expires (1437–41).

3. *I see Death*: Death is not one of the regular Olympian gods, though he figures in the *Iliad*. In this scene he is treated like a bogeyman, an almost grotesque stage villain. This is one feature which makes the *Alcestis* an untypical tragedy.

4. . . . *wintry regions*: the arrival of Heracles is anticipated without naming him; the audience would know who was meant when they heard the name of his task-master Eurystheus.

5. *be it Lycia . . . Ammon has his shrine*: Lycia is in southern Turkey; the oracle of Ammon lay in the Libyan desert. The exotic names suggest vast remoteness.

6. *Phoebus' son*: Asclepius, the great healer, mentioned by Apollo in the prologue. He was slain by Zeus for transgressing the limits of his craft by recalling the dead to life.

7. *Hestia's altar*: Hestia, a rather shadowy figure, was the personification of the hearth and presided over the inner household.

8. *Lord Healer*: Apollo.

9. *Admetus, you see . . .*: to modern readers it seems peculiar that Alcestis not only spends so long dying (a technique paralleled in opera) but also rallies here and makes a much more coherent speech after a phase of delirium and violent emotion. This is a common device in Greek tragedy: what is first treated in lyric is then presented anew, from a different perspective, in rational dialogue. There is a similar sequence when Phaedra first appears in the *Hippolytus*.

10. *I will put an end to them*: Admetus' prohibition here is to be reversed when Heracles appears, determined to enjoy himself.

11. *a statue in your image*: this bizarre idea seems to be a re-use by Euripides of a motif found in Thessalian legend, which he had presented in his own *Protesilaus*. In that play the widowed Laodamia kept an image of her husband in her chamber. Admetus goes further in proposing to embrace the statue in his bed.

12. *Orpheus*: the mythical singer Orpheus descended to the underworld and enchanted even the powers of Hades with his song in an effort to recover his dead wife. The later versions emphasized his failure, but it is possible that Euripides means that he succeeded.

13. ONE OF THE CHILDREN: as far as the extant plays show, only Euripides gave children speaking parts. This is part of the 'democratizing' of tragedy which is referred to in Aristophanes' *Frogs* as Euripides' special achievement (see General Introduction III).

14. *death's debtors*: here and often later in the play the chorus give Admetus consolatory advice, in an effort to soothe his grief and make him see his loss as part of the human lot. These sombre counsels may seem heartless to modern readers, but the point is to contrast the extreme grief of the sufferer with the more measured response of the onlooker.

15. *bequeathed to bards*: it is possible, but not certain, that these lines are 'aetiological' (concerned with origins): that is, like some of the speeches made at the end of Euripides' plays, they foretell religious practice which continued in the poet's own time. The Carneia, a festival of Apollo at Sparta, may well have involved songs about his achievements, including his kindness to Admetus' house. The reference to Athens could even be a glancing allusion to Euripides' own play.

16. *Eurystheus of Tiryns*: Eurystheus, king of Tiryns, was the tyrant who set Heracles the twelve labours. He figures as a character in *The Children of Heracles*.

17. *She is both alive and dead*: Admetus' response, unlike the servant's earlier (141), is artificial: either he means that Alcestis is not yet buried, or that she is still vividly alive in his thoughts. In either case it is inevitable that Heracles will be misled. The audience can relish the deeper irony, that she is dead but will soon return to life.

18. *A woman . . .*: typical ambiguity: Heracles assumes that they were 'just talking about' the woman before he arrived, but Admetus actually means Alcestis, of whom the two of them were talking a moment ago.

19. *. . . the havenless shore*: all the place-names in this stanza refer to parts of the kingdom of Admetus in Thessaly.

20. *Lydia . . . or Phrygia*: this suits fifth-century BC Athens, where

slaves were often imported from overseas, better than mythical Thessaly. Minor anachronisms of this kind are quite common in Greek tragedy.

21. *garlanded and drunk*: Heracles, the strongest of the heroes, was regularly presented in comedy as a lover of food, drink and other physical pleasures, sometimes also as rather slow on the uptake. In tragedy he is usually a more formidable and serious figure, but here, no doubt partly because of the 'satyric' role of the *Alcestis* (see Introduction), he plays the buffoon and offers the servant a plain man's doctrine of hedonism.

22. *Cypris*: Aphrodite, goddess of love. Wine and love-making go together in Heracles' mind.

23. *the Maid and her lord*: Persephone and Hades, who preside over the world of the dead. There was some tendency to avoid using Persephone's name, hence 'the Maid'.

24. ADMETUS: the following passage down to 934 ('the strong arms of death') is in lyrics; thereafter Admetus addresses the chorus in spoken metre (another example of the convention described above in note 9). On the printed page this prolonged lamentation may seem stilted and repetitive, but in performance it would be one of the most powerful scenes in the drama. Ritualized mourning is central to Greek tragedy.

25. *Necessity*: this term, here treated as more or less equivalent to 'Destiny', has a slightly modern, philosophical flavour, which suits the notion of the chorus exploring different religious doctrines.

26. *Orpheus*: here the idea of Orpheus as a religious authority is paramount. Since he had descended to the underworld in search of his wife, he was thought to have possessed special insight into life and death. In Euripides' own time 'Orphic' books of religious teaching were popular.

27. *sons of Asclepius*: the medical profession claimed Apollo's son Asclepius as their ancestor or patron.

28. HERACLES: Heracles plays a trick on Admetus, paying him back for his equally well-intentioned deception. Admetus had pretended Alcestis still lived, Heracles conceals the fact that she is alive again. He also tests both Admetus' hospitality and his determination to stick by his vows that no other woman will dwell in the house. Admetus passes one test but fails the other. How we should judge him remains one of the most difficult issues the play raises.

29. *Gorgon*: the monstrous Gorgon Medusa was so ugly that any creature who looked at her turned to stone. The hero Perseus succeeded in chopping her head off by looking not at her but at her reflection in his shield.

30. *Why is this?*: Heracles answers by describing a religious prohibition, analogous to the rules connected with Greek burial: on the third day food could be offered again at the grave. There are also good dramatic reasons: to allow Alcestis to speak again would almost certainly be anti-climactic. Also, the play can otherwise be performed with two actors, and the player who had been Alcestis is now acting the part of Heracles!

31. *royal son of Sthenelus*: Eurystheus.

32. *Many are the forms . . . today*: this choral tail-piece is repeated at the end of several Euripidean plays, and there is controversy as to whether it belongs in all these places. It suits the plot of the *Alcestis* best of all.

MEDEA

1. NURSE: as often in Greek tragedy, recapitulation of the preceding actions also involves exploration of the causes leading to present disaster. The Nurse refers to the following events: Jason was sent on a seemingly hopeless quest for the golden fleece by his usurper uncle Pelias. In the ship *Argo* he journeyed through dangerous waters to Colchis on the Black Sea, where Medea, daughter of the king, fell in love with him and aided him in winning the fleece. He returned successfully to Greece with Medea, who then tricked Pelias' daughters into killing their father in the vain hope that Medea's spells would rejuvenate him. As a result of this atrocity both Jason and Medea had to live in exile in Corinth; at this point the play's story begins.

2. *O Father dear . . .*: Medea does not refer to her brother Apsyrtos, whom she slaughtered on leaving Colchis to delay pursuit. This is referred to later in the play (166–7; 1333), but would not suit the initial sympathetic treatment of the heroine.

3. *She hates her children . . .*: already Euripides begins to drop hints of the horrific deed to come (as later in this scene, when the Nurse addresses the children). The deliberate killing of the children by Medea may well be his own contribution to the story.

4. *measured tones*: the long speech that follows is remarkable in both tone and content. Medea, previously heard ranting and screaming within, now speaks coherently and argues her case. We see that she is able to control and mask her feelings (as later with Creon and in the second encounter with Jason). The speech also includes general comment on the misfortunes of the female sex which has a remarkably modern flavour, and would no doubt have seemed still more startling

to the male-dominated audience of Euripides. Medea shows her intelligence and expresses the woman's viewpoint with memorable force.

5. *your silence*: the presence of the chorus on stage often makes
promises of this kind necessary (this happens also in *Hippolytus* 714).
The sympathy of the women for Medea makes it natural for them to
agree, but they will later be appalled at the lengths to which her anger
takes her.

6. *Sisyphean wedding*: the adjective means 'Corinthian', as Sisyphus
was an earlier king there. But as he was also a notorious sinner (already
subject to eternal punishment in Homer's *Odyssey*), the implication is
that Jason's remarriage is a criminal act.

7. . . . *of men's*: the chorus declare that men have imposed their viewpoint on posterity because they have in general composed the songs
which preserve memory of the past. Now, they think, Medea's daring
revenge will strike a blow for women, and overturn the reputation
women have for infidelity. Gilbert Murray's translation of the ode was
used by suffragettes early in the twentieth century.

8. *the field of death*: this refers to the tasks Aeetes, Medea's father,
insisted that Jason must perform before taking the fleece. He had to
harness fire-breathing bulls and use them to plough a field in which he
must sow seeds which grew up as armed warriors. Only Medea's
potions guaranteed him invulnerability.

9. *content with them*: the stress Jason lays on offspring in the rest of
his speech shows how decisive Medea's counter-stroke will be.

10. *behaving unjustly*: it is unusual for a chorus to side so emphatically
with one speaker in a debate-scene of this type; this clearly indicates
the weakness of Jason's case.

11. *Enter* AEGEUS: Aristotle in his *Poetics* (ch. 25) complained that
the arrival of Aegeus was inartistic, being a convenient coincidence
unmotivated by anything earlier in the play. Opinions may differ as to
the effectiveness of the scene, but it is important that Aegeus' childlessness further stimulates Medea in conceiving a plan which will give the
maximum pain to her husband. It is in any case likely that the subsequent career of Medea in Athens was already established as part of
the legend (see note 15 below).

12. *prophetic navel*: the Greeks thought of Apollo's shrine at Delphi
as being at the centre of the habitable world.

13. *the wineskin's jutting neck*: the meaning is that Aegeus should
not make love to a woman before reaching his home. Oracles were
proverbially obscure.

14. *Oh, I appeal to you . . .*: the process of 'supplication', a kind of
self-abasement before a potential benefactor, is found frequently in

Greek literature. It has a strong religious element (Zeus was thought to protect the rights of suppliants). An entreaty of this kind is hard to resist.

15. *father sons*: this looks forward to events outside the play: in one version, already current in Euripides' time, Medea lived with Aegeus and bore him a son, Medus. Later, when Theseus, Aegeus' true heir, arrived in Athens after being reared elsewhere, Medea failed in an attempt to murder him and had to flee into exile once more. See the account in Plutarch, *Theseus* (in Plutarch, *Rise and Fall of Athens*, tr. I. Scott-Kilvert, London 1960).

16. *The fate . . . against the gods*: according to legend, oath-breakers were tormented in the underworld by the Furies.

17. *kill my own children*: this is the first time Medea has explicitly declared her intention, and the chorus's reaction shows that this moment marks a major change in their attitude (and ours) to her revenge.

18. CHORUS: the ode praises the beauty and culture of Athens, and expresses dismay at the prospect of Medea finding refuge there after her crimes. The effect on the Athenian audience can be easily imagined. Many of them will also have known the stories of Medea's further crimes when resident there (see note 15 above).

19. *the stock of Erechtheus*: the Athenians.

20. *I shall not weaken my hand*: partly in order to impose greater consistency of character on Medea, partly because of curious features of style and language, several scholars have questioned whether all the remaining part of this speech is by Euripides (see Note on the Text). But the changes of mind and some of the other problems can be overlooked in performance, and it seems best to give the whole speech here, given its central importance in criticism of the play.

21. *a tale of strange suffering to tell*: most of Euripides' plays include at least one long messenger-speech. Since the Greek theatre was limited in the type of action it could present before the audience's eyes, descriptions of battles, chases, miraculous events and so on were regularly described in this way. Often, as here, the messenger-speech is rich in gruesome detail, vividly conveying the offstage horror to the mind's eye.

22. *Pan*: attacks of delirium and other unexplained illnesses are commonly explained by appeal to the supernatural. Pan (and other deities) was thought to send a kind of frenzy; hence 'panic'.

23. *Come, my heart . . .*: this briefer speech is a kind of reprise of the long soliloquy. Here self-address is carried further, with the heart personified; the language seemed strange enough to be parodied by Aristophanes a few years later.

24. *O Earth . . . Fury*: the invocation of Earth is forgotten, and 'your golden race', 'brightness born of Zeus', pick up the reference to the Sun-god. Since the Sun sees all things, he should intervene to prevent the slaughter. The chorus are to be disappointed: in fact, the Sun will act to protect Medea, sending her means of escape (1321).

25. *Should I enter the house?*: it is conventional for the chorus, observers rather than agents in the drama, to consider intervening but then to refrain: a famous case is the scene in Aeschylus' *Agamemnon*, where they hear the king's death-cries from inside. This scene, like Phaedra's death-scene in the *Hippolytus*, imitates Aeschylus' classic play.

26. *Ino*: in the Theban legends, Ino and her husband both suffered from Hera's persecution; in a fit of madness she jumped into the sea with her child. Euripides wrote a play about her, now lost. But in contrast Medea, though passionate, is all too clearly in her right mind.

27. *I fear for my children*: Euripides seems here to be alluding to the version in which the Corinthians killed the children. The hint at a more familiar legend highlights his own innovation and the more terrible outcome in this play.

28. *undo the fastenings*: one of the conventions of the Greek theatre was that internal scenes could be presented on the open-air stage by means of a trolley on which a tableau representing the scene indoors could be wheeled out from within the theatre-building. This device, known as the *ekkuklema* ('rolling-out machine'), was already used by Aeschylus. Here the convention is exploited: we expect the device to be used, but Medea instead appears *above* the stage-building.

29. *punish me*: the idea is that Medea is still polluted by her crimes, and that disaster will strike those close to her; the pollution itself is given invisible substance as a 'spirit of vengeance'.

30. *dared such a thing*: Jason's easy division of the world into virtuous Greeks and villainous barbarians is inadequate; the chorus have already mentioned the infanticide of Ino, and there are plenty of grim crimes by Greeks elsewhere in myth. In the earlier part of the play Medea had spoken with the Corinthian women like one of themselves. Euripides often explores the supposed gap and actual resemblances between Greek and 'barbarian'.

31. *Hera of the Cape*: here Medea adopts a tone appropriate to a god; Euripides often ends his plays with a divine prophecy of future events and particularly with the inauguration of a cult commemorating the events of the play. (Compare Artemis in the *Hippolytus* 1423–30, and note 54; and *The Children of Heracles* 1030, and note 43.) Her superhuman status is also shown by the magical chariot.

32. [*Chorus*]: these lines occur in very similar form in the *Alcestis* and in other plays by Euripides. They fit less well here, but a choral comment ends most Greek tragedies, and although Jason has been made more sympathetic at the end, it is unlikely that Euripides would have allowed him the last word.

THE CHILDREN OF HERACLES

1. *as suppliants*: the concept of supplication is essential to this play, and generally important in Greek tragedy (compare *Medea*, note 14 above). Suppliants throw themselves on the mercy of those who can help them; since the gods are thought to protect the weak, supplication imposes an obligation on others to do the same. Moreover, Iolaus and the others have taken refuge in a sacred place, and it would be sacrilegious to remove them by force, as the herald attempts to do.

2. *carry them off*: violence is unusual on the Greek stage, but it is clear in this scene that the herald manhandles Iolaus and knocks him down. Brutal in any case, these actions are impious within a religious sanctuary.

3. *O men of Athens*: the call summoning help from any member of the community within earshot is an old custom suited to small societies. In Greek tragedy it has almost a ritual quality. Compare Theseus' summons to the men of Trozen (*Hippolytus* 884).

4. *from earliest days*: the Athenians claimed to have lived in Attica throughout their history; this claim of 'autochthony' gave them a special status in contrast with migrating or invading peoples such as the Dorians.

5. *the Agora*: the meeting-place or market, where citizens mixed and engaged in debate.

6. *Mycenae*: although the older settlement of Mycenae and the city of Argos, more prominent in historical times, are distinct, they belong to the same part of the Peloponnese and are often treated as almost synonymous.

7. *when offered*: some scholars think that a few lines have dropped out of the text after this speech.

8. *grounds for hope*: the hope is for the future: the sons of Heracles may prove powerful allies for Athens when they grow up.

9. *yours for the choosing*: these lines, like several other passages in the play, reflect the Athenians' conception of themselves. Athens, like many great powers, prided herself on intervening where injustice was done

to the weak, and the idea is also found in oratory. Naturally not all states regarded this as unselfish altruism.

10. . . . *close to yours*: the argument from family history, and the interest in genealogy, are typical of Greek political discussion. Claims of this kind, based on family connections, might be overruled by other arguments, but no Greek would have thought them irrelevant.

11. . . . *to this world*: these lines refer to two episodes of earlier myth which involved Heracles in danger on Theseus' behalf: the expedition to win the girdle of the Amazon Hippolyta, and the descent to the underworld, where Theseus was imprisoned for a time after attempting with Pirithous to abduct Persephone. It is not clear why Theseus needs Heracles' help in the first case; some scholars think that a further explanatory line or lines are lost.

12. *suppliant boughs*: suppliants carried branches of olive or myrtle, with wool entwined around them, which were laid down on the god's altar; they would remain there until the supplication was granted.

13. *justice*: the reference to legal proceedings may seem surprising in a scene which clearly anticipates war, but the Athenians were proud of their courts and fond of litigation (compare, from very different angles, Aeschylus' *Eumenides* and Aristophanes' *Wasps*).

14. *outwit a god*: the Herald's proposal is that the Athenians should make Heracles' family depart, and the Argives will only lay hands on them after they have left Attic territory. Demophon protests that this is mere casuistry, and would not satisfy the all-seeing gods.

15. *Ares*: the god of war.

16. *land where Alcathous ruled*: Megara, to the south of Attica.

17. *a match for those of Argos*: the idea of different gods backing opposing sides in war goes back to the *Iliad*. Athena naturally supports Athens, her favourite city. Later, at 892ff., the chorus sing of both Athena and Zeus as their supporters.

18. *where the Graces have their happy home*: Athens' reputation for culture and civilized pursuits is projected back into mythical times, as in the well-known chorus of the *Medea* (410ff.).

19. *sacrifices made by priests*: the description of religious rituals accompanying the preparations for war corresponds exactly to practice in historical times. The announcement of the need for a human sacrifice, of course, carries us on to a different plane.

20. *one of Heracles' daughters*: the daughter of Heracles who appears so unexpectedly here is not named in the text, but is called Macaria ('Blessed One') in other sources. The theme of one person (usually a virgin) being sacrificed to save many others, or the whole city, is one

which Euripides used frequently. Her initial remarks about a woman's role, though alien to modern taste, underline her maidenly modesty.

21. *Goodbye, old friend, goodbye*: this speech may seem stilted and lacking in intimacy to modern ears; but dignified formality is what the Greek audience would expect in these circumstances, especially since the daughter is not developed as an independent character: she has been introduced only to die in this way. The claim that she has earned her glory would not give offence in a society so concerned with honour and prestige.

22. *below the earth*: the note of agnosticism is typical of Greek thought: although the myths described Hades in some detail, this was not a fixed picture or laid down in any form of creed. See K. J. Dover, *Greek Popular Morality* (Oxford 1974), pp. 261–8.

23. *support me*: Iolaus' despair and prostration here mark the lowest point of his morale. The subsequent scene will lighten his spirits and pave the way for his rejuvenation on the battlefield.

24. *no longer concerns us*: the point seems to be that old people can have no influence on the events of the battlefield. Iolaus is to prove this false.

25. *taken in battle*: armour captured from enemies was often dedicated in temples; and veterans who had finished their military career might also offer their armour and weapons as a thanks-offering.

26. *The* SERVANT *comes out of the temple with armour*: the scene which follows is hard to interpret. It seems impossible to deny that there is some comedy, with Iolaus' aged enthusiasm contrasted with the cynical reaction of the servant. But the miracle to follow shows that Iolaus is in the right; the god is on their side, and his prayers are answered. Perhaps, after the self-sacrifice of Heracles' daughter, Euripides wanted to reduce the tension before the climax of victory. There are other humorous scenes in his dramas, but this one is unusual in being connected with divine intervention.

27. *I must not stumble . . . good luck's sake*: the meaning is obviously that for him to trip would portend some larger mishap affecting the whole army; but the idea of stumbling as a bad omen, though common in Latin, seems unparalleled in Greek literature.

28. *how well I remember*: after the comedy, there is pathos here, as in the various scenes in the *Iliad* in which Nestor recalls his lost youth.

29. CHORUS: this song combines many of the themes of the play (reverence for the gods, respect for suppliants, divine favour for the righteous, Athenian patriotism), and also alludes to the worship of Athena in historical Athens. In particular, the second antistrophe hints at the rituals of the Athenian festival known as the Panathenaea.

30. *our sovereign lord*: Zeus, as the following stanzas show.

31. *Lady divine*: Athena.

32. *man to man*: single combat, the standard form of confrontation in Homer, is well attested in historical times, though it may have acquired an archaic or aristocratic flavour.

33. *miracle*: even in historical times, strange and supernatural events have been reported after battles. The Athenians, for instance, claimed that an apparition of Theseus led them to victory at the battle of Marathon.

34. *that he does*: Heracles as son of Zeus by a mortal woman was a demi-god, not necessarily assured of immortality after death. Different versions are found in the ancient authors: already in the *Odyssey* we can detect one view which placed him in the underworld, another which held him to be divine and married to Hebe.

35. *A pleasant thing to me is dancing*: the structure of the first strophe follows a conventional pattern: 'A is good, B is good, but especially so is C', where C is the main subject of concern. Sappho uses this device to open one of her loveliest poems.

36. *of the fire*: like Alcmene, the chorus now declare their confidence that Heracles is indeed a god. See note 34 above.

37. *Hymenaeus*: a god who presided over marriage.

38. *true pleasure*: it was commonplace for Greeks to say that one should do good to one's friends and harm to one's enemies. Although moralists such as Plato found fault with the second principle, it was not as controversial as it might seem today. Nevertheless, there were limits, and tragedy (like the *Iliad*) often explores particularly extreme or problematic cases.

39. *alive in battle*: the Greeks had no written code of war like the Geneva Convention; but it was widely recognized that some things (such as mutilation of the dead, or denying burial to the defeated) went beyond acceptable limits. Massacre of prisoners after victory does seem to be rare. In any case, the fact that so much is made of Alcmene's desire to kill Eurystheus makes clear that it is meant to be disturbing.

40. *coward*: the portrayal of Eurystheus is very surprising. Instead of a conventional tyrant we see a more dignified figure whose case has some force, even if his excuses do not satisfy us (it is not usually acceptable for mortals to slough off responsibility simply by ascribing their actions to a god's will). Moreover, it emerges that, if slain, he is to become a 'hero', that is, a supernatural being between god and man, who will protect Athens in future. The simple good-versus-evil plot which seemed to be reaching its conclusion becomes more enigmatic.

Just as Eurystheus is no ordinary 'villain', so Alcmene becomes less attractive in her new position of strength.

41. *the victim . . . hero of noble heart*: this line sums up Eurystheus' ambiguous role. The idea of an invader or foreigner being buried and worshipped in the land of his former foes can be paralleled in Herodotus and elsewhere. See generally E. Kearns, *The Heroes of Attica* (London 1989), ch. 3.

42. *Loxias*: another name for Apollo.

43. *where fate prescribes*: although the tomb and commemoration of Eurystheus are not otherwise attested, it seems likely that this scene establishes an authentic cult, as generally happens at the end of Euripides' plays. (Compare *Medea* 1379, and note 31; and *Hippolytus* 1423–30, and note 54.)

44. *Pallene's holy Maid*: Athena.

45. *against your land*: it is possible that this alludes to the contemporary invasions of Attica by the Spartans and their Peloponnesian allies in the war which had begun in 431 BC. (The Peloponnesian kings, including those of Sparta, claimed descent from the Heraclidae.) But the reference may be vaguer and more general.

46. CHORUS: it seems certain that some lines have dropped out of the text before this final comment by the chorus. After their earlier misgivings, they cannot simply assent to Alcmene's vicious words. But we cannot be sure how much is lost, and reconstruction of the missing lines can only be speculative.

HIPPOLYTUS

1. *Trozen*: in the NE Peloponnese, and not part of Athens' domain in historical times, but closely associated with her in legend. It was there that Theseus grew to manhood and from there that he set out to Athens to find his human father.

2. *the Great Sea*: the Black Sea, which represents the eastern extremity of the world, as 'the boundaries of Atlas' (the Straits of Gibraltar) define the western limit for Mediterranean man.

3. *Amazon*: Hippolyta (occasionally called by another name, Antiope), whom Theseus won as a captive in war. Theseus has other, legitimate sons by Phaedra, though these do not appear in the play. Hippolytus' bastard status is important in relation to his self-esteem and his uneasy relations with Phaedra.

4. *Pittheus*: Theseus' maternal grandfather, former king of Trozen. His grandson seems to have succeeded him in that role.

5. *the foulest of divinities*: it seems important that Hippolytus insults and derides Aphrodite (as he does in the scene with the servant which follows). His crime does not consist of chastity alone, which occupies second place in her complaints.

6. *Pandion*: like Cecrops, mentioned a few lines on, a mythical king of Athens, belonging to remoter legend than Theseus.

7. *she founded a temple to Cypris*: this is an aetiological myth, i.e. one which explains the origins of an existing historical ritual or institution. The playwright often creates or emphasizes these religious links between the mythical past and his own time.

8. *Pallantid blood*: in Athenian legend, Theseus disputed his claims to kingship with his cousins, grandsons of Pandion. The exile forms a kind of penance in which the slayer can be purified of bloodshed. It also enables Euripides to place the action at Trozen, in accordance with tradition, as Theseus is obliged to be away from Athens.

9. *I will reveal the affair to Theseus*: as elsewhere (e.g. in the *Ion*), the poet misleads or allows his audience to anticipate a different development from what actually ensues. Theseus does not in fact learn of his wife's passion until the very end; his curse on Hippolytus is because he believes him guilty of rape. This keeps the audience on their mettle, allowing for an element of surprise.

10. *Reverence*: the word used conveys also a sense of purity and modesty, which fits Hippolytus' self-conscious yet admirable virtue. See the reference to 'shame' by Phaedra (385ff.), who is thinking at least partly of how things appear. The contrast between Hippolytus' and Phaedra's conceptions of what is shameful and honourable is central to the play.

11. *would you listen?*: the scene with the servant is important in guiding our response to Hippolytus' behaviour. If such a loyal retainer feels such misgivings at the young man's conduct, we must assume that it is indeed abnormal and excessive.

12. *Are you possessed, sweet lady?*: madness or delusion was commonly attributed to the influence of some god, often a deity associated with wild nature or ecstatic celebrations (e.g. Bacchus, Cybele or Pan).

13. NURSE: the following exchanges between the Nurse and Phaedra are in lyrics; only when the chorus-leader questions the Nurse (267ff.) do we resume spoken dialogue. This means that the language is freer, the emotional tone more intense. The Nurse is distraught with anxiety, Phaedra (despite her physical weakness) is in a near-hysterical state.

14. *How horrible life is with . . .*: the Nurse's moralizing (compare 253ff.) is rather banal and self-pitying but provides an example of

Euripides' tendency to make characters of lower rank more articulate and interesting than in early tragedy. (Compare the criticisms in Aristophanes: see Introduction, p. xxvi–xxvii.)

15. *Ah, if only . . .*: Phaedra's wild and vivid fantasies involve the places where Hippolytus would often be found; she longs to escape from the palace to a freer existence with him. The audience, who understand her condition, recognize this, but the Nurse is baffled.

16. *seizing hold of my hand?*: this, like touching the knees (next line), is a gesture of supplication. The Nurse desperately throws herself at Phaedra's feet and begs her to reveal the truth. The religious quality of such an appeal imposes a heavy burden on Phaedra.

17. *seized you*: Phaedra's mother, Pasiphae, was filled with a terrible desire for a bull. Eventually she succeeded in coupling with the beast, and their offspring was the monstrous Minotaur, half man, half bull.

18. *Dionysus*: Phaedra's sister was Ariadne, but it is not clear what myth Euripides meant his audience to recall. Clearly, this passion, like Pasiphae's and Phaedra's, is to be regarded as disastrous. In these lines, Phaedra implies that her passion is the result of a taint in her blood: all the women of her family are doomed to unholy desires. In fact, the cause of her passion is external, but it may be that Phaedra's own nature does make her an easier victim.

19. *Ladies of Trozen . . .*: this important speech shows Phaedra more rational and articulate than she was in the preceding scene. Although it is common in tragedy to handle the same material in lyric and then in dialogue (see *Alcestis* 280, and note 9), here the sequence is also psychologically plausible: having unburdened her secret, Phaedra can speak more freely and with more self-control.

20. *the same name*: Phaedra's remarks on shame are mysterious, and have been much discussed. There will never be agreement on all points, but it seems likely that she is distinguishing between virtuous modesty, which is good, and an excessive respect for other people's opinions and feelings, which is bad (Phaedra's own concern for her good name will further illustrate this bad shame later in the play).

21. *the path my mind took*: the following lines are particularly important in showing how different Phaedra in this play is from the conventional lustful woman, as portrayed in the earlier *Hippolytus* (see p. 129).

22. *glorious Athens*: the Athenians prided themselves on the freedom of speech and thought in their society.

23. *to join the gods*: the Nurse's speech in general is full of weak arguments, and at least the first of these examples does not suit her

case. Semele was beloved by Zeus, but died when she rashly asked him to appear in his full glory before her; a mortal could not survive this. In any case, the practice of the gods is not necessarily exemplary for mortals.

24. *I don't know*: this admission by the Nurse gives the game away: she has no potion, but only wants a chance for a word with Hippolytus.

25. *The girl of Oechalia*: the reference is to Iole, daughter of King Eurytus. Heracles, son of Alcmene, sacked the city because of his passion for the girl, and carried her off as his concubine.

26. *for bridegroom*: Semele, princess of Thebes, who was pregnant with Bacchus, was burnt up when Zeus reluctantly fulfilled her wish and appeared to her in his immortal glory. Zeus rescued the unborn child and sewed him in his own side until the time was up; hence Bacchus is 'twice-born'.

27. *You're at the door*: choral intervention in the action is almost unknown in later tragedy, and there seems to have been something of a convention that they did not join the actors on the stage proper (though exceptions can be found). Phaedra is isolated, and must suffer alone.

28. *I clasp your knees and beg you*: again the Nurse has recourse to supplication, but here with limited success.

29. *not my heart*: this line became notorious (compare Aristophanes, *Frogs* 101, 1471); it seems to have been taken up as an example of Euripides teaching immorality, quite unfairly, since Hippolytus does in fact stick by his oath.

30. *O Zeus . . .*: this speech is so violently misogynistic that it can easily turn an audience completely against Hippolytus; the quick temper shown in the earlier exchange with the servant becomes furious indignation here. It is important to remember that Hippolytus thinks Phaedra has actually sent the Nurse as a go-between. Anger, overwhelming any thought of further enquiry, proves his undoing: we should compare Theseus' mistake later on.

31. *without women*: this kind of 'utopian' wish for a differently arranged world is almost a mannerism in Euripides: compare Theseus later (916ff. and note 42), and *Medea* 573ff. It should be obvious, however, that Hippolytus' outburst tells us nothing about Euripides' own attitude to women (cf. Preface).

32. *and your mistress*: Phaedra is present on stage, but Hippolytus seems to ignore her throughout. Without the author's stage directions it is hard to choose between two scenarios: he sees her but ignores her out of revulsion, or she cowers to one side and watches him directing his whole attack on the Nurse. He later says he has just left her (907),

which suggests that the former reading is correct, but Greek drama is not always perfectly consistent in these small details.

33. *no longer shall I die with honour*: Phaedra's concern for her own good name re-surfaces. This leads her to leave behind the untrue accusation of Hippolytus.

34. *to the daylight*: for the chorus's oath of silence, see note 5 on *Medea* 263. This explains their guarded and misleading responses to Theseus in the following scene.

35. CHORUS: the ode begins by expressing the chorus's longing to escape from these disastrous events; but the romantic images of far-off places also remind the audience of the gods' power and the limits that are set to mankind (Phaethon's attempt to drive the chariot of the sun led to his death; mortal sailors cannot journey beyond the Pillars of Heracles, where Atlas stands). The second half of the ode, recalling Phaedra's past and anticipating her imminent death, sums up her tragic story. It also vividly describes the actual hanging, which cannot be represented on stage.

36. *What shall we do, friends?*: the chorus of a tragedy is regularly shown as indecisive and inadequate in a crisis: compare *Medea* 1275, and note 25. Often, as in this play, they are ordinary people, who witness but cannot influence the behaviour of their superiors or masters.

37. PHAEDRA'S *corpse is revealed*: this is done by means of the so-called *ekkuklema* ('rolling-out machine'), a device which the dramatists used to display events indoors. A wheeled trolley was used to bring the interior scene outside; often, as here, those slain within are exposed to view. Compare *Medea* 1315, and note 28.

38. *sent upon me by the gods*: the idea here is that of inherited guilt; Theseus supposes that he suffers for the crimes of an ancestor. This theme is commoner in earlier tragedy, especially that of Aeschylus. In the late fifth century BC it may have seemed a little old-fashioned; in any case, Theseus is wrong in this case (as is Hippolytus later, 1379–83).

39. *a noble wife*: the chorus, as in the *Alcestis*, offer advice which can be little more than cold comfort.

40. *eye of Zeus*: the gods are thought to see all things, and hence to witness all crimes.

41. *one of the three curses*: as this is the first time Theseus has used one of these curses, he does not know whether they will work; hence much more is at first made of the sentence of exile.

42. *prone to error*: Theseus' generalizations keep the action in suspense and Hippolytus remains baffled. Some of them also take the favourite

form of 'utopian wishes': compare Hippolytus at 616ff., and note 31.

43. *let your father see you face to face*: at this point Hippolytus covers his head with his cloak, fearing that the very mention of such a crime may bring him misfortune, or pollute him. Theseus angrily takes this to be a gesture of shame. In the first *Hippolytus*, the young man seems to have done the same thing when brazenly approached by Phaedra, and it has been suggested that this passage is a kind of allusion to that scene in the earlier play: Euripides shows how he can put the same device to quite different use.

44. *scribblings*: Orpheus, the mythical poet, was also regarded in classical times as a sage and mystical teacher. So-called 'Orphic' writings were circulating in Euripides' time, and some of these probably advocated vegetarianism, as the Pythagoreans did. But Hippolytus is a hunter and meat-eater; Theseus is simply deriding him for his alleged purity, and piles on whatever other insults he can think of.

45. *Sinis of the Isthmus . . . Sciron*: these were bandits slain by Theseus in his youth.

46. *no alternative but to speak out*: Theseus' speech, like his character, is passionate and emotional. Hippolytus' is couched in much more rational and argumentative terms, and has several features which recall the language of the Athenian law-courts. This seems deliberate: the young man's priggish and pedantic manner serves to fuel his father's anger.

47. *what the prophets say?*: in historical as in mythical times, where evidence is inadequate men might turn to the gods for guidance (as is constantly done, for example, in Xenophon's *Anabasis*). Asking an expert to interpret the movements of birds in flight was one form of divination. Theseus is at fault for not pursuing such a course, as Artemis later comments.

48. *Aphaea*: a title of Artemis.

49. *curse of my father*: the curse was not mentioned in the dialogue between Theseus and Hippolytus, but it is easy enough to suppose that one of the latter's companions told him about it. Euripides does not want to waste time on explanations after the event.

50. *The goddess* ARTEMIS . . . THESEUS: after the chorus's prayer to Aphrodite we might perhaps expect that goddess to reappear. The epiphany of Artemis, her enemy and opposite, makes for a greater symmetry in the play: the two goddesses frame and comment on the human action.

51. *tears*: the gulf between divine serenity and human suffering is powerfully stressed.

52. *curse the gods*: a murdered man would leave a curse on his human

murderer; but what happens when the murderer is divine? This daring line is typical of Euripides: he extends traditional religious beliefs in unconventional ways. But the authority of the gods is reasserted with Artemis' rebuke.

53. *on earth*: Artemis takes revenge by bringing about the death of Aphrodite's beloved, the beautiful Adonis.

54. *nameless silence*: as in the *Medea* and *The Children of Heracles*, the events of the play will be commemorated in cult. This kind of 'aetiology' is found in most of Euripides' closing scenes. The ritual in memory of Hippolytus is also mentioned by the geographer Pausanias (2. 32).

55. *near to you now*: the gods are immortal, and must not be present when men and women perish. Birth or death within a temple is sacrilege.

56. *so many hunts*: resignation, reproach, or simple statement of fact? Each actor will give his own interpretation, and audiences will respond in different ways. The fact remains that the final lines of the play are given up to the intimate parting of father and son.

Bibliography

The standard Greek text, which forms the basis for this translation, is the new Oxford Classical Text edited by J. Diggle (3 volumes, 1981–94); this supersedes the much-used edition by G. Murray in the same series. As this edition is arranged chronologically, all the plays translated in this Penguin Classic figure in Diggle's vol. 1. The Oxford Text includes detailed information about the manuscripts and other textual details, but no translation or notes.

Those wishing to consult the plays in Greek will find the best guidance in the following annotated editions:
Alcestis, ed. A. M. Dale (Oxford 1954); see also the shorter edition by
    D. J. Conacher (Warminster 1988): includes translation.
Hippolytus, ed. W. S. Barrett (Oxford 1964); also the shorter edition
    by M. R. Halleran (Warminster 1995): includes translation.
Medea, ed. D. L. Page (Oxford 1938); D. J. Mastronarde (Cambridge
    2002); also the school edition by A. Elliott (Oxford 1969).
The Children of Heracles (Heraclidae), ed. J. Wilkins (Oxford 1993);
    W. Allen (Warminster 2002): includes translation.

The Loeb Classical Library, which publishes bilingual editions of most classical authors, is currently bringing out an edition of Euripides by David Kovacs (1994–), arranged chronologically: at the time of writing five volumes have appeared, taking the sequence as far as *Orestes*. This edition replaces an older and wholly unsatisfactory edition by A.S. Way. Those who need to consider the detail of the Greek text should note that Kovacs presents his own text, which often differs from Diggle's.

Other translations available include those by various hands in the series edited by D. Grene and R. Lattimore, *The Complete Greek Tragedies* (Chicago 1941–58). Otherwise, complete versions of Euripides are hard to find, though the major plays are often translated individually or in smaller selections. A parallel enterprise to our own is the series published by Oxford University Press, with translations (prose) by James Morwood and introductions by Edith Hall. These are grouped thematically rather than chronologically; the emphasis in the introductions is on reception and performance history. Three volumes have appeared, of which the first (1997) contains *Medea* and *Hippolytus* alongside *Electra* and *Helen*.

General works on Greek tragedy

Goldhill, S., *Reading Greek Tragedy* (Cambridge 1986).

Hall, E., *Inventing the Barbarian: Greek Self-definition through Tragedy* (Oxford 1989).

Heath, M., *The Poetics of Greek Tragedy* (London 1987).

Jones, J., *On Aristotle and Greek Tragedy* (London 1962).

Knox, B. M. W., *Word and Action: Essays on the Ancient Theater* (Baltimore 1979).

Lesky, A., *Greek Tragedy* (Eng. tr. London 1954).

Sommerstein, A., *Greek Drama and Dramatists* (London and New York 2002): a helpful guide to the genre, including much factual data and a selection of translated passages from the dramas themselves and other relevant texts.

Taplin, O., *The Stagecraft of Aeschylus* (Oxford 1977). Despite the title, relevant to all the tragedians.

Taplin, O., *Greek Tragedy in Action* (London 1978).

Vernant, J.-P. and Vidal-Naquet, P., *Myth and Tragedy in Ancient Greece* (New York 1988): amalgamates two earlier collections of essays.

Vickers, B., *Towards Greek Tragedy* (London 1973).

Easterling, P. E. and Knox, B. M. W. (eds.), *The Cambridge History of Classical Literature*, vol. 1 (Cambridge 1985), includes expert essays on the Greek theatre and on each of the three tragedians (Knox covers Euripides); these chapters, together with those on satyric drama and comedy, are reissued in paperback as *Greek Drama*, ed. Easterling and Knox (Cambridge 1989).

Useful collections of work include:

Easterling, P. E. (ed.), *The Cambridge Companion to Greek Tragedy* (Cambridge 1997).

McAuslan, I. and Walcot, P. (eds.), *Greek Tragedy (Greece and Rome Studies* 2, Oxford 1993).

Pelling, C.B.R. (ed.), *Greek Tragedy and the Historian* (Oxford 1997).

Segal, E. (ed.), *Oxford Readings in Greek Tragedy* (Oxford 1983).

Silk, M. (ed.), *Tragedy and the Tragic* (Oxford 1996).

The Greek theatre

Csapo, E. and Slater, W. J., *The Context of Ancient Drama* (Michigan 1995): this excellent source-book translates and discusses many ancient texts relevant to theatrical conditions in the Greek and Roman world.

Pickard-Cambridge, A. W., *The Dramatic Festivals of Athens*, 2nd edn, revised by J. Gould and D. M. Lewis (Oxford 1968; reissued 1988). Authoritative, but quotes extensively in the original Greek.

Green, J. R., *Theatre in Ancient Greek Society* (London 1994).

Green, R. and Handley, E., *Images of the Greek Theatre* (London 1993).

Rehm, R., *Greek Tragic Theatre* (London 1992).

Simon, E., *The Ancient Theatre* (English tr. London and New York 1982).

Historical and cultural background

Andrewes, A., *Greek Society* (London 1971); originally published as *The Greeks* (London 1967).

Davies, J. K., *Democracy and Classical Greece* (London 1978; revised and expanded 1993).

Religion and thought

Bremmer, J. N., *Greek Religion (Greece and Rome New Surveys* 24, Oxford 1994).

Burkert, W., *Greek Religion* (Eng. tr. Oxford 1985).

Dodds, E. R., *The Greeks and the Irrational* (Berkeley 1951).

Easterling, P. E. and Muir, J. V. (eds.), *Greek Religion and Society* (Cambridge 1985).

Mikalson, J., *Athenian Popular Religion* (Chapel Hill 1983).

Mikalson, J., *Honor thy Gods: Popular Religion in Greek Tragedy* (Chapel Hill and London 1991). Helpful, but perhaps emphasizes too strongly the gap between literature and the realities of cult and worship.

Parker, R., *Miasma: Pollution and Purification in Early Greek Religion* (Oxford 1983).

Studies of Euripides in general, and of the four plays in this volume

Allan, W., *Euripides, Medea* (London 2002).

Clauss, J. J. and Johnston, S.I. (eds.), *Medea: Essays on Medea in Myth, Literature, Philosophy, and Art* (Princeton 1997).

Collard, C., *Euripides (Greece and Rome New Surveys* 14, Oxford 1981). An excellent short account with many examples and full bibliographical guidance.

Conacher, D. J., *Euripidean Drama: Myth, Theme and Structure* (Toronto and London 1967).

Hall, E., Macintosh, F., and Taplin, O. (eds.), *Medea in Performance, 1500–2000* (Legenda, European Humanities Research Centre, Oxford 2000).

Halleran, M. R., *Stagecraft in Euripides* (London and Sydney 1985).

Knox, B. M. W., 'The *Hippolytus* of Euripides' in *Word and Action* (see above), pp. 205–30 (originally in *Yale Classical Studies* 13, 1952).

Knox, B. M. W., 'The *Medea* of Euripides' in *Word and Action* (see above), pp. 295–322 (originally in *Yale Classical Studies* 25, 1977).

Michelini, A. N., *Euripides and the Tragic Tradition* (Madison, Wisconsin and London 1987). This includes valuable chapters on the history of interpretation, and detailed 'readings' of four plays, including *Hippolytus*.

Mills, S., *Euripides, Hippolytus* (London 2002).

Morwood, J., *The Plays of Euripides* (Bristol 2002).

Murray, G., *Euripides and his Age* (London 1913): influential but very outdated.

Zuntz, G., *The Political Plays of Euripides* (Manchester 1955): includes detailed account of *Heraclidae*.

Special aspects

Barlow, S. A., *The Imagery of Euripides* (London 1971).

Conacher, D. J., *Euripides and the Sophists* (London 1998).

Jong, I. J. F. de, *Narrative in Drama: The Art of the Euripidean Messenger-speech* (*Mnemosyne* Suppl. 116, Leiden 1991).

Kovacs, D., *Euripidea* (*Mnemosyne* Suppl. 132, Leiden 1994). Includes text and translation of many passages concerning Euripides' life, works and reputation in his time; also textual notes on various points in *Alcestis* and *Medea*.

Lloyd, M., *The* Agon *in Euripides* (Oxford 1992).

General reference works

Hornblower, S. and Spawforth, A. (eds.), *The Oxford Classical Dictionary* (3rd edition, Oxford 1996): detailed and authoritative. For some readers the abridged and illustrated version, *The Oxford Companion to Classical Civilization* (1998), will be more suitable.

Howatson, M., *The Oxford Companion to Classical Literature* (Oxford 1989): useful particularly for summaries of myths.

Glossary of Mythological and Geographical Names

Information given here is only occasionally reproduced in the notes to specific passages.

Acamas like Demophon, son of Theseus and sharing power in Athens after the latter's death.

Acastus son of Pelias of Iolcus, and brother of Alcestis.

Achaean often used as meaning simply 'Greek', but strictly a region of the northern Peloponnese.

Acheron one of the rivers of the underworld.

Admetus son of Pheres, king of Pherae in Thessaly (NE Greece). His hospitality to Apollo led to the ambiguous favour the consequences of which are explored in the *Alcestis*.

Adrian off the Gulf of Venice, at the northern limit of the Adriatic.

Aegean the part of the Mediterranean sea separating Greece from Asia Minor.

Aegeus son of Pandion and king of Athens, who gives refuge to Medea; father of Theseus.

Aethra wife of Aegeus and mother of Theseus.

Alcathous son of Pelops, king of Megara (to the south of Athens) in early mythical times.

Alcmene wife of Amphitryon and mother of Heracles by Zeus.

Alpheus river running by the great cult-site of Zeus at Olympia, in the NW Peloponnese.

Amazon one of a race of warrior women, usually man-hating. Theseus' son Hippolytus was the result of a liaison between Theseus and one of the Amazons.

Ammon an Egyptian deity whose oracle in the Libyan desert was famous among the Greeks, who often identified the god there with their own Zeus.

Aphrodite daughter of Zeus, goddess of love and desire.

Apollo son of Zeus and Leto, brother of Artemis; one of the most powerful and dignified of the Olympian gods. He was famous for his good looks, his powers as an archer, his musical gifts and above all his power of prophesying the future through his oracles, of which that at Delphi was the most famous.

Ares god of war, usually regarded as a cruel and threatening figure.

Argo the ship of Jason and the Argonauts.

Argos city in the northern Peloponnese, often conflated in tragedy with the older site nearby, Mycenae.

Artemis daughter of Zeus and Leto; sister of Apollo, and like him an archer; virgin goddess, associated with hunting and wild animals; patroness of Hippolytus.

Asclepius, Asclepius' Rock Asclepius was son of Apollo, a great healer who overstepped the limits by recalling the dead to life. For this he was slain by Zeus with a thunderbolt. His rock, referred to in the *Hippolytus*, was probably near Epidaurus, where in historical times he had a great sanctuary.

Athens main settlement in Attica, in central Greece.

Atlas a giant who supported the sky on his shoulders; usually described as standing in the far west, near Gibraltar.

Bacchus = Dionysus, god of wine.

Bistonians, Bistones a Thracian tribe.

Boebe a lake in eastern Thessaly, part of Admetus' domain.

Carneia a harvest festival celebrated at Sparta and in other states of Dorian descent. The 'Carneian month' embraced part of August and part of September. Apollo was worshipped during this festival.

Cecrops early mythical king of Athens, allegedly half man, half snake.

Cephalus native of Athens beloved and abducted by the goddess Dawn.

Cephisus major river flowing to the west of Athens.

Chalybes legendary metal-workers dwelling on the south coast of the Black Sea.

Charon the sinister ferryman who, in mythology, transported the dead across the river Styx to their eternal abode in the underworld.

Clashing Rocks one of the supernatural obstacles faced by Jason on his quest for the golden fleece – massive rocks which moved in the water to smash any ship passing between them. They were vaguely located in the Bosphorus area. He succeeded in passing this barrier, apparently with Medea's aid on the return journey.

Cocytus one of the rivers of the underworld; its name means 'lamentation'.

Colchis realm of king Aeetes, father of Medea; located at the far end of the Black Sea. It was from his expedition to this distant kingdom that Jason brought back both Medea and the golden fleece.

Corinth one of the chief cities of the Peloponnese: its position immediately to the south of the Isthmus gave it advantages in both war and trade.

Corybantes male priests associated with the wild rituals of Cybele and Bacchus.

Creon in the *Medea*, king of Corinth and father of the (unnamed) princess whom Jason is now wooing.

Crete in the SE Mediterranean; largest of the Greek islands, in mythical times the realm of King Minos, father of Phaedra.

Cyclops (plural *Cyclopes*) monstrous one-eyed giants, threatening to mortals but often presented as subjects of Zeus, for whom they forged supernatural armour and weapons, above all the thunderbolt.

Cycnus a son of Ares, robber and murderer, who was killed by Heracles.

Cypris, the Cyprian Aphrodite, goddess of love, who was born from the sea near Cyprus, and was especially worshipped there.

Dawn goddess personifying this natural phenomenon, conceived as young and beautiful; fell in love with the human Cephalus (and in other stories Tithonus).

Demeter goddess of fertility in nature, presiding over the crops and other products of the earth; mother of Persephone.

Demophon son of Theseus, and king of Athens after his death.

Dictynna 'lady of the net', a title of Artemis the huntress.

Diomedes of Thrace a Thracian king, son of Ares, and king of the Bistonians. His man-eating horses were captured by Heracles as one of his labours. He should be distinguished from Diomedes son of Tydeus, one of the Greek heroes at Troy.

Dionysus son of Zeus by Semele; god of wine and other natural forces; often seen as a wild and irrational deity, bringer of madness.

Dirce major river of Thebes in Boeotia.

Electryon a king of Mycenae, father of Alcmene and hence grandfather of Heracles.

Enetic see Venetian

Epidauria the area around Epidaurus, a small state in the NE Peloponnese, south of the Isthmus.

Erechtheus early mythical king of Athens; hence 'Erechtheids' = 'Athenians'.

Eridanus a mythical river in the far west of the Mediterranean. The name was later given to the Italian Po.

Eros the personification of Love in boy's form, conceived as son and constant companion of Aphrodite (his father varies in different versions, but sometimes he is referred to as son of Zeus). The more familiar name 'Cupid' is Latin in origin.

Euboea a large island off the coast of Attica and Boeotia.

Eurystheus son of Sthenelus; tyrannical king of Argos, persecutor of Heracles and his family.

Eurytus king of Oechalia, father of Iole, who was seized as a captive by Heracles when he sacked Oechalia.

Euxine a Greek name for the Black Sea, meaning 'hospitable' – a euphemism used to avoid bad luck. Similarly, the terrifying Furies could be referred to as 'the kindly ones'.

Four Towns ('Tetrapolis') an area of Attica in which in early (i.e. pre-classical) times the centre of power may have been located. Marathon was one of the four towns; the others were Oenoe, Probalinthos and Tricorythos.

Fury a daemonic and dangerous creature who was thought to persecute evil-doers in life and after death; hence any horrific and avenging figure, especially female.

Gorgon a type of hideous female monster with snakes for hair, so horrible that to look at one outright would turn a man to stone. The most famous Gorgon, Medusa, was slain by Perseus, who chopped off her head by looking not at her, but at her reflection in his shield.

Graces, the personifications of beauty and other fine qualities, conceived in female form; often associated, like the Muses, with the arts.

Great Sea the Black Sea, symbol of the eastern extremities of the known world.

Hades (a) one of the three most powerful Olympians, the others being Zeus and Poseidon – they divided up the universe, and Hades drew the underworld as his domain; (b) the underworld itself.

Hebe divine consort of Heracles, personification of youthful beauty.

Hecate a sinister goddess associated with darkness, witchcraft and ghosts.

Helios the Sun-god, often identified with the fiery orb he controls.

Hera queen of the gods and consort of Zeus; presides over marriage; often associated with Argos, one of her favourite cities; persistent enemy of Heracles.

Heracles son of Zeus and Alcmene; greatest of the Greek heroes, famous for his many victories over monsters and barbaric peoples; enslaved by Eurystheus and compelled to perform twelve labours; after his death, deified and married to Hebe.

Hermes of the Nether World Hermes was conceived as escorting the dead on at least part of the way to the underworld, before entrusting them to Charon's ferry.

Hesperides literally 'daughters of evening'; nymphs dwelling in the far west, where they inhabit a garden where golden apples grow.

Hestia goddess of the hearth and hence almost a symbol for the home.

Hippolytus bastard son of the Athenian king Theseus by an Amazon prisoner-of-war; in Euripides' play, a young man of self-conscious purity, devoted to the goddess Artemis.

Hyllus son of Heracles.

Hymenaeus a deity who presided over marriage and its ceremonies, often invoked in song at such occasions.

Ino sister of Dionysus' mother Semele; driven mad by Hera, she jumped into the sea with one of her children; both died, but in some versions were transformed into sea-deities.

Iolaus nephew of Heracles, and former companion on his labours.

Iolcus town near Mt Pelion in NE Greece; rightfully the domain of Jason's family, but usurped by Pelias.

Isthmus the narrow stretch of land connecting central Greece with the Peloponnese.

Jason son of Aeson, Greek hero, leader of the Argonauts on their quest for the golden fleece. His treacherous abandonment of Medea and its consequences are the focus of Euripides' play.

Larisa town in Thessaly, to the north of Admetus' residence at Pherae.

Leto mother of Apollo and Artemis by Zeus.

Libya in Greek literature, this name is often loosely applied to any part of North Africa west of Egypt.

Loxias a title of Apollo, perhaps meaning 'crooked' or 'slanting', with reference to his ambiguous oracles.

Lycaon a son of Ares who challenged Heracles to single combat.

Lycia Greek-speaking region to the south of modern Turkey.

Lydia part of Asia Minor.

Maia a nymph who was mother of Hermes.

Maid, the = Persephone, consort of Hades. Although she had a kinder face, as daughter of Demeter and bringer of fertility, she is often regarded with awe, and 'the Maid' is a way of avoiding use of her name.

Marathon district in NW Attica, the territory of Athens, at some distance from the city proper. In historical times the site of the great battle with Darius' invading force, which the Greeks repelled.

Medea daughter of Aeetes and granddaughter of the Sun, princess of Colchis; fell in love with the Greek Jason, whom she helped and married; when he jilted her for a Greek princess, she took her revenge.

Minos king of Crete and father of Phaedra.

Molossia a region in Epirus, in NW Greece.

Munichus one of the harbour-areas near Piraeus, the port of Athens.

Muses nine in number, goddesses of the arts and especially poetry; daughters of Memory.

Mycenae in very ancient times, a great centre of power and wealth in the Peloponnese. By Euripides' time it was eclipsed by Argos, with which, in *The Children of Heracles*, it is virtually identified.

Ocean in early Greek thought, conceived as a vast river circling the entire world, and often personified as the greatest of river-gods.

Oechalia a town, rather vaguely located: in some versions in Euboea. It was sacked by Heracles. 'The girl of Oechalia' means Iole, whom Heracles desired and took as a captive on that occasion.

Olympus a mountain in northern Greece, on the borders of Macedonia and Thessaly. As a result of its majestic height, it was considered the home of the gods, though the name is sometimes used more loosely, to describe a remote heavenly realm.

Orpheus a gifted poet and musician whose singing could spellbind even wild beasts and who endeavoured to charm the powers of the underworld into releasing his dead wife – in some versions successfully. He was also seen as the teacher of religious doctrines and purity (including vegetarianism): hence Theseus' jibes in the *Hippolytus*.

Othrys a mountain to the south of the Thessalian plain.

Pallantid of the family of Pallas, an Athenian, son of Pandion, who clashed with Theseus over control of Attica.

Pallas = Athena.

Pallene a region of Attica to the east of Athens, on the northern slopes of Mt Hymettus; location of an ancient temple of Athena.

Pallenis a title referring to the goddess Athena's temple in Pallene, a district of Attica.

Pan son of Hermes; half goat, half man, this lesser deity is a figure of the wild and is often thought to induce frenzy and fits of madness (hence 'panic').

Pandion early mythical king of Athens, grandson or great-grandson of Erechtheus.

Pelian of or from Mt Pelion in Thessaly.

Pelias uncle of Jason, whose father he had supplanted in seizing the throne of Iolcus in Thessaly; he sent Jason on the quest for the golden fleece, hoping he would die in the attempt; eventually killed by his daughters through Medea's trickery. He was also the father of Alcestis.

Pelion great mountain in Thessaly.

Peloponnese the massive peninsula which forms the southern part of Greece, including such major cities as Mycenae, Corinth, Argos, Tiryns, Sparta.

Pelops son of Tantalus and founder of the Pelopid line, after which the Peloponnese is named; father of Atreus and Thyestes.

Perseus one of the great heroes of Greek myth, slayer of the Gorgon Medusa. He was an ancestor of the even greater hero Heracles.

Phaedra wife of Theseus, cursed by an uncontrollable passion for Hippolytus.

Phaethon a rash youth who dared to ride the chariot of the Sun-god, his father, with disastrous results. The chariot went out of control, and Zeus was forced to destroy him to prevent the world from being engulfed in fire.

Pherae town in Thessaly in northern Greece, ruled by Admetus.

Pheres father of Admetus, to whom in the *Alcestis* he has passed on rule over Pherae.

Phoebus = Apollo.

Phrygia part of Asia Minor.

Pierian of or associated with the Muses, who were born in Pieria.

Pirene famous fountain at Corinth.

Pittheus father of Theseus' mother Aethra, and former king of Trozen. In the *Hippolytus* he is thought of as honourably retired from this role.

Pluto another name for Hades, lord of the underworld and husband of Persephone.

Poseidon god of the sea and also of other threatening natural forces such as earthquakes; father of Theseus.

Pythian associated with Pytho (= Delphi), and hence with Apollo, whose oracle was there.

Pytho another name for Delphi, the sanctuary of Apollo where his oracle was located. The name derives from 'Python', a great snake which Apollo killed when he won control of Delphi; hence he is known as 'Pythian Apollo'.

Saronic Gulf the sea to the east of the isthmus connecting northern Greece with the Peloponnese.

Sciron a villainous figure who attacked travellers on a cliff and hurled them into the sea below; he was killed by Theseus, who encountered him while travelling from Trozen to Athens. The 'rocks of Sciron', where the incident was located, were on the isthmus west of Megara.

Scylla a six-headed sea-monster who attacked wanderers, including

Odysseus, and devoured sailors who were not fast enough to escape.

Semele mortal woman beloved by Zeus, by whom she became pregnant with Dionysus (Bacchus). Deceived by the jealous Hera, she rashly asked to see Zeus in his full divine glory, and was consumed in fire. The baby was rescued by Zeus.

Sinis a bandit slain by Theseus in his youthful journey from Trozen to Athens.

Sisyphus, Sisyphean Sisyphus was one of the great sinners in Greek mythology, condemned to push a gigantic rock up a hill down which it always fell again. He was the founder of Corinth, and in the *Medea* 'Sisyphean' is used for 'Corinthian'.

Sparta in historical times the most important city of the Peloponnese and regularly opposed to Athens. This antagonism is often projected back into the mythical period.

Sthenelus a hero of a family noted for rashness and arrogance; father of Eurystheus.

Thebes chief city of Boeotia, north of Athens.

Themis a rather shadowy goddess, but with an important and weighty role as personification of what is right and just. Usually regarded as one of Zeus' consorts.

Theseus son of Aegeus or of the god Poseidon; most famous of the mythical kings of Athens.

Thessaly region of NE Greece.

Thrace a region to the extreme north-east of the Greek mainland, beyond Macedonia; southern Greeks regarded it as primitive and savage.

Tiryns a city in the Peloponnese, east of Argos.

Trachis small city in northern Greece, where the children of Heracles vainly took refuge.

Trozen or Troezen town near Epidaurus in NE Peloponnese, and not part of Athens' domain in historical times, but closely associated with her in legend. It was there that Theseus grew to manhood and from there that he set out to Athens to find his father.

Tuscan (Etruscan) loosely used by Euripides to mean 'Italian' or 'western'. In the *Medea* Scylla is described as 'Tuscan' because Odysseus' wanderings were thought to have taken him near Italy and Sicily.

Venetian in Greek 'Enetic' – from a region at the north of the Adriatic. In Euripides' time Venice itself was not yet founded.

Zeus the most powerful of the Olympian gods and head of the family of immortals; father of Apollo, Athena and many other lesser gods, as well as of mortals such as Heracles.

Zeus of the Agora Zeus in his capacity as god of good counsel, debate and decision. The *agora* ('gathering-place') is thought of as a place for discussion (compare the Latin *forum*).

THE STORY OF PENGUIN CLASSICS

Before 1946 ...'Classics' are mainly the domain of academics and students, without readable editions for everyone else. This all changes when a little-known classicist, E. V. Rieu, presents Penguin founder Allen Lane with the translation of Homer's *Odyssey* that he has been working on and reading to his wife Nelly in his spare time.

1946 *The Odyssey* becomes the first Penguin Classic published, and promptly sells three million copies. Suddenly, classic books are no longer for the privileged few.

1950s Rieu, now series editor, turns to professional writers for the best modern, readable translations, including Dorothy L. Sayers's *Inferno* and Robert Graves's *The Twelve Caesars*, which revives the salacious original.

1960s The Classics are given the distinctive black jackets that have remained a constant throughout the series's various looks. Rieu retires in 1964, hailing the Penguin Classics list as 'the greatest educative force of the 20th century'.

1970s A new generation of translators arrives to swell the Penguin Classics ranks, and the list grows to encompass more philosophy, religion, science, history and politics.

1980s The Penguin American Library joins the Classics stable, with titles such as *The Last of the Mohicans* safeguarded. Penguin Classics now offers the most comprehensive library of world literature available.

1990s The launch of Penguin Audiobooks brings the classics to a listening audience for the first time, and in 1999 the launch of the Penguin Classics website takes them online to a larger global readership than ever before.

The 21st Century Penguin Classics are rejacketed for the first time in nearly twenty years. This world famous series now consists of more than 1300 titles, making the widest range of the best books ever written available to millions – and constantly redefining the meaning of what makes a 'classic'.

The Odyssey continues ...

The best books ever written

PENGUIN CLASSICS

SINCE 1946